Commissioner Roosevelt

Commissioner Roosevelt

The Story of
Theodore Roosevelt and
the New York City Police,
1895–1897

H. PAUL JEFFERS

JOHN WILEY & SONS, INC.
New York · Chichester · Brisbane · Toronto · Singapore

Copyright © 1994 by H. Paul Jeffers
Published by John Wiley & Sons, Inc.

Library of Congress Cataloging-in-Publication Data

Jeffers, H. Paul (Harry Paul).
 Commissioner Roosevelt : the story of Theodore Roosevelt and the
 New York City police, 1895–1897 / H. Paul Jeffers.
   p. cm.
 Includes bibliographical references and index.
 ISBN 0-471-02407-4 (acid-free paper)
 1. Roosevelt, Theodore, 1858–1919. 2. Police chiefs—New York
 (N.Y.)—Biography. 3. Police administration—New York (N.Y.)—
 History—19th century. I. Title.
 HV7911.R65J45 1994
 363.2′092—dc20   94-18144
 [B]

Printed in the United States of America

10 9 8 7 6 5 4 3 2 1

*For my friend and colleague in news
through 25 years of covering the good and bad
of New York's cops and politicians,
Ed Rickards*

I have the most important, and the most corrupt, department in New York on my hands. I shall speedily assail some of the ablest, shrewdest men in this city, who will be fighting for their lives, and I know well how hard the task ahead of me is.

—THEODORE ROOSEVELT, MAY 5, 1895

Contents

Preface

When I was growing up in Phoenixville, Pennsylvania, and exploring the shelves of the town's library, I encountered two men who became my life's heroes. One seemed so amazing that he ought to have been fictional: Theodore Roosevelt. The other I knew to be imaginary, yet I felt as if he really lived: Sherlock Holmes.

In 1978, as I pondered the daring task of writing my first mystery novel, I combined the two into a detective yarn dealing with a politically motivated murder in New York City in 1880. This was the year TR graduated from Harvard, and Holmes, according to his "biography," was in the city as a touring actor, honing skills of makeup and performance that would prove to his advantage as the sleuth of Baker Street, commencing the following year.

I picked 1880 out of cowardice. I did not wish to stumble into grievous error by writing about TR fifteen years later when he was Police Commissioner and Sherlock Holmes when he would have had fourteen years of history jotted down by Dr. John H. Watson. I called the book *The Adventure of the Stalwart Companions.*

Having taken on TR in the pages of a fiction, I hoped for a nonfiction author to write about his two years in Mulberry Street so I could read it. There existed Roosevelt biographies that devoted a chapter or so to the subject, but I wanted to know more. Ultimately, when no such work devoted to Mulberry Street appeared to be at hand or forthcoming, and by then having done some nonfiction authoring myself, I decided to write it.

For general illumination I turned at the start to TR's memoirs and general biographies. But what is frequently absent in autobiographies, official records, and other sources is detail and color of everyday things: the weather on a given date, what someone was wearing, a mood, a look, the decor of a room, smells, sounds, and the whole panoply of life and its events as they are played out. For these one must turn to history shot on the wing—that is, contemporary journalism.

For as complete a day-by-day account of Theodore Roosevelt's two years as police commissioner there exists no better contemporaneous source than *The New York Times.* Even in 1895–1897 it prided itself on being a newspaper of record. The detailed coverage was astonishing and captivating to read. Articles proved to be painstakingly complete, enlightening, occasionally surprising, and frequently amusing and witty. As one whose adult life was in large part spent in a journalism career, I was awed by the ability of these gatherers of news a century ago to produce transcripts of meetings, courtroom proceedings, interviews, descriptions of action, dialogue, and news events, and with an obvious respect for the English language that one does not always encounter in the journalism of today, especially in electronic media.

Reading 100-year-old next-day accounts of the events of TR's two years as police commissioner, I found myself beside him as he shouted *Hier bin ich* while relishing being lampooned by German-Americans who resented his taking away their Sunday beer; tramping along on the midnight rambles as he caught slacking coppers flatfooted and then called them on the carpet in his second-floor office for their derelictions; feeling outraged with him and Jake Riis as they inspected slums; eavesdropping on the squabbles with the mystifying antagonist of the second act of this drama, Andrew Parker—all through the unerring eyes, words, wit, and humor of reporters with nothing to aid them but notebooks and pencils.

Having written the book that I hoped would turn out to be the one I had always wanted to read, about TR and his Mulberry Street blues, I searched for a gemlike quotation to end it and to sum him up. Finally, I settled on a passage written by Vincent Starrett about that other personality of the 1890s whom I met in a library long ago—Sherlock Holmes—whose name I have substituted with that of the main character of this book.

"Let us speak, and speak again, of TR. For the plan fact is, that the imperishable Mr. Theodore Roosevelt is still a more commanding figure in the world than most warriors and statesmen in whose present existence we are invited to believe."

Commissioner Roosevelt

Prologue

Mr. Steffens Gets an Assignment

Dodging horses, omnibuses, carriages, a few bicycles, and a swarm of pedestrians as he dashed across Broadway, twenty-six-year-old Lincoln Steffens found himself badly in need of work. Just back from several years studying in Europe, the lean and lanky figure with a wife to support had been welcomed back to the America of 1892 by a startlingly energizing letter from his father in California.

The elder Steffens pointed out that when his son had finished school and had wanted to go to college he had paid his tuition at Berkeley. "When you got through there, you did not care to go into my business," he went on. "You preferred to continue your studies in Berlin. I let you."

After that came Heidelberg and Leipzig. Then Paris and a year of studying among the French. Next he had to have half a year of the British Museum in London. The father had assented.

"You must know about all there is to know of the theory of life," said the senior Steffens, "but there's a practical side as well. I suggest that you learn it, and the way to study it, is to stay in New York and hustle."

He enclosed a hundred dollars, "until you can find a job."

Believing he possessed the makings of a writer, Steffens tried his hand at authorship. To his surprise and encouragement he sold a short story he had dashed off in three days. *Harper's Magazine* paid him fifty dollars. Emboldened, he tried again but without repeating the success. Running out of his father's money, he dressed up daily in a beautiful morning coat with top hat to answer advertisements for anything connected to writing, only to promptly discover that

1

people looked with suspicion on his claim to a college education, and not only from one college, but five.

Dispiritedly turning to a business associate of his father with connections to the newspapers of Park Row, he obtained a letter of introduction to an editor of the New York *Evening Post*. Housed in a ten-story, red brick building at Broadway and Fulton Street across Manhattan's busiest intersection from the city's oldest church, St. Paul's, and a short walk from City Hall, the paper had been founded in 1801 by Alexander Hamilton with the intention of strengthening the Federalist Party. Its first editor, William Coleman, proved himself to be a crusader with plenty of righteous causes to champion, from quackery and patent medicines to the cruel hoaxes known as lotteries that picked the pockets of the poor. After Coleman, carrying on such campaigning on behalf of the public interest, William Cullen Bryant led the *Post* to declare against slavery as early as 1840, then broke with the Democrats by supporting the newly organized Republican Party in 1856, and backed Lincoln for president of the United States four years later. As editor he had been the first to suggest that a vast, open, derelict piece of Manhattan real estate stretching north from Fifty-ninth to 110th Street, known as "Shantytown," be cleared and turned into a great promenade and open-air resort.

Twenty years after Frederick Law Olmstead and Calvert Vaux transformed that vision into Central Park and three years after Bryant's death, in 1878, railway builder Henry Villard took over the newspaper and placed it in the hands of E. L. Godkin, as editor in chief. Irish-born, English in both his culture and political liberalism, and against bad government and "yellow journalism," he put out a conservative three-cent evening paper that assiduously shunned the seamy scandals, sensationalism, and crime found in the one-cent papers. In 1892 his political targets were Tammany Hall of the Democrats, and their boss, Richard Croker, and the Republican state machine of Boss Thomas C. Platt.

City editor of the *Post* on the morning Steffens presented himself was Henry J. Wright. "I don't need any more reporters," he said huffily, "but you can come in next Monday and sit down out there with the reporters, and as I get a chance, I'll try you out."

Having told his wife he had found a job, Steffens took his place in the city room on the appointed day and waited while all those around him bustled with journalistic activity as reporters received assignments. Untried but undaunted that day, he returned the next and waited again, catching a glimpse of Mr. Godkin as the famed editor passed by the door and ignored him, as did all the "interesting fellows" who actually had news to cover and who seemed to know all the mysteries of the great city outside.

"They did not talk much," Steffens would recall thirty-nine years later in his autobiography, "but I overheard enough to infer that they were familiar and bored with sport, politics, finance and society. I was awed by the way they would, upon a few words from the city editor, dart or loaf out of the room, be gone an hour or so, come in, report briefly, and then sit down, write, turn in their copy carelessly, and lie back and read, idly read, newspapers."

More than anything he had ever wished in his life, he longed to be like them.

Several days later, Wright came into the room around one o'clock, looked around, saw no one but Steffens, exclaimed impatiently and went out. Returning a moment later, he muttered, "See here, Steffens, there's a member of a stockbrokerage firm missing. Disappeared utterly. Something wrong. Go and see his partner and find out why the man is gone, whether there's money missing, too."

When he interviewed the broker, the man admitted, "My partner has not only skipped, he has taken every cent there was in the office, in the banks, and—then some."

Judging Steffens to be "reliable, quick and resourceful," Wright immediately hired him as a regular reporter, launching Steffens on "a series of daily adventures, interesting, sometimes thrilling" that in the course of a few months took him to all parts of the city, calling on all sorts of men and women, meeting politicians and businessmen, covering fires, accidents, fights, strikes, and meetings. He found journalism in New York to be "a great swimming hole into which every day I dived, here, there, anywhere, and swam around for something or somebody worth getting." He came to love the business, politics, and streets of the brawling city that cared neither for him nor for itself.

On the strength of his success with the absconding broker, he was called upon to fill in for the ailing *Post* reporter whose beat was Wall Street, in time to cover the Panic of 1893. Reporting one of the great periodic depressions in the history of the United States, he pictured himself "sailing through the storm on the bridge with the officers of the ship" with the cool eye and detachment of the uninvolved observer. "Having no prejudice for or against finance," he said, "I had no judgment, no point of view. I was only a reporter reporting."

When the regular Wall Street reporter reclaimed his beat Steffens found himself consigned again to general reporting, until another afternoon when Wright beckoned him to the city desk to ask a question that was so startling it left Steffens almost breathless: "How would you like to cover police headquarters?"

Located in a large stone building at 300 Mulberry Street in the heart of the city's most atrocious tenement district, the police department headquarters housed the four members of the board of police commissioners, inspectors, and captains who commanded the rank and file of the force and the detective bureau. Source of all crime news, headquarters was the clearing house for eager reporters seeking details of the misdemeanors and felonies of the more than 1.5 million people living upon forty-two square miles (twenty-two of them being the island of Manhattan), stretching from the Battery to Yonkers.

In this melting pot of disparate immigrants from all over the world the 1890 census had listed 400,000 Irish, nearly that many Germans, 25,000 Italians, and 10,000 Chinese. Largely Roman Catholic and poor, the population declined at an annual death rate of twenty-five per one thousand.

To maintain law and order in this conglomeration of humanity the police department operated thirty-six police stations with a force of about 3,600 patrolmen, roundsmen, and officers.

For Steffens "the police" represented a dark and mysterious layer of the life of the great city that he had not penetrated. Contemplating Wright's enticing offer, he envisioned himself going to Mulberry Street as he had gone to Wall Street, as he had gone to Europe, and as he had come home to America, "with the suppressed ardor of a young student and with the same throbbing anxiety that an orator feels just before he rises to speak." But speaking to Steffens at the moment was his city editor, Henry Wright, forcefully laying down the rules for the exciting new assignment in cautioning terms that clipped the fledgling police reporter's wings. "The *Evening Post* is not turning into a one-penny yellow sheet," the editor warned. "The *Post* does not cover crime. You are not going up to Mulberry Street to report murders and robberies. Pay no attention to crime. You are being assigned to cover the activities of the Reverend Parkhurst."

Anyone who read one of New York's fifty daily newspapers, two hundred seventy weeklies and periodicals, and three hundred fifty journals and magazines had heard of the slight, respectably bearded minister of the staid Madison Square Presbyterian Church. The Rev. Dr. Charles H. Parkhurst had been the biggest news story in the city since Sunday, February 14, 1892, when he had ascended into the pulpit of the Gothic brownstone church at Madison Avenue and Twenty-fourth Street to deliver a sermon entitled "Ye Are the Salt of the Earth." By its end the preacher had astounded the congregation with the charge that "in its municipal life, our city is thoroughly rotten."

The government, he exclaimed, constituted "a damnable pack of Administrative bloodhounds that are fattening themselves on the ethical flesh and blood of our citizenship." City leaders, he declared to the thunderstruck upturned faces in the pews, had become "a lying, perjuring, rum-soaked, and libidinous lot of polluted harpies" who under the guise of governing the city were "feeding day and night on its quivering vitals."

Turning his attention to the chief elected official at city hall, he pointed a rhetorical, accusatory finger at Mayor Hugh J. Grant: "Every effort to make men respectable, honest, temperate and sexually clean is a direct blow between the eyes of the mayor and his whole gang of drunken and lecherous subordinates."

Directing a lightning bolt in the direction of District Attorney De Lancey Nicoll, he charged that the office pledged to maintaining the law showed "no genius in ferreting out crime," prosecuting only when it had to, and "with a mind so keenly judicial that almost no amount of evidence was accepted as sufficient to warrant an indictment."

Even more shocking, Parkhurst accused "the guardians of the public peace and virtue, vulgarly known as the police," with being a force of corrupt bribe takers. "Your average policeman, or your average police captain," he said in outraged tones, "is not going to disturb a criminal, if the criminal has means. It is the universal opinion of those who have studied longest and most deeply into the municipal criminality of this city, that every crime has its price."

What had provoked such an outburst of hellfire, brimstone, and damnation from a clergyman renowned for his mild manner and frequently sleep-inducing, harmless sermon? What had possessed a fifty-year-old, slightly built, and near-sighted scholar with a degree from Amherst, and a command of Greek, Latin, and Sanskrit to use his secure and prestigious ministry to the cream of New York society to rail against the personalities of city government, and to brand them a generation of vipers?

While some of Parkhurst's Presbyterians may have speculated as to whether their pastor had experienced a mystical Epiphany to catapult him into the pulpit that Sunday morning, the genesis of the tirade had been Dr. Parkhurst's assumption two years earlier of the leadership of the Society for the Prevention of Crime. Organized in 1878, this association of progressive citizens had as its purpose the improving of social conditions that they deemed to be the corrosive roots of youth involvement in crime and vice.

Finding the Society virtually moribund, Parkhurst launched himself into a study of "the gambling evil and the social evil." What he discovered was not only unexpected but appalling. Rather than walking into the welcoming arms of a police department eager for his help, he discovered that an organization he had "supposed existed for the purpose of repressing crime had for its principal object to protect and foster crime and make capital out of it."

Demanding that the Society henceforth deal with the police as its "arch-antagonist," he insisted in April 1891 that he become the society's president and that it adopt a policy toward the police department of "making with it no alliance and giving it no quarter." He even provided a motto: "Down with the police."

Having set such a course, he headed inexorably to the sermon he delivered several months later. Courageous though it had been, Lincoln Steffens viewed Parkhurst's decision to publicly attack the police as quite perilous. "They were dangerous allegations; libelous," he noted. Unless they could be proved true.

Because the accusations had been laid at the feet of the top officials of the city, Parkhurst's charges amounted to indictment of the political organization that put them in office—Tammany Hall, traditional archenemy of successive editors of Alexander Hamilton's paper, and now nemesis of Steffens' boss, E. L. Godkin.

Regarding Rev. Parkhurst's tirade, Steffens noted with disarming understatement, "The *Post* was interested."

Calling upon Parkhurst, he informed him of his assignment and suggested that they both might benefit if they were to work together and exchange confidences. Interpreting Steffens' presence as at least tacit endorsement by the *Post* of his efforts to clean up city government, Parkhurst readily agreed to cooperate with Steffens. Spending several mornings describing his plans and methods to the attentive reporter, the meek-looking, fearlessly crusading preacher embellished his sermon's allegations with illuminating portraits of the leading personalities of the police department, and the depth and breadth of their corruption.

As the eager young newspaperman drank in the minister's tales, he became convinced that Dr. Parkhurst knew what he was talking about—although the minister had not been able to produce proof sufficient to persuade a grand jury to return indictments of the persons he had denounced in his sermon.

"After a few talks with Dr. Parkhurst," Steffens wrote in his autobiography, "I felt that I knew both the police officers and their worst crimes, and so, with no little dread and a solid foundation, I went one morning early to police headquarters with my card to present to the Superintendent of Police."

In professional reputation, public esteem, and personal fame not even the late-blooming notoriety of Rev. Parkhurst approached that of Thomas J. Byrnes. Indeed, no detective, including those of England's heralded Scotland Yard and the renowned agency of Allan Pinkerton—whose motto was "We never sleep," and whose symbol was a wide-open eye that ultimately provided the American lingo of hard-boiled crime writers with the term "private eye"—had reaped the accolades of the fifty-year-old top cop of the New York City Police Department.

By the time Steffens called upon Byrnes in 1893, the man the *New York Times* called the greatest thief taker in the history of the New York police had been head of the detective bureau since its inception. Born in Ireland on June 15, 1842, he had emigrated to America as a child, received little formal education, and had spent his growing years on the streets of the Fifth Ward where he ran with a gang of street brawlers attached to Hose Company No. 21 of the city's volunteer fire department. At the outbreak of the Civil War he enlisted in Ellsworth's Zouaves and fought at the first battle of Bull Run. Leaving the army after two years when the Zouaves disbanded, he returned to New York and looked to the police department for employment. Appointed a patrolman on December 10,

1863, he was assigned to the Third Precinct station house in Chambers Street. Five years later, having proved his mettle as a thief taker and peacekeeper, he was promoted to the rank of roundsman. Again proving his competence, he was rewarded with elevation to captain in 1870. After another decade of exceptional performance he was invited to put away the blue outfit of the uniformed force to be fitted for the cutaway suit and top hat of the Detective Bureau. Ten years later he stood in command of it.

Summoning reporters to his office in 1884, he boasted of the crime-fighting record his detectives had achieved under his leadership. "During the four years before I took charge of the detectives 1,943 arrests were made and 505 years of convictions secured," he told them, "whereas, for the four years I have been in charge 3,324 arrests were made and 2,428 years in conviction were secured."

He then led the newspapermen across the hall for a guided tour of what he called "the Mystery Chamber." A roomful of the memorabilia and souvenirs of cases solved by the men of the detective bureau, it was described by Richard Wheatley for readers of *Harper's New Monthly Magazine* in 1887 as "a shuddering horror," offering photographs that were "speaking likenesses" of all sorts of criminals "glaring from the walls." Displayed in cabinets and on shelves he found the implements of human crime and depravity, ranging from a sledgehammer and powder-flasks used to plunder the Manhattan Bank of nearly three million dollars in cash, bonds, and securities in 1878—a case which Byrnes solved—to "pipes, lamps, liquid raw opium and pills used for smoking in opium joints."

Crediting Byrnes, Wheatley asserted, "Crooks are now afraid of their shadows; great robberies have ceased, and minor crime has been reduced over eighty percent."

How did Byrnes achieve such results? He told Wheatley, "I make it a point to meet some of these men (criminals) in their resorts, and learn from them the whereabouts of their friends, and what they are doing. One crook of consequence generally knows what other good men are doing. In this way I keep posted, and know in what part of the country all the sharp men are. In the long-run the honest officer is a match for the smartest thief."

So confident had Byrnes become in his reputation as a superb policeman that in 1888, as Scotland Yard's entire detective force searched in vain for Jack the Ripper, he boasted that if London's killer of prostitutes who called himself "Saucy Jack" turned up in

New York he would be caught "soon enough," presumably by Tom Byrnes himself.

"My business is shrouded in mystery," he told one interviewer, "and the more difficult it is to unravel the harder I work."

But not all this success came about because of superlative sleuthing. As frequently as Byrnes and his detectives employed their minds to crack a case, they resorted to intimidation and physical abuse of suspects. They coined a term for it: "the third degree." Defending the technique, Byrnes told *Collier's* magazine, "I believe in any method of proving crime against a criminal," to which the writer of the article added, "His very manner, the size of him, the bark in his voice, his menacing shoulders and arms would terrorize the average crook."

Should Byrnes detect in a criminal suspect an above average intelligence, the third degree was likely to be modified to put the suspect, in the Chief of Detectives' words, "into the state of mind of the man in Poe's story 'The Telltale Heart,' wherein he can't help believing that proof of his guilt has been discovered and that his cross-examiners are mocking him by pretending not to be aware of it. The third degree should be a psychic rather than a physical process."

Having cultivated an intimate knowledge of New York City's criminal element, and every den of iniquity in each of its most sinister and dangerous neighborhoods—from the gang-breeding Five Points on the East Side to the aptly-named Hell's Kitchen on the shore of the Hudson River—Byrnes had gotten to know burglars, robbers, swindlers, confidence men, forgers, shoplifters, pickpockets, receivers of stolen goods, cut-throats, and killers by sight and by name. Consequently, when he rose to head the detective force in 1880, he set out to enshrine that knowledge by the creation of a catalog of photographs of such miscreants, thereby adding to the law enforcement dictionary the pithy term "Rogues' Gallery." In 1886 he included many of those photos, along with colorful essays on the criminals and their crimes, in a best-selling book, *Professional Criminals in America.*

Within one thick volume for detectives, vulnerable businessmen, and ordinary people to study were bank sneak Rufus Minor; forger Charles Becker; John Larney, alias Mollie Matches, pickpocket; Emil Voegtlin, boarding house thief; highwayman Daniel Hunt; Mary Hoey, Ellen Clegg, Lena Kleinschmidt, Mary Connelly, and Margaret "Mother Hubbard" Brown, pickpockets all; and William Burke, a bank sneak with the dubious distinction of sharing the nickname of the late and unlamented New York City-born, western desperado, Henry McCarty—better known as William Bonney, and even more widely recognized as "Billy the Kid."

"Aware of the fact that there is nothing that professional criminals fear so much as identification and exposure," Byrnes wrote in the preface to the book, "it is my belief that if the men and women who make a practice of preying upon society were known to others besides detectives and frequenters of the courts, a check, if not a complete stop, would be put to their exploits."

Now, six years after the publication of the tome and at the zenith of his fame, as Lincoln Steffens sojourned uptown from Broadway and Fulton to Mulberry Street to introduce himself to Byrnes as the police reporter for the *Evening Post,* the Rev. Dr. Parkhurst was daring to suggest that men of Byrnes's Detective Bureau were no less criminal than those they were expected to arrest, and perhaps worse.

Steffens approached the great detective's domain with unbounded curiosity, some trepidation, and a little embarrassment. "It was his hour for receiving citizens with complaints, his inspectors, captains, heads of departments with reports and 'the press,'" Steffens wrote in his memoirs. "His small outer office was crowded with people, uniformed and in plain clothes."

As he presented his card to the chief's favorite sergeant, Mangin, and was told to wait, he could not fail to hear a tall, handsome police inspector with a lavish handlebar mustache and a "clear and distinct" voice. "A reporter from the *Evening Post,*" the inspector bellowed with clear disdain. "The *Post* has always despised police news, true police news, but now when we are under fire they are to have a man up here to expose and clean us all out, us rascals." With a sneer and a stroke of the mustache, he added, "We'll see how long he stays."

As the inspector turned away, Steffens asked Sergeant Mangin the man's name. Mangin answered, "Inspector Williams." Steffens recognized the name as one of those ranking police officers whom Parkhurst cited for either malfeasance or personal corruption.

Second only to Byrnes in reputation as a dynamic policeman, truly feared among the city's criminal element, and heralded in the penny papers as "the toughest cop on the force," Alexander S. Williams had developed a powerful physique as a youth working as a ship's carpenter. He brought his strength to his work as a cop. Assigned to patrol the dangerous Houston street area, he made it his first business to locate the two toughest characters in the neighborhood. Tracing them to their hangout, the Florence Saloon, he goaded them into a fight, promptly knocked them out with his nightstick and hurled them through the saloon's plate glass window. When their pals swarmed after him, he stood his ground and felled them with his nightstick, earning the nickname "Clubber."

Appointed a captain in 1871 and placed in command of the Twenty-first precinct in the heart of the Gas House district—one of the most lawless sections of the city—Williams employed his trusty club so ruthlessly that he was able to hang his watch and chain on a hitching post at Third Avenue and Thirty-fifth Street, then lead a band of amused reporters around the block to find on their return the items were not only there but untouched.

Rewarded in 1876 with a transfer, he moved to the Twenty-ninth precinct, encompassing the theater district known as the Rialto. Compared to the grinding poverty of the Gas House area the glittering blocks were rich in potential for personal profit through bribery and other forms of graft. Gleefully, he informed a friend, "I've had nothing but chuck steak for a long time, and now I'm going to get a little of the tenderloin." Whether this is the source of "Tenderloin," meaning that portion of a community that is rampant with vice and corruption, is open to debate.

One aspect of Clubber Williams' penchant for phrasing is not in doubt. It was he who coined a maxim of policing that is still jotted down in the notebooks of first-year criminal law students more than a century later: "There is more law at the end of a policeman's night stick than in any ruling of the U.S. Supreme Court."

"Oh, Clubber Williams, I know about him," Steffens said to Sergeant Mangin while the supplicants in Byrnes's outer office laughed at Williams' taunting of the reporter from the detested *Evening Post*. Deciding to call Williams' bluff, Steffens strode defiantly toward the famed Inspector and announced, "I shall stay here till you are driven out."

After gasping at such audacity, the occupants of the room fell silent and expectant while a pale, aghast Sergeant Mangin dashed through the open door to Superintendent Byrnes's office. Bidden to enter the inner sanctum out of turn, Steffens found the figure standing to greet him a disappointment. Tom Byrnes, the famous police chief, was not the awe-inspiring figure he had imagined.

Thirty years on the force and ample dinners had dulled the edges of the burly, robust, broad-shouldered, two-fisted and granite-jawed punisher of the wicked who had joined the department straight out of the Union Army. His thinning hair and lush mustache were more gray than dark. But through the slits of the eyes in the puffy face Steffens detected, as they studied and read him, undimmed alertness and cunning.

Indicating a chair, the Superintendent said, "The *Evening Post* is welcome at police headquarters. A fair paper, it will be just and true to the facts. You will seek the truth, and the truth you will report, as you find it." He paused a long moment. "But you can not get the truth from Dr. Parkhurst nor from any enemy of the police."

Steffens fidgeted anxiously.

"Yes, yes, I know you must see Dr. Parkhurst," Byrnes said with a tolerant tone. "But you must listen to us, too, to me. You will want the news. Well, sir, I control the news from the police department. I can give and I can *withhold* the news."

Feeling blackmailed, Steffens bolted for the door.

"No, no, keep your seat," Byrnes implored. "Please. I am only endeavoring to say to you that I am going to put you on the same basis here as the old reporters who have been with us for years, most of them, and in return I ask you, in all fairness, not to print the stuff you get from the enemies of the police without submitting it to me for correction or—at any rate—for comment."

As the words slipped slyly from the lips of this policeman with the reputation as a master of men, Steffens saw in Byrnes "no complications at all." The boss of the police, he realized, was quite a simple character to understand. He made no bones about his power and his aim. He was a man who could buy you or beat you, as you might choose, but get you he would.

To counter the blatant threat to keep news away from the new man from the *Evening Post,* Steffens said, "The *Post* has no use for ordinary police news. I was sent here to see what I might see, hear what might be said, and print what I can prove—*of politics.* That is all. I am willing to tell you whatever of importance I mean to report. If you will see me promptly. I can not allow any delays in news, of course."

As Byrnes listened, he drummed his fingers on his desk; then, rising after Steffens stopped talking, walked to a window, drummed his fingers on the glass with his nails, turned suddenly, with a look of displeasure and grunted, "All right."

A touch of a button summoned Sergeant Mangin.

Hustled out of the office, Steffens found himself facing an elderly man whom he know to be a reporter for a morning paper. "You have made a bad start," the man said gravely. "You have made an enemy of Clubber Williams. I hope you have made a friend of Tom Byrnes. With Williams against you, you will need him."

"What do I need friends for?" Steffens replied. "They would only embarrass me in what I am here to do."

"I know your city editor, Harry Wright," the reporter went on, "and I know that he will expect you to get some news. I can help you, if you will work with me for a while and take my advice till you know the ropes yourself. You'll need an office. The best place for a police reporter is in the buildings across the street. From there you can watch police headquarters, see who comes and goes, and run across in a moment for any news which might turn up. But all the rooms across the street are taken. It would be better for you to have a desk in my office. You'll have to pay for half the telephone and light rates of course."

Steffens hardly heard the offer. His thoughts were riveted on all that had just happened. Questions flashed through his mind. How did this man know so much about him? How did Clubber Williams know? Everybody at police headquarters seemed to know why he was there. Astonished and worried and repelled by the reporter's overtures regarding help and half an office, he wanted to get away from "this friend" and out of the headquarters as quickly as possible.

Still accompanied by the unwanted friend as he left the building, he heard a voice bellowing, "Max! Max!"

Looking for the source of the blaring, he spotted a shaggy-looking, older man charging down Mulberry Street and asked the persistent self-imposed friend, "Who's that?"

"Oh him," the reporter replied with a sigh of disapproval. "That's the *Evening Sun* man. Jake Riis."

Here, too, was an individual whose name, like Williams' and Brynes's, had reaped city-wide acclaim. Not only a famous newspaperman and author of a best-selling book, *How the Other Half Lives,* a scathing exposé of the abysmal life of city slums, Jacob Riis had become a well-known character in one half the life of New York.

Steffens decided he liked his looks. Watching Riis, he observed the *Sun's* Mulberry Street man joined in the middle of the street by a little round, happy figure to whom Riis shouted, "There you are Max!"

"That is Riis's assistant," explained Steffens' lingering, still unwanted, but knowing companion. "His name is Max Fischel."

The two *Sun* men disappeared into the opposite building, 303 Mulberry. A moment later, they appeared again in the window of an upper floor, settling at desks and down to work. Deciding then and there he had to meet Riis, Steffens dashed across the street, into 303, and up the stairs. Locating Riis, he presented a card identifying him and his newspaper.

"Glad you've come," Riis exclaimed. "The *Post* can help a lot up here. And you've begun well."

Steffens gasped, "Begun well? I haven't begun yet."

Riis roared a great laugh. "Oh yes, you have. Max says you banged Alec Williams and disappointed the old man himself. That's the way to handle them. Knock 'em down. They are afraid of me, not I of them, and so with you. You have started off on top. Stay there. Play alone. Don't throw in with the likes of that fellow you were with a while ago. He's part of what I call the combine. They will beat you with news stories for a while. So will I, of course. The whole police force will help beat you. But you'll soon learn the game and hold your own. I'll show you around."

Of the rest of that day in the company of Jacob A. Riis, Lincoln Steffens wrote in his memoirs, "He broke into all the offices, police and health, walked right in upon everybody he thought I should know, laughed, made them all laugh, and introduced me, not by name, but as the new *Evening Post* man."

As they left the building, at the front end of the hall they observed two policemen half forcing, half carrying, a broken and bandaged man in the traditional clothing of an Orthodox Jew into the office opposite that of Williams. There were officers and citizens all about, but Riis pointed to the man as he stumbled through the open door and shouted, "There you have a daily scene in Inspector Williams' office. That's a prisoner. Maybe he has done something wrong; anyway he's done something the police don't like. But they haven't only arrested him, as you see. They have beaten him up. I'll tell you what to do while you are learning our ways up here, Steffens. You hang around this office every morning, watch the broken heads brought in, and as the prisoners are discharged, you ask them for their stories."

Williams had heard. Rising from his desk, he pointed at the door and shouted something to someone within the office. The door closed with a bang. Jake Riis laughed. But there was no merriment. Only rage. And in the laugh Steffens understood, more than any sermon by Dr. Parkhurst might convey, the sorry state of the New York Police.

Chapter 1

I Have Read Your Book

When Isaac J. Hunt laid eyes on the outfit sported by another newcomer to the New York state legislature in January 1881, he thought, *The man is a joke, a dude.*

Carrying a gold-headed walking stick, the young assemblyman from New York City presented a toothy grin in a square-jawed face adorned with side-whiskers and a large head topped by a tall silk hat. Fashionably tight trousers flared out over his shoes. A silk cord dangled from nose glasses. Thrusting a hand toward Hunt, the splendid sartorial specimen blurted, "Hello, my name is Theodore Roosevelt."

Twenty-four days later he delivered his first address to the legislative body in what one newspaper described as "a Dundreary drawl." A veteran assemblyman noted that young Roosevelt had spoken with some difficulty, "as if he had an impediment in his speech," although another journalist wrote of hearing "sensible and well-delivered remarks" that had resulted in "many hearty congratulations from the older members." A third reporter told his readers, "This young gentlemen has been dubbed 'Oscar Wilde' by admiring colleagues, who were much amused by his elastic movements, voluminous laughter and wealth of mouth."

Picking up a rumor that some elders of the legislature were plotting a special kind of welcome for him, the freshman tracked down the suspected organizer of the scheme, an oxlike New York saloon keeper named "Big John" McManus.

"Look here," TR snapped. "I understand you fellows want to toss me in a blanket. Am I right?"

McManus grinned. "Well, what if *you* are?"

"Just this. I serve notice now that if you try anything like that

I'll fight. I'll bite, kick, and do anything that my teeth, fists and feet can do."

The blanket party never materialized.

That Roosevelt could ever utter such a bellicose warning and have it unchallenged would not have been believed by anyone who knew him as a child of such poor health that it was doubtful he would grow into manhood. Born on October 17, 1858, he was small, weak, and asthmatic. Descended from the Scottish, English, and Huguenot stock of his mother, Martha Bullock, and the Dutch of his father and namesake, a scion of one of the early settlers of New Amsterdam, the second child of Theodore and Martha Roosevelt was nicknamed "Teedie." His sister Anna, four years older, was called "Bamie." Corinne, born two years after Teedie, answered to "Conie." Younger brother Elliott, born four years after Teedie, managed to grow up without benefit of a nickname.

Next door to the brownstone mansion at 28 East Twentieth Street lived an uncle, Robert Roosevelt, and a flock of cousins.

Too frail to attend a public school, Teedie went to Professor McMullen's nearby private school or received tutoring at home. Confined to bed much of the time by ill health, he added to this education by reading voraciously, especially books on travel and nature as well as the novels of Charles Dickens and James Fennimore Cooper.

With sporadic attention, he began a diary. The writing down of his adventures and ideas became considerably more regular as he grew older. By the time his parents took the family to Europe in 1869, the diarist in him was emboldened enough to title his record of his continental travels, *Journal of Theodore Roosevelt of U.S.A. New York*.

In a notebook dated 1875, written in the new Roosevelt home on Fifty-seventh Street, the former sickly child of Twentieth Street wrote the title *Roosevelt Sporting Calendar* and listed data on broad and high jumps, pole vaults, and dashes. These feats had been carried out in a gymnasium built for his use in the palatial new residence. He also recorded his physical characteristics: 5 feet, 8 inches tall; chest (expanded), 34 inches; weight, 124 pounds.

At age eighteen, this increasingly robust individual presented himself for matriculation at Harvard. Going with him to Cambridge were the words and hopes of his father: "Theodore, because we have a little money, you must not grow up hoping to depend on that. I shall expect you to work and make your own way in life."

Two years later, as Theodore crammed for sophomore midterm examinations, he received word that his father lay near death of peritonitis. Actually, the man Theodore called "Greatheart" and "the one I loved dearest on earth" suffered from cancer of the bowel. He died in agony on Saturday, February 9, 1878, at the age of forty-six.

Returning to Harvard, the heartbroken son studied science diligently, took up boxing, and courted Alice Hathaway Lee, "an enchanting creature . . . of singular loveliness . . . unfailing sunny temperament . . . exceptionally bright" and "the life of the party." In the winter of his senior year, February 1880, his friends were informed that he and Alice had become engaged.

TR had by then abandoned the notion that his future lay in science or journalism, deciding, instead, to study law. That autumn he enrolled at Columbia University and married Alice.

Deciding to get into politics, he rejected the argument of some friends who told him politics were "low" and not controlled by "gentlemen" but run by "saloon keepers, horsecar conductors, and the like" who would be "rough and brutal and unpleasant to deal with." But in TR's view a heavy moral obligation rested upon the man of education to do his full duty by his country. He felt those who had enjoyed the privilege of having attended college were "honor bound to take an active part" in political life "without regard to the effect it has upon his own fortunes." And in the pursuit of politics, he also saw the necessity of being bound by a high ideal and the willingness to strive to realize it. Political activity "must be disinterested and honest, and it must be given without regard to his own success or failure." In exhibiting virtues of righteousness and tolerance and gentleness, the young man going into politics would also have to show, he believed, "sterner virtues of courage, resolution, and hardihood, and the desire to war with merciless effectiveness against the existence of wrong."

The party he chose was that of the man he most admired for all those qualities, his father. But he discovered it was "no simple thing" to find a Republican clubhouse that would take him. One did not simply declare oneself a member of a political party in 1880. A man had to be regularly proposed for and elected into a clubhouse. Often rejected but undaunted, he ultimately found himself welcomed into the Republican Association that met in Morton Hall. A barnlike room over a saloon, it had furniture of "the canonical kind, dingy benches, spittoons, and a dais at one end with a table and a chair and a stout pitcher for iced water." On the wall hung a portrait of General Ulysses S. Grant.

"I went around there often enough to have the men get accustomed to me and to have me get accustomed to them," he wrote in his memoirs, "so that we began to speak the same language, and so that each could begin to live down in the other's mind what Bret Hart has called 'the defective moral quality of being a stranger.'"

Among those with whom he shattered barriers was "one of the lesser captains" of the club. In Joe Murray he discerned "a straight man," fearless and staunchly loyal, a man to be trusted in any position demanding courage, integrity, and good faith.

Presently, Murray concluded TR was just the man to go up against a veteran political heavyweight, Jake Hess, for the nomination for a seat in the assembly in the elections of 1880. When Hess went down to defeat, he enthusiastically enlisted in Murray's campaign to send Theodore Roosevelt to Albany.

Recalling his first effort at soliciting votes, Roosevelt wrote in his autobiography, "At first they thought they would take me on a personal canvass through the saloons along Sixth Avenue. The canvass, however, did not last beyond the first saloon. I was introduced with proper solemnity to the saloon keeper (and) he began to cross-examine me, a little too much in the tone of one who was dealing with a suppliant for his favor."

The proprietor let it be known that he expected that Roosevelt would treat the liquor business fairly, to which TR replied, "I hope to treat all interests fairly."

When the saloon owner expressed the opinion that the cost of licenses was too high, TR answered that he believed the license fees were not high enough. Finding that the conversation threatened to turn stormy, Murray and Hess hurried their candidate outside.

"Teddy, go back to your friends on Fifth Avenue," Murray advised. "Jake and I will look after your interests on Sixth Avenue."

After the ballots were tallied, Roosevelt found himself "triumphantly elected." He arrived in Albany as the youngest member of the legislature and the representative of the wealthiest district in Manhattan. Initially viewed as a New York City version of the foppish Oscar Wilde, a lowly legislative freshman, and, worse, a Republican in a house controlled by Democrats, he assumed his place expecting little opportunity to be effective. However, he quickly discovered that family ties were stronger than politics.

His proud Uncle Robert reached out to a fellow Democrat, a friend, and one of the most powerful figures in the assembly, Michael C. Murphy. Assuring the uncle he would "look after" the nephew, the chairman of the City Affairs Committee astonished the novice assemblyman and everyone else in Albany by appointing him a seat on the committee. "It was," Roosevelt recorded in his memoirs, "a coveted position."

Observing the newcomer on the job, the Albany correspondent of the *New York Times,* George Spinney, noticed Roosevelt's ability to huddle in his seat with a book in his hand yet keep track of business on the legislative floor, leaping to his feet with a comment or, more often, a question. "He went to the bottom of everything," Spinney said. "He seemed to be constantly asking, prying into things, following the trail of debate with the pertinacity of a ferret." By the end of the first session, said Spinney, "he knew more about state politics than ninety percent of the others did."

Sitting on Murphy's powerful committee, TR also attained an education in the politics of New York City and the organization that controlled its every aspect—Tammany Hall. But he was a Republican in a Democrat-controlled—and by extension a Tammany-controlled—legislature. Reelected in 1882, he remained in the minority, though he had managed during his first term to impress other Republicans enough to elect him minority leader.

A year later, at the end of the 1883 session, the *New York Times* declared, "The rugged independence of Assemblyman Theodore Roosevelt and his disposition to deal with all public measures in a liberal spirit have given him a controlling force on the floor superior to that of any member of his party."

That November, voters handed Republicans a stunning victory and control of both houses of the legislature. By all odds, TR appeared a shoo-in for speaker of the assembly. But a bit of backroom deal making by senior powers in the party denied him the honor. Disappointed at first, he found the loss to be, in the end, to his benefit. To assuage his feelings, the man who beat him to the speakership offered him membership on the three most powerful committees: banks, militia, and cities.

Named chairman of the latter, the representative from the

Twenty-first Assembly District of Manhattan immediately introduced bills to reorganize the way New York City government operated. Fulfilling his pledge to the Sixth Avenue saloon keeper who in 1880 had griped about the cost of licenses, he sought increased fees. A second measure limited the city's borrowing of money from unorthodox sources. The third aimed to reform the basic structure of city government, investing real power in the office of mayor and curbing the powers of aldermen, whom he described in a speech on the floor of the assembly as "creatures of the local ward bosses or of the municipal bosses."

Simultaneously, he introduced a resolution for the establishment of a Special Committee to Investigate the Local Government and County of New York, then lost no time in gaveling it to order for its first session. It convened on Friday, January 19, 1884, in the old Metropolitan Hotel. A venerable city landmark at Broadway and Prince Street and long a stronghold of Tammany Hall power brokers, it had once been leased by Boss William Marcy Tweed for his son, who spent half a million dollars redecorating it. As the hearings began, reform-minded citizens and enemies of Tweed's legatees waited anxiously for Roosevelt's questioning to begin.

What they witnessed was a procession of grim men with faulty memories. Others, such as the city sheriff, were combative. Asked about the costs of transportation in his office, the official expressed offense at Roosevelt's "going into a gentleman's private affairs."

Thumping a big fist on the table, TR roared back, "You are a public servant. You are not a private individual. We have a right to know what the expense of your plant is. We don't ask for the expense of your private carriage that you use for your own conveyance. We ask what you, a public servant, pay for a van employed in the service of the public. We have a right to know. It is a perfectly proper question."

While such public posturing and evasion had been expected, the chairman of the committee did not anticipate the extent to which his antagonists were prepared to go to stymie the work of the investigation. He learned it in the person of a member of the committee. Described in Roosevelt's memoirs as "a very able" man who hailed from a rural area of the state, the assemblyman, when he reached New York City, "felt as certain Americans do when they go to Paris—that the moral restraints of his native place no longer applied." Shadowed by the police and "caught red-handed by a plainclothesman doing what he had no business to do," the embarrassed and terrified committee member found himself a victim of police blackmail.

"Thenceforth those officials who stood behind the Police Department had one man on the committee on whom they could count," TR recalled. "I never saw terror more ghastly on a strong man's face than on the face of this man on one or two occasions when he feared that events in the committee might take such a course as to force him into a position where his colleagues would expose him if the city officials did not."

Appreciating the likelihood of traps being set for more than one member of the committee, Roosevelt wrote that he scrupulously heeded Josh Billings' advice that "it is much easier to be a harmless dove than a wise serpent." He offered enemies no opportunities.

Citing the dilemma of the indiscreet committee member in his autobiography, he later proposed a personal code that subsequent politicians seemed never to have learned, namely, that "no man can lead a public career really worth leading, no man can act with rugged independence in serious crises, nor strike at great abuses, nor afford to make powerful and unscrupulous foes, if he is himself vulnerable in his private character."

As the committee struggled against obstacles set before them by powerful and unscrupulous foes, one observer leaning forward in gleeful anticipation in his chair in the seats reserved for the press was Jacob Riis of the *Sun*. Impressed by Roosevelt, he came forward to introduce himself and compliment him and the committee on its work. Yet years of experience covering the very men who were being investigated had shown Riis that one committee and a few weeks of questioning were unlikely to result in rooting out the entrenched evils that beset city government. Two decades later in *Theodore Roosevelt, the Citizen,* he wrote, "There was enough to investigate but [the public] had not yet grown a conscience robust enough to make the facts tell."

In the midst of the investigation of corruption in the city of his Dutch ancestors and his birth, the energetic battler for reform found himself battered by a personal disaster that would have wrecked lesser men. It began at noon on February 12, 1884, with good news, a telegram informing him he had become the father of a daughter. This happiness was eclipsed, however, when he arrived in New York City to be met by his brother and sisters. Elliott, Bamie, and Conie carried the devastating news that their ailing mother's frail health had taken a sudden turn for the worse. She was dying.

Then fell another blow. Informed that his wife Alice's condition had also deteriorated, he learned that she, too, might die. A few hours later, at two o'clock in the morning, February 13, his mother passed away. Alice Hathaway Lee Roosevelt died twenty-five hours later.

"Seldom, if ever, has New York society received such a shock as yesterday," said the *World*. The *Tribune* opined, "The loss of his wife and mother in a single day is a terrible affliction."

TR wrote in his diary, "The light has gone out of my life." Following their burials on the sixteenth, he inscribed, "For joy or sorrow, my life has now been lived out."

The next day the baby girl, Alice Lee, was christened, to be cared for by Anna.

The day after the baptism, TR went back to Albany and threw himself into work at an even more feverish pitch.

The deplorable facts concerning the city of New York discovered by his investigation, he reported to the legislature, were that the government was riddled with corruption. In one million words of testimony filling 2,590 pages, the committee unearthed a system of blackmail and extortion, hush money paid to the police, gross abuses in the sheriff's office, and a pattern of political influence that prevented criminal prosecutions.

Given special attention in the report was the "vicious" and "farcical" system of appointments to the police force in which all applicants were required to obtain recommendations from members of the four-man board of police commissioners, thus assuring political control of the police. The board itself was rebuked by Roosevelt for its failure to enforce the laws against prostitution, gambling, and the sale of liquor.

Drafting seven bills directed at correcting or rooting out these failings, the chairman of the cities committee next had to bully them through the legislature. That he succeeded was, in the view of a now-admiring Isaac Hunt, due to TR, whom he called a "presiding genius" and an "eagle in the midst of the storm."

Reporting passage of the "Roosevelt reform bills," the newspapers that had ridiculed him for so long now trumpeted him. "Theodore, the Cyclone Hero of the Assembly," said one. Another bore the headline "A Big Day for Roosevelt." A third proclaimed "Roosevelt's Brilliant Assault on Corruption." A Philadelphia publication looked northward admiringly and proclaimed, "The career of this young man, who has gone boldly and honorably into public life, ought to shame thousands who complain that politics are so dirty that no decent gentleman can engage in them." *Harper's Weekly* offered a cartoon depicting Roosevelt presenting Governor Grover Cleveland with a scroll of laws. The caption declared, "Reform Without Bloodshed."

Despite the praise and a general expectation that Theodore Roosevelt would be a name to be reckoned with in the future of New York and national politics, TR was depressed and pessimistic. He said in a letter to the editor of a newspaper in Utica that he had "little expectation of being able to keep on in politics" and that he would not mind going back into private life.

"I shall probably be in Dakota," he predicted in the letter dated April 30, 1884, "and I think I shall spend the next two to three years in making shooting trips, either in the Far West or in the Northern Woods."

The author of *The Naval War of 1812*, written while he was serving his first two terms in the legislature, TR added, "And there will be plenty of work to do writing."

First, however, there was the Republican National Convention to which he was committed to attend as a delegate. With his friend Henry Cabot Lodge of Boston, he backed Senator George F. Edmunds of Vermont for the presidential nomination. When it was offered to James G. Blaine, TR growled to a reporter, "We ought to support any good Democratic nominee." Blurting, "I am through with politics," he headed west.

It was not his first venture into the wild and woolly wilderness. Accompanied by Elliott, a veteran of western adventure, he had spent the summer after his graduation from Harvard tramping and hunting in Illinois, Iowa, and Minnesota. He went again in 1883, trekking alone into the Territory of Dakota via the brand-new Northern Pacific Railroad.

Greeted in 1880 by a fellow wearing nose glasses and booming "Dee-lighted to meet you" through a toothy grin, the townspeople of a place called Little Missouri had not known quite what to make of TR. The local paper, the *Bad Lands Cowboy*, reported "Theodore Roosevelt, the young New York reformer, made us a very pleasant call Monday in full cowboy regalia. New York will certainly lose him for some time, at least, as he is perfectly charmed with our free Western life."

Having been charmed enough in 1883 to buy into a cattle ranch, he returned in 1884 prepared to work as vigorously as the native cowhands. "There was much hard work and some risk on a round-up," he recalled in his memoirs, "but also much fun." And through it all he bore up stoically to strangers calling him "four eyes."

Informed on one occasion that "Jake Maunders is talking it around that he's going to kill you," he remarked quietly, "Is that so?" and went to fetch his horse.

Confronting Maunder at the man's shack, he said bluntly, "I hear you want to shoot me. I came over to find out why."

Astonished and evidently cowed, Maunder blurted, "Why, Mr. Rosenfelder, that's a mistake. I never said nothing of the sort."

Presently, "Rosenfelder" found himself serving as deputy to Sheriff Bill Jones, "a gun-fighter and also a good man with his fists" who had once been on the police force of Bismarck. Asked by TR why he had given up the job, Jones replied that he had hit the mayor over the head with a gun.

"The mayor, he didn't mind it," Jones continued to TR's delight, "but the superintendent of police said he guessed I'd better resign."

Whether Roosevelt told Sheriff Jones tales of misbehaving police officers back home in New York City, TR did not record in his reminiscences of his years in the West. However, he did make note of being impressed by "the advantage the officer of the law has over ordinary wrong-doers."

Departing the Dakota Territory for six months of the fall and winter of 1885, he visited daughter Alice, sisters, brother, and other relatives and looked after Eastern business affairs, including a house on Madison Avenue and one called Sagamore Hill at Oyster Bay on the north shore of Long Island.

In October, at the age of twenty-seven, he encountered twenty-four-year-old Edith Carow, whom he had known growing up. Now, in the adjectives of biographer Edmund Morris's *The Rise of Theodore Roosevelt,* she impressed him as a mature, complex, exciting, and alarmingly attractive woman. Edith found him equally intriguing. Acutely aware of the proprieties expected of a man who had been so recently widowed, they kept their love a secret, going so far as to tell no one that he proposed marriage to her in November.

Following the winter social season, he returned to Dakota. Soon after, early on the morning of March 24, 1886, the deputy sheriff and his two partners discovered that a boat belonging to them had been stolen during the night by a ne'er-do-well named Redhead Finnegan. A long-haired gunman of vicious reputation who also had a charge of horse stealing lodged against him, he and two other "hard characters" lived in a shack some twenty miles above Roosevelt's ranch and, TR suspected, had for some time been "wishing to get out of the country, as certain of the cattlemen had been openly threatening to lynch them."

Setting out to track the boat thieves in the aftermath of a severe blizzard, TR and his partners pursued the trio in bitter cold and hindering drifts until, on April 1, they spotted their quarry beside an ice-clogged river. Leaping from the cover of underbrush, guns drawn, the pursuers "took them absolutely by surprise."

Ordered to hold up their hands, two of the thieves did so immediately. Only Finnegan hesitated, "his eyes fairly wolfish" as TR approached to within a few paces. Covering Finnegan's chest so as to avoid overshooting, Roosevelt repeated the command. When Finnegan "saw that he had no show," he cursed TR, let his rifle drop, and thrust up his hands in surrender.

After enduring several more days of bitterly cold weather until he could deliver the prisoners to authorities, TR remarked, "There is very little amusement in combining the functions of a sheriff with those of the Arctic explorer."

As a fee for his deputy sheriffing and the arrests, plus a mileage allowance, he was paid fifty dollars.

Spring 1886 passed with a combination of the hard, physical work of the annual cattle roundup and writing a biography of Thomas Hart Benton, while his reputation as a man equal to the West grew. Addressing a July Fourth celebration in the town of Dickinson, he drew roars of approval.

"Like all Americans," he told the admiring audience under the wide Dakota skies, "I like big things; big prairies, big forests and mountains, big wheat fields, railroads, and herds of cattle too, big factories, steamboats and everything else. But we must keep steadily in mind that no people were ever yet benefitted by riches if their prosperity corrupted their virtue."

Three years had passed since he had declared himself done with politics as a means of championing virtue and left New York. For reform-minded New Yorkers who had been heartened by Assemblyman Roosevelt's vigorous attacks on the entrenched corruption of Tammany and its subalterns in the police department, the news of his departure for the wilds of the Dakotas had come as a blow of crushing disappointment, especially to the *Sun*'s man in Mulberry Street.

Landing in New York City in 1870 at the age of twenty-one from Denmark, Jacob August Riis had knocked around the East Coast in semipoverty for seven years, the latter months in hopes of getting a foothold on a metropolitan newspaper, only to be told he was "too green." In 1877 his luck had changed in the form of a job on the *New York Tribune*. Discovering "there is no corner in all New York where the wind blows as it does around the *Tribune* building," he spent the winter months chasing news, on probation as a reporter. Deemed suitable, he was offered the police beat at twenty-five dollars a week.

Moving into his office in a building opposite police headquarters, he immediately assessed the men with whom he would be working, starting with the other reporters. One prided himself on being a sleuth, feeding on detective mysteries. Another who thrived on covering fires knew the history of every house in town and ran any risk of being burned to death to get the facts of the latest conflagration. Still others yearned for ever-bloodier murders to splash across the front pages. Each and every one depended on the police as the source for stories.

"The police reporter on a newspaper, then," Riis recorded in his memoirs, *The Making of an American,* "is the one who gathers and handles all the news that means trouble to someone: the murders, fires, suicides, robberies, and all that sort, before it gets into court. He has an office in Mulberry Street, across from Police Headquarters, where he receives the first intimation of the trouble through the precinct reports. Or else he does not receive it. The police do not like to tell the public of a robbery or a safe 'cracking,' for instance. They claim that it interferes with the ends of justice. What they really mean is that it brings ridicule or censure upon them to have the public know that they do not catch every thief, or even most of them. They would like that impression to go out, for police work is largely a game of bluff."

This was a sport in which Riis eagerly joined, spelling out for anyone who cared to listen the only rule: "The reporter, who through acquaintance, friendship, or natural detective skill, can get that which it is the policy of the police to conceal from him, wins."

Although Riis could take a light-hearted attitude toward the contest of wills between himself and the police during the years between his posting in Mulberry Street in 1877 and the Roosevelt committee's police investigation in 1884, he regarded reporting crime news and activities of the police as the highest form of journalistic idealism. "The reporter who is behind the scenes sees the tumult of passions, and not rarely a human heroism that redeems all the rest," he wrote. "It is his task so to portray it that we can all see its meaning, or at all events catch the human drift of it, not merely the foulness and the reek of blood. If he can do that, he has performed a signal service [that will] speak more eloquently to the minds of thousands than the sermon preached to a hundred in the church on Sunday."

A year after being sent to Mulberry Street by the *Tribune,* Riis's competitiveness, if not altruism, had stimulated an offer to continue covering the police beat for the *Sun.*

By the time Theodore Roosevelt settled into his New York houses in the summer of 1886, the combative Dane had been for the official occupants of police headquarters a familiar presence and the bane of their existence for sixteen years.

Although from dramatically different perspectives—one a wealthy, reform-minded politician and the other a poor reform-minded newspaperman—both looked forward, but on the sidelines, to autumn and the election of a mayor. Of enormous interest and excitement for Riis was the appearance for the first time in New York history of a political party to challenge the Democrats and the Republicans—the United Labor Party. It chose as its candidate a brainy social critic, Henry George, author of *Progress and Poverty.* Published in 1879, the book had proposed a system of taxation of land related directly to speculation in real estate.

As George exhibited signs of garnering a substantial vote, Riis observed, "The world that owned houses and lands and stocks was in a panic. The town was going to be sacked, at the very least. And, in wild dread of the disaster that was coming, men forsook party, principles, everything, and threw themselves into the arms of Tammany, as babies run in fear of the bogey man and hide their heads in their mothers' laps."

To counter the appeal of George's Labor ticket, Tammany Hall turned to a candidate with a relatively enlightened attitude toward the working man, despite the fact that Representative Abram S.

Hewitt was an industrialist. Equally uncomfortable with the idea of a Mayor George and with the unlikely dream that a split in the city's workingmen's vote in a three-way race might let a Republican slip into city hall, Republican leaders astonished everyone in candidate preference, and no one more so than the man to whom they offered the nomination, Theodore Roosevelt.

Believing in duty to his party but convinced he would be engaging in a hopeless contest, he accepted the role and campaigned vigorously against George ("mainly wind," TR called him) and his old nemesis, Tammany. The outcome was a disaster. Hewitt won with 90,552 votes, George tallied 68,110, Roosevelt got 60,435. Worse than coming in third was the realization that a large number of Republicans had ignored party loyalty and deserted him to vote for George.

On Saturday, November 6, 1886, he and his sister Anna sailed for England. Edith Carow was already there. On December 2, "Edie" became his second wife. Their next three years would be taken up by traveling and TR's work on the monumental *The Winning of the West,* his twice-a-year visits to the Dakota ranch (increasingly a failing enterprise), intervals in New York, and becoming parents of Theodore, Jr.

In March 1889, President Benjamin Harrison appointed the boy's father to the Civil Service Commission. That year a second son, Kermit, was born. Two years later came Ethel. Writing one of his frequent "Dear Bamie" letters to Anna from Washington, TR in 1894 described dining out three or four times a week and having people to dinner once or twice "so that we hail the two or three evenings when we are alone at home and can talk or read, or Edith sews while I make ineffective bolts at my third volume [of *The Winning of the West*]."

A few months later, the third son and fifth child was born, Archie. Extremely concerned about family finances, TR wrote to Bamie, "If I can, I shall hold this position [member of the Civil Service Commission] another winter; about that time I shall publish my next two volumes of *The Winning of the West;* I am all at sea as to what I shall do afterwards."

While these activities, a burgeoning family, and ruminations concerning his future occupied him in the nation's capital in the years following his defeat in the contest for the mayoralty, New York City had plunged into the 1890s. In a spirit of exuberance and explosive growth, it looked both outward and upward. The visitor crossing to Manhattan on one of the North River ferries gazed at a city silhouette described with the words "skyline" and "skyscraper." Rising above the low rooftops of tenements and soaring beyond the spires of churches were the tall red tower of the Produce Exchange, the sharp-pointed *Tribune* Tower, and the gold dome of the new Pulitzer Building (home of the *World*). Beyond them ascended the towers of the Brooklyn Bridge, built in 1883, and a symbol of the outward sprawl of a city grown too vast and important to be confined to one narrow island and ready at last to embrace an idea that dated back to 1868. In 1890, a commission had been appointed to look into how to effect a *greater* New York by governmentally amalgamating the city with Brooklyn, Richmond (Staten Island), Queens, and the Bronx.

As pressure grew to stretch New York beyond its encircling rivers, so did the need for more working space to make efficient use of the downtown section of Manhattan, its center of commerce. The answer was to put offices on top of offices. Fortunately, as the need to go up manifested itself, technology kept pace in the form of steel construction and elevators.

Elbowed out by new commercial buildings, residences had to shift uptown, followed by retail merchants and cultural and entertainment amenities. In this increasingly far-flung urban environment, city planners recognized a need for a transportation system. Mayor Thomas F. Gilroy in 1894 complained, "The rapid transit system is no nearer solution than it was two years ago." Appointed to come up with answers, a Rapid Transit Commission promptly sent its engineer, William Barclay Parsons, to spend a year in Europe studying transit systems.

But the greatest problem of the city's future was signified by a new structure on Bedloe's Island in the heart of the upper harbor. Dedicated in the year in which Theodore Roosevelt lost the mayoralty, the Statue of Liberty Enlightening the World had been inscribed with a poem by Emma Lazarus, "Give me your tired, your poor, your huddled masses yearning to breathe free; the wretched refuse of your teeming shores. . . ." At the start of the 1890s, thousands of such people were eager to grab the offer.

Joining the million and a half people already crowded into New York, more than double the number of residents of a quarter century earlier, the new immigrants arrived through another patch of harbor real estate, Ellis Island. It opened its gates for the first time on January 1, 1892. But those who passed through were different from those who preceded them. Before Lady Liberty held up her torch, an overwhelming majority of immigrants (about 85 percent) had hailed from northern and western Europe. Now they were pouring across the Atlantic Ocean from central and southern Europe. Whether Russian Jews or Italians, they set foot in New York invariably poor and headed for their respective ghettos, the Jewish Lower East Side and Little Italy.

A policeman leaving headquarters on Mulberry Street who desired (or had been ordered) to reach either of these teeming neighborhoods required no system of rapid transit. He could walk. So could the reporters of the "police shack" directly across the street, though they did so only in pursuit of a news story with which to shock or titillate readers, usually a ghastly murder. But for the man from the *Sun,* Jacob Riis, a different kind of story drew him to the ghettos.

Going after it in the years immediately after the bridge spanned the East River, and the Statue of Liberty and Ellis Island drew a flood of new faces to the city, he sought to capture his story not only through his skill with words but in the lens of a camera. Mastering photography, he trudged into the ghettos to capture and show to a bustling, burgeoning New York at the start of the 1890s the city's ugly underbelly.

How the Other Half Lives (1890) captured in text and photographs the abysmal existence of those living and working in the tenements. Not since Charles Dickens tramped through the horrors of the Five Points had anyone with a gift for language and image— and a sense of moral outrage—ripped aside the veil that masked the festering reality of New York's poor. Depicting the dark basements and windowless rooms, Riis introduced the world beyond to lodging houses where a bit of floor to sleep on cost five cents a night, a two-room flat was home for an entire family and a lodger, and rooms were factories where tenants shredded tobacco and rolled cigars during waking hours, seven days a week.

Providing photographs of a garment-making sweatshop in "the Hebrew quarter," he wrote, "You are made fully aware of it before you have traveled the length of a single block in any of these East Side streets, by the whir of a thousand sewing machines worked at high pressure from earliest dawn till mind and muscle give out together. Every member of the family, from the youngest to the oldest, bears a hand, shut in the qualmy rooms, where the meals are cooked and clothing washed and dried besides, the live-long day. It is not unusual to find a dozen persons—men, women and children—at work in a single, small room."

The same conditions applied to Little Italy. Running north and south from a twist of direction in Mulberry Street, known as the Bend, or Mulberry Bend, to Houston Street, between Broadway and the Bowery (the western boundary of the Jewish ghetto), the area had been the domain of Irish and blacks and stood almost on the ground of the old Five Points. Snapped by Jake Riis's telling lens, the Bend in 1890 appeared as a narrow, curving cobblestoned roadway lined on both sides with pushcarts and dreary-looking tenements.

Two years after Riis's book appeared, the Italian dramatist Giuseppe Giacosta walked Mulberry Street and observed women in doorways, on the steps of staircases, on little wooden and straw stools, almost in the middle of the street, carrying on all the pursuits of their "pathetic domestic life." He wrote, "They nurse their young, sew, clean the withered greens which are the only ingredient of their soup, wash their clothes in grimy tubs, untangle and arrange one another's hair. They chatter, but not in the happy and playful mood of Naples, but in a certain angry importuning that stings the heart."

Riis's exploration of how this other half lived delved as well into the rampant vice and crime of the ghettos which was within an easy walk for any policeman and, in the case of Little Italy, surrounded police headquarters. He reported on the saloons dispensing pints of beer to small children to tote home for their parents, and countless drunks, derelicts, and gangs eager to prey on anyone who presented a tempting target—all of this within sight of the police and known to politicians if not to the uptown privileged "other half," who not only did nothing about it but profited from it.

As pervasive as sweatshops and saloons, Riis found, was the payoff to the cop and his boss, the crooked politician. Yet none of this was new. Official corruption had not suddenly blossomed in 1890. Assemblyman Theodore Roosevelt's committee on cities had exposed it during the hearings at the Metropolitan Hotel half a dozen years earlier. Nothing had resulted.

Might anything come of Riis's book?

Arriving at the *Evening Sun*'s downtown offices shortly after publication of the book, Riis found someone had left a calling card with a note across the front. Reading the bold signature, he felt a surge of optimism.

"I have read your book," Theodore Roosevelt had written, "and I have come to help."

Riis wrote of receiving the card, "It was like a man coming to enlist for a war because he believed in the cause."

If the cause were to have any chance of succeeding, the first front in the war would have to be opened in Mulberry Street.

Chapter 2

Mulberry Street Blues

A persuasive case can be made that the city of New York began with a swindle. For generations school children have been taught that a slick trick was played on unsuspecting Indians by the director of the Dutch West India Company, Peter Minuit. In 1626 he purchased the island of "Manna-hatin" for sixty guilders worth of trinkets, about twenty-four dollars. What Minuit did not know at the time, however, was that his masterful real estate deal had been struck with the Canarsie tribe, residents of Long Island: they held no title to the land they sold to the Dutch. In due course, the intruders from Amsterdam who thought they had pulled a sharp one on the locals were forced into negotiating a second, more costly deal with the true landlords.

This dubious beginning notwithstanding, the Dutch built at the tip of Manhattan a settlement they called New Amsterdam. To protect it from marauders they built a fortified wall at its northern edge. The settlement flourished, prompting city fathers in 1652 to promulgate an ordinance foreshadowing a problem that would vex succeeding generations for more than three hundred years: reckless traffic. The edict banned speeding. Enforcement of all the laws rested in the hands of a Schout Fiscal, a sheriff/attorney who had power to hang criminals. In 1658 a small force of men was added to patrol the streets at night. Carrying wooden rattles for sounding the alarm, they became the first city police.

Considerably expanded, New Amsterdam and New Netherlands lasted until 1664 when King Charles II of England staged a land grab of his own, bestowing the territory on his brother James, the Duke of York. Forcing the Dutch to hand over the deed and the keys to the city, the Englishmen marched in on September 6, 1664, and promptly changed the name of the place to New York. The following year a new form of local government was installed with a mayor, aldermen, a sheriff, and the English jury system. This government held sway until the army of King George III finally conceded that they had wound up the losers in history's first successful anti-colonial war. They pulled up stakes and sailed home to England in 1783.

Left behind was a population of approximately twenty-five thousand New Yorkers, not all of whom were committed to law-abiding lives. To police them the fledgling city government maintained a nightwatch of twenty-eight men (three shillings per night) under the command of one captain (eight shillings per tour of duty). Additional pay could be earned through a bounty system paying a shilling for each warrant served, arrest made, and defendant conveyed to the jail. They also shared in any fines exacted. Because many of these watchmen had daytime jobs they passed their nightly duty tours sleeping. (Hardly conducive to good police work, napping on the job continued to be a problem for the police department. Three centuries later it was called "cooping" and was not limited to nighttime.)

Should a crime occur in daylight, the matter was handled by a pair of constables in each city ward and a handful of court marshals. Best known of these stalwarts was Jacob Hays. Named High Constable in 1802 by Mayor Edward Livingston and reappointed by each succeeding mayor for nearly fifty years, he amounted to a one-man police force. Particularly skillful at breaking up riots, he cautioned against calling in the army. "If you send for the military," he warned, "they will kill someone, and that will bring trouble; then there will be the trouble of burying them; and that will be the greatest trouble of all." The first recorded detective of the New York police, he also pioneered the use of informants, and maintained a large file on criminals, their habits and their haunts. Police departments across the country sought Hays out for advice and assistance.

With little protection against lawbreakers, post-Revolution New Yorkers watched the crime rate soar. In an attempt to cope, the city raised the bounties paid to its lawmen. When this extra money proved insufficient, concerned citizens appealed to the state legislature to offer even more financial incentives. One proposed that the *esprit* of the police might be improved if the men wore uniforms. In 1820 the symbol of police pride and authority was limited to a hat patterned on the leather headgear of firemen, but with a distinctive identifying badge pinned to it. The public immediately named these officers "Leatherheads." To ensure police authority the force toted a thirty-three-inch club far harder than their hats.

With New York's population burgeoning (350,000 in 1843) and crime keeping pace, a committee of aldermen studied the status of law enforcement and recommended consolidation of the nightwatch, daytime constables, and marshals into a cohesive entity. However, because all these jobs were political appointments, the plan languished for a year until the state legislature passed the Municipal Police Act. The law was due in great measure to the urging of a bookseller who turned vigilante to ward off thieves, and then became a magistrate—George W. Matsell. The act established the New York City Police Department, and Matsell became its first superintendent.

The act also authorized a genuine uniform: a singlebreasted blue frock coat, buttoned to the neck with the initials M.P.—for Municipal Police—and a copper badge, giving rise instantly to the sobriquette "copper." Unfortunately, New Yorkers found the idea of uniformed authority anathema, as Londoners had hated the notion of their metropolitan police dressing up like soldiers. Like the English, many New Yorkers saw in the blue uniform an inviting target. Scores of coppers were attacked and the blue suits were abolished by law after a year.

Contentious attire aside, the new police proved themselves effective in battling the criminal element. At the end of their first six years the unified force of 1,000 men had made 144,364 arrests, including 13,896 for assault and battery; 20,252 for disorderly conduct; 29,190 on drunk-and-disorderly charges; 14,545 pickpockets; 64 murderers; 68 rapists; and 187 on the charge of bastardy. They also had rounded up 11,347 vagrants who apparently elected not to take advantage of a section of the 1845 law permitting indigents to obtain overnight accommodations within police stations.

Although these statistics suggest a city of law and order, the New York of the midnineteenth century was far from a peaceable place. Indeed, there existed sections of the city in which the police dared not venture, no matter the criminal offenses reported. The worst of these neighborhoods was Five Points in the "bloody ould sixth ward," so-named for the intersection of five streets bounded by Broadway, Canal Street, the Bowery, and Park Row. (Ironically, this section of lower Manhattan was later taken over to house city, state, and federal courts and New York City's most famous jail, the Tombs.)

"Let us plunge into the Five Points," wrote Charles Dickens, the English author of *Oliver Twist, Great Expectations,* and *A Christmas Carol,* in *American Notes,* following a tour of America. "This is the place; these narrow ways diverging to the right and left, and reeking everywhere with dirt and filth. Such lives as are led here, bear the same fruit as elsewhere. The coarse and bloated faces at the doors have their counterparts at home and all the whole world over. Here are hideous tenements which take their names from robbery and murder."

Among the places visited by Dickens was Murderer's Alley, a portion of a cesspool of crime and vice centered on a tenement called the Old Brewery. It also housed a room called the Den of Thieves. Stories of horrors abounded. An investigator found in 1850 that no person had been outside the den for more than a week, except to pounce upon and rob an unfortunate passerby. When a child who made the mistake of showing a penny she had begged was murdered, her body lay in a corner of the den for five days before her mother buried it in a shallow grave, without the police ever being notified.

In *The Gangs of New York,* a twentieth-century newspaperman and author, Herbert Asbury, noted, "murders were frequent; it has been estimated that for almost fifteen years the Old Brewery averaged a murder a night" with few of the killers ever punished, "for unless the police came in great force they could not hope to leave the Old Brewery alive."

The Five Points also bred gangs. Swarming among the mean streets and teeming tenements were the Dead Rabbits, Chichesters, Roach Guards, Plug Uglies, and Shirt Tails. Out of them flowed some of the worst criminals of the pre- and post-Civil War years and, later, such twentieth-century gangsters as Al Capone, Lucky Luciano, and Bugsy Siegel. But in 1849 it was a band of toughs led by Isaiah Rynders, known as the Bowery Bhoys, who presented the incipient police force with the greatest challenge to its authority. The test came not in the Five Points but amidst the sedate surroundings of Astor Place. The occasion was a production of Shakespeare's *Macbeth,* starring the distinguished British actor James Macready.

Both outraged that an English actor dared to take the stage in

New York, and nursing a professional grudge, the American star Edwin Forrest unleashed a publicity campaign against Macready. "Workingmen: Shall Americans or English Rule in This City?" asked posters that blossomed all over town. By the date of Macready's debut in "the Scottish play," resentment against him had become rampant. But this animosity was not to be confined to outdoor demonstrations. Somehow, Rynders' Bowery Bhoys got into the Astor Place Theater on the night of May 7, even though Macready was not on the bill. They wreaked havoc.

Consequently, for the English thespian's appearance three evenings later, Superintendent Matsell's police were on hand inside the theater to drag out troublemakers. Because uniforms had been banned by law, and with only their small badges to set them apart from the crowd, the cops proved difficult to discern from the people they were trying to arrest. Delightedly pointing out the rowdies from the stage, Macready held a truncheon of his own.

As word of arrests reached the large, unruly crowd outside, Matsell's three hundred twenty coppers found themselves with a fullscale riot on their hands. Heedless of High Constable Jacob Hays' warning four decades earlier, a panicked Mayor Caleb S. Woodhull called for intervention by the state militia. Pelted with paving stones and anything else within reach of the rioters, the harried soldiers did exactly what Jacob Hays had predicted, opening fire with muskets, at first over the heads of the mob, then point-blank into it. When the smoke cleared twenty-one people lay dead in the street.

Aside from the horrifying realization that people had been killed because of feuding actors, the people of New York faced the distressing realization that in coping with its first riot, the police force had failed. But no one felt more disgraced than the police themselves. Morale plummeted.

Desperate to stem the collapse of pride among the members of the force and hoping to rekindle public confidence, Matsell turned to the controversial issue of uniforms. He felt that uniforms on his men might have helped quell the Astor Place catastrophe. Bolstered by similarly concerned citizens, he pressed the rank and file to accept the idea of uniforms. They refused, until he warned if they did not accept the uniform they would be dropped from the force.

Shown one of the outfits, patterned somewhat on the tunic of Britain's "Bobbies," one of the most recalcitrant cops muttered, "Well, if that be what they call the uniform, it is a first class thing."

The "first class thing" consisted of a blue coat with a velvet collar and nine black buttons, gray trousers with a black leg stripe and a cloth cap. Later, Matsell proposed the black buttons be replaced with brass ones.

"The dress was the first major step in establishing discipline," wrote Gerald Astor in *The New York Cops, An Informal History,* published in 1971. "For the first time the cop was separated from his peers in New York. The pattern of isolation and submission of authority that exists today dates from the acceptance of the uniform. The police department was not simply a rabble of peace keepers; it was an organization of visible symbols."

Evidence of the impact of the uniform, Astor believed, was in the force's arrest record in the next six months, two thousand eight hundred more than the previous half year, for a total of twenty-five thousand. The upturn, Astor wrote, was a result of "the greater pride in work policemen took as a result of the new uniform."

To become a member of the force a man had to be a citizen, able to read and write, know the first four rules of arithmetic, present a doctor's certificate of good health and fitness, have twenty-five character references and, most important, had to receive approval by a committee of three politicians, all of them Democrats serving with the blessing of the political machine known as Tammany Hall.

Founded in 1789 by Aaron Burr and William Mooney, the Society of St. Tammany had been envisioned as a patriotic benevolent club whose goal was to promote democracy. By midnineteenth century it had become a champion of the masses, largely Irish in membership, and the engine driving the Democratic Party. Given the numbers of immigrants living in New York City whose votes Tammany Hall warders could deliver at the polls, the machine dominated municipal government and controlled all patronage. Nowhere in the city was Tammany's grip more iron than in the Police Department.

Deluged with citizen complaints that the cops were a band of corrupt lackeys and "the worst in the world," Republicans in control of the state government in Albany in 1857 reacted by taking over the police. Amending the city charter, they widened the reach of the police by creating a new police district and naming it the metropolitan police, encompassing the counties of New York (Manhattan), Kings (Brooklyn), Richmond (Staten Island) and Westchester (the Bronx). Ordered to disband the municipal police, Tammany's man at city hall, Mayor Fernando Wood, declared the legislation to be un-

constitutional and refused to comply. The state responded by ordering one of its police commissioners, Daniel D. Conover, to arrest the
mayor on charges of inciting to riot and violence.

With a warrant in hand and accompanied by a band of sturdy
Metropolitans, including a tough cop by the name of George Wal-
ling, Conover headed for city hall to do his duty. Awaiting them were
stalwarts of the municipals and a mob of Tammany loyalists. As
described by onlooker George Templeton Strong, a lawyer and diarist, the mayor's force was "a miscellaneous assortment of suckers,
soaplocks, Irishmen and plug-uglies" who hissed and booed the Metropolitans, then waded in with fists and clubs.

Driven back, the metropolitans ran into a bit of luck in the form
of a contingent of the national guard's seventh regiment. With flags
flying, they were on their way to board ships bound for Boston and a
celebration of the anniversary of the Battle of Bunker Hill. In a
matter of minutes they obeyed the orders of their commander, Maj.
Gen. Charles W. Sanford, and altered their route to descend on city
hall. While his troops surrounded it he barged up the steps, into the
mayor's private office and arrested "Fernandy." Who was right?
Courts ruled for Wood. But it was a fleeting victory. The state's
highest tribunal came down on the side of Albany and the municipals passed into history. Meanwhile, until the matter was sorted out
by lawyers and judges, the gangs of Five Points, Hell's Kitchen, and
other pockets of lawlessness ran rampant. By the end of summer
scores of gangsters and others had been killed, including ten in a
pitched battle spanning the July Fourth holiday. The biggest gang
fight in New York City history, it ended only with the recall of the
seventh regiment from Boston. Not until riots protesting the draft
during the Civil War would New York streets be so bloodied.

As peace settled on city streets that autumn, the new police
force numbered a little over one thousand in a sprawling city of
more than eight hundred twenty thousand people, a ratio of one cop
per 804 citizens, and more immigrants pouring in each day to join
the ranks of Tammany.

With state sovereignty secured, the legislature's next step in
imposing its authority over the city police came in 1870 with enactment of a law creating the police department of New York. At its
head would be a board of four commissioners. Appointed by the
mayor, they were to be chosen on the basis of political affiliation
and would each serve a term of six years.

Revisiting the police in 1875, an investigating committee of the state assembly found a dismaying situation in which the crime rate rose, criminals went free, the police got their jobs through political influence, and the general public held the police force in utter contempt. According to a contemporary historian of the department, Augustine Costello, the conception of a policeman was that of "a bloated drunken ugly fellow, who depends on graft and political influence to retain his sinecure situation and who perfunctorily does his 60 minutes to the hour from pay day to pay day and from one blackmailed rum hole to another."

Despite these revelations, the report of the assembly investigation was left to gather dust and the police of the city to continue as before, until May 1884 and the establishment of yet another committee to investigate all the departments of the city government. Its chairman was to be a brash, young Republican prodigy from the twenty-first "silk stocking" district of Manhattan: Theodore Roosevelt.

Chapter 3

"TR is enough."

"I have always had a horror of words that are not translated into deeds, of speech that does not result in action—in other words, I believe in realizing them, in preaching what can be practiced and then in practicing it." Writing these words in his autobiography, Theodore Roosevelt looked back two decades to *How the Other Half Lives* and on its author approvingly. Jacob Riis, he recalled, "had drawn an indictment of the things that were wrong, pitifully and dreadfully wrong, with the tenement homes and the tenement lives of our wage workers."

In 1886 Roosevelt wrote an illuminating essay for *The Century* that amounted to a manifesto for reformers. Entitled "Machine Politics in New York City," it analyzed the power of entrenched political organizations and found that the men "having control and doing all the work have gradually come to have the same feelings about politics that other men have about the business of a merchant or manufacturer; it was too much to expect that if left entirely to themselves they would continue disinterestedly to work for the benefit of others. Many a machine politician who is today a most unwholesome influence in our politics has forgotten that his business affects the state at large, and regards it as merely his own private concern."

As examples Roosevelt cited an assemblyman who had served several terms in the legislature while his private business was to carry on corrupt negotiations between excise commissioners and owners of "low haunts" who wished liquor licenses. The president of a powerful semipolitical association was a professional burglar whose receiver of stolen goods was an alderman. A second alderman had been elected "while his hair was still short from a term in State Prison." A school trustee had a conviction for embezzlement. A prominent official of the police department had received an endorsement in obtaining his appointment to Mulberry Street from politically connected owners of disreputable houses.

When Roosevelt called upon Jacob Riis more than six years after he had conducted the hearings at the Metropolitan Hotel nothing had changed. Boss Croker still called the shots at Tammany. Byrnes, Williams, and the clubbers continued to hold sway at 300 Mulberry Street. The people had not yet grown "a conscience robust enough" to rise up in fury and kick the rascals out. Despite prickings by Roosevelt and Riis, two more years were to go by before any voice upraised in outrage would capture their attention.

When one spoke, at last, in February 1892, the denunciation of the city's evils had issued from the last mouth and the last place Jacob Riis could have expected: Rev. Charles Parkhurst's in the Presbyterian pulpit of a Madison Avenue church. Nor could Riis have predicted, as he went about covering the police and TR returned to Washington and his duties as a member of the Civil Service Commission, that he, the cantankerous police reporter for the *Sun,* would discover a kindred spirit in a newly arrived man from the *Evening Post.*

Welcoming Riis's friendship and tutelage in the intricacies of covering the police in 1893, Lincoln Steffens had found himself amazed that Riis showed little interest in reporting stories that propelled others across Mulberry Street to scoop up all the facts possible from the police. To gather this raw data Riis sent his assistant, Max Fishcel, and often let Max write routine items that Riis deemed appropriate for the pages of the *Evening Sun.* Stories of most interest to Riis, Steffens noticed, were those containing a human interest angle, especially if they contained any semblance of official tyranny, abuses or miseries imposed on the poor of the city by officials and tenement landlords. If he did report a suicide, fire, or murder he wrote his stories with heart and understanding. Having attended the scene of a story of fire or other disaster in the slums of the East Side, Riis looked up the landlord and demanded explanations as to why he permitted such conditions to exist. Not at all interested in vice and crime on which others in the press shack doted, Riis cared deeply about stories of people and the conditions in which they lived.

Steffens recognized this difference between his journalism and Riis's, but never quite as dramatically as in the murder of a woman in Mulberry Bend. Steffens looked at the dead woman, the blood, her wretched tenement apartment, and wrote about the killing as a sketch in which the murderer was saved from being beaten to death by an irate mob of avengers. Riis wrote it as a melodrama with a different villain and a moral. "Mulberry Bend," he said in his story, "must go."

Despite Riis's years of covering the police, Steffens was astonished to discover that Riis was naive about one aspect of human behavior, which presented itself one morning in the form of Max roaring up the stairs of 303 Mulberry after a routine check of the night's activities by the police.

"There was a big raid on a bunch of fairies," Max bellowed.

Riis blinked with amazement. "Fairies?"

"They raided one of the fairies' resorts last night," said Max, breathlessly.

"Fairies," Riis exclaimed in disgust. He threw down his pencil and strode from the office, leaving the story to Max Fischel to write.

That there had been a raid on a secret gathering place for homosexuals, Steffens noted in his autobiography, was attributable to "a failure of someone to come through with the regular bit of blackmail" required to ensure the "fairies'" premises were protected by the police. "So with prostitution, so with beggars, so with thieves," Steffens said.

Among the lessons the younger reporter gleaned from the old warhorse of Mulberry Street was that newspapers, literature, and public opinion did not always picture men and life as they were. Living proof was found in the person of Rev. Parkhurst. Picking up Monday morning papers containing accounts of his latest sermon demanding that the police enforce laws forbidding the sale of alcohol on Sundays, an amazed Lincoln Steffens read descriptive reports and caricatures of Dr. Parkhurst that depicted him as a wild man, ridiculous, sensational, unscrupulous, or plain crazy. Rather, Steffens found him to be "a tall, slim, smiling gentleman, quiet, determined, fearless and humorous." Asking himself if the other papers might be right and if he had gotten the Parkhurst story wrong, Steffens sought out Riis.

Picking up his hat, Riis said, "Let's go over and have a talk with Byrnes."

A few minutes later, the Superintendent of Police paced the floor of his office in evident consternation. Halting in front of Riis, he demanded, "Is the *Sun* backing Parkhurst? I know the *Post* is, but as I read the *Sun* . . ."

"Never mind the *Sun*," snapped Riis. "Say what you are going to do about Parkhurst's charges about the unwillingness of your men to close down illegal saloons. That's the news of the day. The *Sun* prints the news."

Byrnes bristled. "Come back at two o'clock."

Returning on the dot, Riis and Steffens found Byrnes in his office in full uniform. Before him at attention stood an array of inspectors. Without a look in the direction of Riis and Steffens he addressed his top policemen sternly. "Did I not command you last Monday on this very spot in this same office to enforce the letter of the laws regulating the saloons in this city and to close them one and all at the legally fixed hours for closing?"

The inspectors remained silent.

Crouching low before them, his fists balled, Byrnes cried, "Well, and what I want to know now is, did youse did it?"

Although Steffens knew Byrnes to be an uneducated man who had emigrated from Ireland and had struggled to learn to speak English well, he could not suppress amusement at the lapse in Byrnes's syntax. He snorted a laugh.

Byrnes unbent and turned in fury toward Steffens. "Get out of here!" As Steffens headed for the door, Byrnes glared at Riis. "Both of you."

Riis followed Steffens out, both chuckling.

The following Saturday night, many saloons shut their doors in compliance with the law. But not all. As Steffens saw it, the saloon owners, not the police, had decided which were to close and which to remain open. For the next few weeks he noted that different saloons seemed systematically to obey and disobey the law. He observed few raids by the police on the establishments and none on the most notorious watering holes.

"Why were these lawbreakers so strong?" he asked. Why was there such an opposition to what he deemed the simple, superficial reforms demanded by Parkhurst? As the minister forced such results as the voluntary closing of some saloons, he was hated more and more openly by people whom Steffens expected to approve: bankers, businessmen, and even other clergymen.

Deeply puzzled, he turned to one of the men he had gotten to know when he had covered Wall Street. James D. Dill's reply was a hard kick in the shin. With Steffens howling in pain, Dill asked, "Why does your mouth cry out when only your shin is hurt?"

In Dill's reply Steffens realized that decent people of the city who agreed with Parkhurst were afraid he was going to so undermine confidence in public institutions that the entire city would be hurt. Furthermore, what had the minister offered in the way of proof to justify kicking the city in the shin?

Denouncing Parkhurst's allegations as "the most vindictive utterance from the pulpit I have ever heard," District Attorney De Lancey Nicoll posed the same question to Parkhurst before a grand jury. Unable to present specific evidence of the charges he had made in his sermons, Parkhurst felt the sting of the grand jury's presentment on March 1, 1892. It expressed "disapproval and condemnation of unfounded charges . . . which can only serve to create a feeling of unwarranted distrust in the minds of the community with regard to the integrity of public officials."

Vowing to "never again be caught in the presence of the enemy without powder and shot in my gun-barrel," Parkhurst took the rebuke as "severe schooling." Rather than capitulate to "a whole jungle of teeth-gnashing brutes" he made up his mind that "it was a question of whether the hunter was going to bag the game or the game make prey of the hunter."

Determined to collect the evidence he had lacked before the grand jury, he hired a former police detective, Charles Gardner, and enlisted the aid of a young member of the congregation, John Erving, to conduct him, like Dante, into the Inferno he had tried to describe from the pulpit.

A tall, good-looking blond and society dandy, young Erving provided suitable clothing to disguise the clergyman as a man out for a good time around town. Leaving Gardner's West Eighteenth Street apartment on the night of Saturday, March 5, 1892, they set out for Tom Summers' Saloon on Cherry Street. Sipping whiskey, Parkhurst watched small girls buy liquor at ten cents a pint to take home to their parents. Later the trio of undercover investigators arrived at a bordello at 342 Water Street where the Reverend managed to fend off the implorings of two persistent prostitutes. Still later he narrowly escaped being dragged upstairs in a second whorehouse by a two hundred-pound woman who begged him to call her Baby.

Four nights later the triumvirate explored the bar of the East River Hotel at Water and Catherine Street and observed a pair of on-duty uniformed cops imbibing intoxicants, compliments of the management. Parkhurst discreetly jotted down their badge numbers. Then he ordered a round for the house, providing drinks for the sixteen patrons and running up a tab of eighty cents.

Subsequent excursions carried the minister and his knowing guides to the Bowery and into "tight houses," so-called because the women in them wore tights. Strolling along Mulberry Street within sight of police headquarters, they resisted invitations from no less than fifty streetwalkers. Retreating to a saloon on Third Avenue, Parkhurst got the scare of his life by being greeted by an old chum from Amherst, but Parkhurst's fright was surpassed by the owner of the place. Recognizing the minister's name, he immediately ordered him and his companions to get out.

Said Parkhurst to Gardner as they emerged to the street, "Show me something worse."

Gardner commenced a whirlwind tour of dens of iniquity distinguished one from the other by the nationality or race of those who ran or worked in them. Chinatown offered gambling on the game of fan-tan and an opium den in which a white man and his Chinese wife shared smoking of the narcotic with their eight-year-old son. A section around Sullivan and West Houston Streets was known as Coontown. Frenchtown bordered on Washington Square and offered block after block of houses of ill-fame.

On West Third Street stood an establishment that especially irked the disguised clergyman, the Golden Rule Pleasure Club. But the sacreligious name proved far less scandalous to him than the club's patrons, young men with rouged faces and dressed as women.

On his final night out Parkhurst had to travel only three blocks from his church to inspect a bawdyhouse operated by Hattie Adams. Gardner paid fifteen dollars for three of Hattie's eight girls to dance for them. Having completed their terpsichore, they stripped naked and played leapfrog while Rev. Parkhurst quietly sipped beer in a corner. Leaving Hattie's, they visited a "French circus" on West Fourth Street where Parkhurst observed "the most brutal, the most horrible exhibition" he had ever seen.

The following Sunday he took to the pulpit bearing affidavits from Gardner and Erving attesting to their adventures, naming thirty houses of prostitution in the Nineteenth Precinct alone. In a voice brimming with revulsion he told his riveted congregation, "Many a long, dismal, heart-sickening night, in company with two

trusty friends, have I spent . . . going down into the disgusting
depths of this Tammany-debauched town. And it is rotten with a
rottenness . . . that would be absolutely impossible, except by the
connivance, not to say the purchased sympathy, of the men whose
one obligation before God, men, and their own conscience, is to
shield virtue and make vice difficult. To say that the police . . . who
are paid nearly five million dollars a year . . . do not know what is
going on is rot."

Addressing himself to his critics, he cried, "You have been winc-
ing under the sting of a general indictment and have been calling
for the particulars. This morning I have given you the particulars—
two-hundred and eighty-four of them. Now, what are you going to do
with them?"

Many parishioners felt disgust, not with their minister's evidence, but with what he had done to obtain it. Newspapers, including Riis's *Sun* (to his consternation), turned on Parkhurst for in-
stigating and paying for obscene performances.

The authorities reacted by doing nothing, refusing to issue warrants that Parkhurst demanded they serve on the keepers of disorderly houses and other dens of vice. When a grand jury was convened it offered only the *opinion* that the police force might be
either incompetent or corrupt. "The general efficiency of the Department is so great," the grand jurors' lengthy report lamely
stated, "that it is our belief that the latter suggestion is the explanation of the peculiar inactivity."

The grand jury handed up only two indictments—of bordello
madams, not of police or city officials.

Though he never ventured again into saloons and whorehouses,
Parkhurst remained undaunted and unrelenting, railing for nearly
two more years against the alliance between the underworld, the
police, and Tammany. Ultimately as public opinion mounted behind
the Parkhurst campaign, leaders of the Republican legislature in
Albany smelled blood in the political waters. They announced the
establishment of a committee to investigate the police. However,
their motive appears to have been less than fully public spirited.
Republican boss Thomas Platt may have been trying to get even
with Tammany boss Dick Croker for freezing Republicans out of
their customary patronage after the 1892 municipal election. Platt
also nursed resentment of Croker's refusal to back a bill in the

legislature to create a bipartisan police commission that would have let the Republicans step up to the trough.

Whatever his motive, Platt authorized a probe of Parkhurst's allegations. Appointed to head the committee was State Senator Clarence Lexow of Nyack, a Columbia law graduate and holder of a Ph.D. from the University of Jena. The body would consist of five Republicans, an "independent" Democrat, and one Tammany appointee. Counsel for the committee was to be John W. Goff. As a lawyer with impeccable credentials and not a whiff about him of political chicanery, he was the personal choice of Parkhurst.

Lexow gaveled the committee into session on March 9, 1894, in the third floor chamber of the Court of Common Pleas, Part III. At 52 Chambers Street, the New York County Courthouse had been built by Boss Tweed and was doomed to bear that ignominious name in perpetuity. The hearings would be held in two stages, lasting all the way to Christmas.

A decade had gone by since a similar committee chaired by Theodore Roosevelt had settled down to business at the Metropolitan Hotel. During those years the population of the city had swelled to almost two million. Ranks of the police, who prided themselves on the self-appointed sobriquette "the Finest," numbered four thousand.

After taking testimony concerning election irregularities attributable to either malfeasance, nonfeasance, or outright unlawfulness on the part of the police, the committee turned to the subject that most interested the flock of reporters who represented city newspapers practicing "yellow journalism." In a steady and colorful stream appeared men and women associated with the vices that Parkhurst had witnessed firsthand.

Early in the procession came brothel-keeper Charles Priem. Had he ever paid money to the police so as to avoid being raided?

"Oh God, yes," Priem responded, rolling his eyes and provoking laughter in the audience.

At first the payoff had been twenty-five dollars a month. Then the "rent" doubled. When a Captain Cassidy left for another precinct and was replaced by Captain Adam Cross a raid was pulled— the only one in Priem's six years in business. A payment of five hundred dollars to Cross assured no more trouble, providing the fifty-dollar stipend was paid monthly. With the naming of Captain

William Devery to succeed Cross, another five hundred dollars changed hands.

Was Priem still in business?

He was not, he said. Because of "the Parkhurst trouble," the police had suggested he desist. However, he told the committee, he expected to resume business as soon as the investigation was over. The audience tittered with delight at the brazen honesty.

A pair of madams followed Priem to deny they had ever paid the police. But the next witness, Augusta Thurow, testified to paying five dollars a month to the collector for the police for each girl employed in her establishment.

When committee counsel Goff greeted another bordello keeper, Matilda Hermann, with, "I am very glad to meet you," Matilda retorted, "I am very *sorry* to meet you, Mr. Goff."

Day after day the committee listened to tales of official corruption across the spectrum of human vice. With groundwork laid, the panel summoned the second most famous personality in the department, Inspector Alexander S. Williams.

When queried about his selective closings of disorderly houses while in command of the Tenderloin district, the cop who claimed to have taught more law breakers the lesson of the night stick than anyone on the force, replied, "I proceeded against some of the eighty-three disorderly houses in my precinct, but I made no attempt to close them all."

Goff asked, "Why?"

"Well, they were fashionable."

"Then you, the police officer charged with carrying out the laws, and paid by the people for so doing, say that you left the houses open because they were fashionable?"

"Yes," said Williams, flatly.

An astonished Chairman Lexow interjected, "Don't you know that that is an extraordinary answer?"

"Well," said Williams, "I haven't any other."

Deciding to freely admit what everyone knew, Clubber told the committee about his bulging bank accounts, a home in the city, a mansion in Connecticut and ownership of a yacht.

How had he managed all this on his salary?

He said with a straight face that he had been fortunate in speculating on some "lots" of real estate in Japan.

Calling Superintendent Thomas Byrnes to the third floor of the

Tweed courthouse, the members of the committee looked upon a pillar of policing, renowned and respected all over the world, yet under a cloud. Of Byrnes the Rev. Parkhurst had declared, "Either he was acquainted with the character of the police force or he was not acquainted with it. If he was not acquainted with it he stands thereby convicted of base negligence or of colossal incompetence. If he was acquainted with it, his assault upon our efforts to improve the force was sneaking, vicious and malignant."

The committee wished to hear how Byrnes, with the assistance of Wall Street financier Jay Gould and others, had acquired some three hundred fifty thousand dollars in securities and real estate. Byrnes's explanation was tortured and unsatisfying, but nonincriminating. In four days of testimony the most the committee managed to wring from him was an admission that it was a custom of the police department to tolerate gambling dens, brothels, and illegal saloons so long as the police shared in the profits. However, he could provide the committee with no personal knowledge of such abuses by anyone under his command, he said.

If the chief of police did not know what had been going on under his nose, suggested the *World,* he was not a good enough detective to detect Limburger cheese without eating it.

Returning to Mulberry Street, Byrnes left the spotlight to a cop who knew chapter and verse of the gospel of corruption in the police as well as the Rev. Parkhurst could quote from the Holy Bible. Tall, rosy-faced, and wearing the uniform of Captain as he strode into the courtroom, Captain Max Schmittberger seemed to be the epitome of the American Dream come true. Born of poor German immigrant parents in Hoboken, New Jersey, he had apprenticed as a pastry cook and would have been happy in that profession. But one day a customer who happened to be a Tammany leader suggested that the strapping youth would fit well into a policeman's uniform.

"It won't cost you a cent, either," said the Tammany man, though Schmittberger did not understand at that time that there was a price for an appointment to the force. Should a cop seek to advance to a higher rank he would learn that he was expected to pay again. In the event his ambition included becoming Captain at an annual pay of two thousand seven hundred fifty dollars the price began at twelve thousand dollars. Neither did Schmittberger know then that, having attained a captaincy, such an individual could rely on recouping the money rapidly through the department's exceedingly well-organized system of bribe-seeking and blackmail. For anyone able to buy his way to the rank of Inspector, the initial cost might reach twenty thousand dollars, a sum easily earned back from whoremasters like Priem and madams like Matilda. But all that was the future as Schmittberger took up the Tammany man's suggestion and applied to the police.

For the examination required of applicants by law and police regulations, he crammed with a Tammany tutor and passed easily. Because of his good looks he found himself assigned to a highly visible post in the middle of busy Broadway and Thirty-fourth Street in the heart of the Tenderloin. There, his cleancut figure invariably persuaded citizens that, with such a fine young man in the ranks, the police department could never be less than an upright and righteous guardian of decency and the law.

"They used to put in good words for me with my captain," Max would recall for Lincoln Steffens years later. "Gosh, but I did like being a policeman."

Presently assigned to a night beat in "the colored quarter," the eager and enthusiastic patrolman liked the activity and enjoyed watching "the niggers" sing and dance—though by the end of the night some of them "cut one another with razors." One night soon after the new posting he was amazed when a girl dashed out of a house, blurted, "Here, officer," and pressed a ten-dollar bill into his hand. Astonished and puzzled, he reported the incident to a veteran officer at the end of the tour of duty.

"Don't you see," said the older cop with a wink, "that's what the captain put you on that fat job for, to make a little on the side. That girl works in a cat house. That ten bucks is your monthly cut for looking the other way."

Incredulously, Schmittberger muttered, "The captain knows about this?"

"He knows everything, knows what every post in the precinct is worth. His putting you where you are shows he likes you and wants to feed you up. He thinks you're too damned skinny."

Suspecting he was being toyed with, Schmittberger took the ten dollars to the captain and reported how it had been gotten. Told to keep it, the naive and idealistic policeman thus began his education in the system of payments, bribery, and blackmail that were the bedrock of the department. In due course he found himself promoted to ward man, a supervisory position with the added responsibility

of collecting graft for the precinct's captain from gamblers, prostitutes, saloons, and all the other lawbreakers who desired and had
the cash to stay in business.

In going along with the system and being good at it, he rose to
the official rank of captain and the unofficial role as collector in
Inspector Alexander Williams' Tenderloin. Covering an area from
Fifth to Ninth Avenues between Twenty-eighth and Forty-eighth
Streets, it encompassed theaters and vaudeville houses, hotels, restaurants, saloons, the best gambling "resorts," and the top of the
line in houses of prostitution—all prepared to pay the police to
operate without encumbrances of any kind.

So subtle and incremental had been this immersion in the environment of corruption, from that first ten dollars to the thousands
he had collected through the years, that in the view of Lincoln
Steffens, Schmittberger "never realized what he was doing until the
Lexow Committee exposed him to himself."

One day at police headquarters as the Lexow Committee produced shock after shock, Schmittberger saw the light. He grumbled,
"They've got us." A few days later he sat before the committee and
hit the investigators, the public, and the press on the third floor of
the Tweed courthouse with the first in a bombardment of shells that
exploded during several days of shocking admissions.

He described having been ordered as an up-and-coming cop to go
into all the barrooms, gambling houses, and whorehouses on his
beat to collect and sometimes force payment of bribe money for
protection. Frequently amounting to twenty-thousand dollars a
month, the cash was counted by him and his precinct captain, who
then divvied it into sacks for the precinct inspector and the two ward
men. Lower ranks were expected to gather their own loot, as Schmittberger learned in the form of his first "tip."

Gratuities were also received openly in the station house, he
testified, pressed into the hungry hand of the sergeant. Later in the
"fat" precinct of Alexander Williams' Tenderloin, the take for Clubber and Captain Schmittberger was enormous.

"THE CROWNING EXPOSURE," blared one newspaper. "ALL
THE CITY EXCITED," headlined another. In smaller print a third
declared, "Frightful Revelations About Our Commissioners, Inspectors and Captains." One bannered, "A Flood Of Light On Williams."

"Schmittberger's amazing revelations were the talk of the town
last night," reported the *Tribune*. "In the hotel corridors, the social

clubs, the political organizations, the theaters, the fine cafes in the fashionable streets and avenues and rumshops and 'dives' of the East and West side—every place in the city where people come together the one topic of discussion was the shocking confession."

Through seventy-four sessions, 10,576 pages of testimony, and 678 witnesses lasting almost a year the Lexow Committee presented a mosaic of personal and institutional corruption. The famous men of the police force had been exposed. Besides Chief Thomas Byrnes and Inspector Alec Williams, they included former Police Chief Joe Murray and Captains William McLaughlin and William Devery.

New Yorkers studying the report found themselves gazing in disbelief at an exhibit consisting of the police department's "budget." In addition to the government's official appropriation of $5,139,147.64, the department counted on brothel contributions of $8,120,000.00; saloon contributions of $1,820,000.00; gambling house receipts totalling $165,000.00; collections from merchants, peddlers, and others to the tune of $50,000.00; and $60,000.00 in fees squeezed from new members of the force. These sums brought the grand total to $15,354,147.64.

Public disgust at this sordid portrait of greedy police had become evident even before the Lexow hearings adjourned. It was, said Lincoln Steffens, "like a fire." Long in advance of Captain Max Schmittberger's confession the Council of Good Government Clubs had called for a public protest meeting at the Madison Square Garden Concert Hall on the evening of September 6, 1894. It drew three hundred outraged citizens and ended with the formation of a "Committee of Seventy" to coordinate a nonpartisan effort to oust Tammany in the November mayoral election.

"The time has come for a determined effort to bring about such a radical and lasting change in the administration of the City of New York as will ensure the permanent removal of the abuses from which we suffer," proclaimed a broadside issued by the new committee.

Who was the individual to lead such a crusade? In looking for him, more than one set of reform-minded eyes gazed longingly toward Washington, D.C., to the last individual to have twisted the Tammany Tiger's tail: Theodore Roosevelt. That he remained committed to local reform was apparent in an essay that he contributed to *The Forum* in July. "Sometimes, in addressing men who sincerely desire the betterment of our public affairs," he wrote, "I feel tempted to tell them that there are two gospels which should be preached to every reformer. The first is the gospel of morality; the second is the gospel of efficiency. The men who wish to work for decent politics must work practically, and yet must not swerve from their devotion to a high ideal."

Readers of the essay interpreted it as Roosevelt's way of declaring his availability as a candidate for mayor. Compared to Lumuel Quigg, these TR enthusiasts were Johnny-come-latelies. The savvy New York congressman and member of the Committee of Seventy had already begun plumbing the possibility of Roosevelt leaving the Civil Service Commission to try for City Hall.

TR promptly reminded his friend Quigg, "I have run once."

In August a family tragedy overshadowed thoughts of local politics when TR's beloved but alcoholic brother Elliott suffered an epileptic fit and died. Less than a month later TR headed West on a hunting excursion. But only two weeks passed before he was back on Sagamore Hill in Oyster Bay, depressed, ill, and beset again by pleadings from friends and hopeful civic reformers like Lem Quigg that he run. However, one voice speaking out forcefully against the idea, largely for financial reasons, was the one most able to sway him, his wife's.

Though he wished to run and believed not running would prove to be a political mistake, he heeded Edith's wishes. His reason for turning down the candidacy that he provided to his political allies, such as Henry Cabot Lodge, was that he simply did not have the funds to run. The Republicans turned to a banker and dry-goods merchant with ample finances but no political experience: William Strong.

"He was the good businessman who would throw out the rascally politicians and give us a good business administration," wrote Lincoln Steffens approvingly. Sharing the ticket with Strong as candidate for city recorder would be John Goff, the Lexow Committee's brass-knuckled counsel. The team beat Tammany's slate by more than forty-two thousand votes.

Headlined the *Times*, "The Tammany Tiger Has Been Flayed Alive." According to Steffens, however, Boss Dick Croker regarded any obituary for Tammany as premature. Throwing an arm around Steffens' shoulder as the anti-Tammany votes came in, Croker said, "One trip of inquiry into any Tammany ward would have told you that Tammany voters were going to vote against us this year. Our people could not stand the rotten police corruption. They'll be back at the next election. They can't stand reform either."

The next day as Steffens walked into police headquarters he encountered Clubber Williams. Holding newspaper stories of the big victory for the reformers, the policeman who embodied all they despised glared at Steffens with hate in his eyes. Through a sneer the inspector demanded of the man from the *Post*, "Well, are you satisfied now?"

Recognizing that Williams was still in uniform, still a member of the force, and would be until Strong took office on the first of January 1895 and appointed a new board of commissioners to clean up 300 Mulberry Street and run men like Williams out of it, Steffens replied, "Not yet."

Turning to his closest associates in matters having to do with the police—Parkhurst and Riis—Steffens suddenly found a dichotomy where there had been unity in thinking. Dr. Parkhurst worried deeply about the structure of the police under the new mayor. He suspected Strong would not live up to the promise of his name and show the strength needed to avoid making deals that might compromise reform in Mulberry Street. The test of Strong's will, Parkhurst believed, would come in the appointments he made to the four-member police commission.

Under the now repudiated Tammany regime the board members had been nothing more than figureheads who received their posts through deal-making between Tammany's Boss Croker and Republican boss Tom Platt. Only loyal machine men got the jobs, evenly divided between the parties. "They had full power under the law," wrote Steffens, "but actually they had nothing to do with anything but routine expenditures and details of policy. The uniformed police governed themselves in cahoots with certain politicians and associations of liquor dealers, gamblers and other lawbreakers."

If the Lexow Committee's work was not to become an exercise in futility, the nature of the police board would have to undergo a dramatic change.

"Everybody was pulling and hauling upon (Strong) to do this or not do that, to name this man and not to name the other," said Steffens. "The police board he had to appoint was the bone of contention among the groups who thought and said they had 'made him mayor.'"

Complicating the matter, the Republican legislature had made up its mind to drastically amend the state law under which the New

York Police Department was organized. Furthermore, Albany had in mind enacting the Power of Removal Act to facilitate dismissal of Tammany department heads. Until these matters were ironed out in the legislature, whoever Mayor Strong appointed to the board of police commissioners faced a period of uncertainty until the new laws took effect.

These factors, and the bidding for Strong's attention on the matter of police board appointments, troubled Parkhurst. But in Jacob Riis, Steffens discovered a single and simple mind on the question of who should run the show in Mulberry Street. For Riis there could be only one: Theodore Roosevelt.

However, the Mayor-elect had a different job in mind for TR. Shortly before Christmas, 1894, he asked Roosevelt to become his Street Cleaning Commissioner.

Roosevelt declined the invitation, although exactly how he expressed the decision to Strong is not known; TR's reply does not survive. But he stated in his autobiography, "I did not feel that I had any especial fitness."

In a letter to Riis he made it clear there had been aspects of the street-cleaning commissionership that had tempted him. "I would have been delighted to smash up the corrupt contractors, and put the street-cleaning force absolutely out of the domain of politics," he wrote. Although it would be admirable if New York were to have clean streets, "indeed, it is an essential thing to have them," he penned to the author of *How the Other Half Lives,* "but it would be a better thing to have our schools large enough to give ample accommodation to all who should be pupils and to provide them with proper playgrounds . . . to take the children off the streets so as to prevent them from growing up toughs."

The job of running the street-cleaning department would go to Colonel George F. Waring, a man of sterling reputation with a background in engineering and more than acceptable to Riis's reform spirit.

In turning down the street-cleaning department Roosevelt kept alive in the heart of Riis the vision of Riis's favorite politician running the police department. To Steffens' fretting over the four men Strong would choose to head the police and purge the force of Clubber Williams and others like him, Riis asserted, "Roosevelt is the man for president of the police board, and God will attend to his appointment. I do not care who the other commissioners are. TR is enough!"

Chapter 4

The Gospel According to Teddy

With its Louis XVI pillasters between arched windows, New York's graceful City Hall, designed in the postcolonial style by Joseph F. Mangin and John McComb, had been completed in 1811 after ten years of work and a cost of half a million dollars. Before noon on Tuesday, January 1, 1895, the last Republican to raise his hand on its marble front steps and take the oath of office as Mayor of New York had been George Opdyke in 1861. Now that rare distinction descended upon the shoulders of the lushly mustachioed and full-bearded William Lafayette Strong. A gentleman of grace and Christian fellowship, he lauded his Tammany predecessor, Thomas H. Gilroy, whose administration had just been repudiated, as "the best presiding officer I have ever met."

As Strong greeted and shook hands with hundreds of well-wishers to the point that his fingers were rubbed raw, the individual who might have stood on city hall's steps and gotten a sore hand remained in the nation's snowy capital, by his own admission, eating and drinking too much, but thoroughly enjoying dealing with "big interests and big men."

As a member of the Civil Service Commission and presenting a dashing figure with his robust physique, nose-glasses, mustache, enormous smile, and colorful background as frontiersman and author, TR found himself a much-sought-after prize guest on Washington's circuit of dinners, breakfasts, balls, and receptions. When not engaged socially or in dealing with Civil Service reformation he continued the writing of *The Winning of the West,* Volume IV, and collaborated with friend Henry Cabot Lodge on a book for boys,

Hero Tales From American History. Always on the lookout for new aspects of what he called "the strenuous life," he took up skiing. In less energetic hours he dropped in at the Cosmos Club to debate and lecture on politics, world affairs, nature, sports, and literature.

Among his rapt audience on one occasion was Rudyard Kipling. Curled up on the seat opposite, he "listened and wondered until the universe seemed to be spinning around and Theodore was the spinner." When the author of *Plain Tales From the Hills, Soldiers Three,* and *Gunga Din* took the United States to task for its brutal treatment of its native Indians, Roosevelt countered by thanking God that he, Roosevelt, did not have "one drop of British blood" in him. Disagreements notwithstanding, he delighted in showing Kipling grizzly bears at the zoo and introducing him to his own literary and political friends. Commenting to Roosevelt on the state of politics in New York City, Kipling noted TR's hometown seemed to have a government of the worse elements of the population, tempered by occasional insurrections by its respectable citizens. (One imagines TR responding with a booming laugh and "Dee-lightful.")

Keeping in touch with the current "insurrection" through correspondence from New York friends and the newspapers, he could not escape the fact that "respectable citizens" expressed their opinion and hope that Theodore Roosevelt's name might appear on the list of prospective police commissioners being considered by Strong to replace Charles H. Murray and Gen. Michael Kerwin, two holdover Republicans whom the reform movement expected to be removed. Despite the fact that Murray's term was not due to expire until May 1, 1900, and Kerwin's had another year to run, Strong had pledged to replace them with his own men, although Murray, Kerwin, and others insisted Strong did not have legal authority to do so without a revision of the law by the state legislature. Republicans in Albany promptly provided the authority, although, as will be seen, they lived to regret it.

When Strong announced on April 2 that one of the positions had been offered to Edward Mitchell, the United States District Attorney, a reporter turned to the second Republican seat on the board and asked Strong, "Have you communicated with Civil Service Commissioner Roosevelt upon the subject?"

"No, I have not communicated yet with Mr. Roosevelt," the mayor replied.

Taking note of the word "yet," the *New York Times* in its story the next day said, "The Mayor said this in a way that led those who heard him to believe that Mr. Roosevelt would be asked to take the other place."

On the same day (April 2) the *Times'* man in Washington put the question directly to Roosevelt. Would he confirm that he had received a letter from Strong offering him a commissionership?

"I have not received such a letter," Roosevelt replied. "There is nothing in the matter."

The following day the *Times* ran a story on the question and answer under a headline that could be interpreted as rhetorical or as an endorsement: "IF NOT MR. ROOSEVELT, WHO?"

The article reported Roosevelt's friends as saying "he would much prefer to retain his office in the Civil Service Commission, which is much to his liking."

Most of TR's friends believed this to be true; however, the man who had declined Lemuel Quigg's invitation to leave the Civil Service Commission to run for mayor in 1894 was not as happy in his work as he appeared to be. Despite vigorous efforts to win extension of the civil service in the federal government he had met considerable frustration. Always a controversial figure, he had become embroiled in several contentious situations under the two presidents who appointed him, Benjamin Harrison and Grover Cleveland. "As far as my own work is concerned," he said, "the two Administrations are much of a muchness."

Only a few days before the *Times* had composed its ambiguous headline, "If not Mr. Roosevelt, who?" TR let Lemuel Quigg know he would like to become one of the Mulberry Street commissioners. And on the very day of the *Times'* headline and story, April 3, he sent a wire telling Quigg that Henry Cabot Lodge would be coming to see him to confirm that he would "accept subject to honorable conditions" appointment to the Board of Police Commissioners.

He added, superfluously, for Lemuel Ely Quigg was not a politician to prematurely reveal a wining hand, "Keep this strictly confidential." It did not matter. Both New York and Washington were alive with speculation and rumor, buzzed about as fact.

Five days later, Mayor Strong at last got around to "communicating" with Roosevelt. "I am about to appoint two Republican police commissioners in place of Messrs. Murray and Kerwin," he stated, "and your name has been suggested to me by many of your friends as a suitable person for that position, and I write to know if you would like to have me consider your name favorably."

Yes, indeed, he would like it, TR replied.

Writing to his sister Anna, he looked through the glass of his future darkly and with remarkable prescience. "I shall have, if I go, much hard work. Moreover, it is a position in which it is absolutely impossible to do what will be expected of me; the conditions will not admit it. I must make up my mind to much criticism and disappointment."

These were not maudlin cliches, for in April, 1895, no man in America appreciated the depth and breadth of the problems besetting New York and other large American cities more than Theodore Roosevelt. Nor had anyone become more prominent in a movement for "reform" that had swept the country in the shape of nearly two hundred local reform associations, calling themselves the National Municipal League. In 1894 he had addressed the Philadelphia convention of the National Conference for Good City Government. His subject, as passionately discussed as any sermon by Parkhurst, had been the gospels of "efficiency" and "morality." Bad men and bad systems, he preached, were the root of the corruption of civic virtue. To prevent the bad men from running things, he said, it was necessary that citizens demand merit as a condition for government service and reject patronage and political "pull."

So respected and renowned was he that a British scholar, diplomat, and social reformer, James Bryce, consulted him in the writing of *The American Commonwealth,* a study of conditions in American cities, published in 1888. "There is no denying that the government of cities is the one conspicuous failure of the United States," Bryce asserted, citing "extravagance, corruption and mismanagement" as the reason why he found "not a city with a population exceeding 200,000 where these poison germs have not sprung into a vigorous life."

Two years after Bryce's book, when Jacob Riis presented *How the Other Half Lives,* TR had dashed to the *Sun* to slap onto the crusading newspaperman's desk his calling card and the pledge, "I have come to help." Now, in 1895, he saw an opportunity to do so, however risky the task might prove, and to correct his mistake in not taking up Lemuel Quigg's offer to run for mayor himself the previous November. That he had erred mightily he had admitted to Henry Cabot

Lodge. He told his trusty friend and advisor he would literally have given his right arm to make the race, win or lose. But he had felt he had no choice but to forgo "the golden chance, which never returns," because of his wife's opposition. Now, in making himself available for a membership on the Board of Police Commissioners, he saw a second chance; perhaps not golden, but certainly precious.

Pleas with friends for confidentiality notwithstanding, the imminent appointment of Roosevelt as police commissioner pervaded both New York and Washington. But the deal had not yet been done. As much as he wanted the position, TR insisted on a few conditions. Acceptance depended on "decent colleagues." The mayor promised "first rate men . . . suited to your taste in every way."

When might the deed be done? Strong intimated a starting date of May first. Accordingly, TR informed President Cleveland of his intentions in a letter of resignation dated April 17, but not to be announced immediately. One week later the *New York Times* reported "on the authority of statements from New York" and a "report from Washington" that, in the unequivocal words of a front-page headline, "He will be police commissioner." A second banner added, for the record, "He refuses to confirm or deny." Citing an unnamed "close friend of Mr. Roosevelt," the story below quoted the source as saying "in two days at the outside (Roosevelt) would announce his decision."

A sidebar biography of TR described him as an "affable and gifted author, field sportsman, and legislator," a reformer who proved himself to be "conspicuously able." After a listing of his governmental positions and accomplishments, the newspaper noted that the thirty-seven-year-old "explorer, hunter and ranchman" was "President of the Boone and Crockett Club of this city, a member of the London Alpine Club, a trustee of the American Museum of Natural History and a member of the Board of State Charities Aid Association." It added that he had kept up the "standard desired by his father" in supporting the Newsboys' Lodging House.

Regarding the effect Theodore Roosevelt could be expected to have on the police force, the *Times* referred to another unnamed friend of Roosevelt who had been quoted in the *Washington Star:* "Strict honesty, attention to duty, and an observance of the rules and regulations of the department will govern the tenure of office of every man in it, high or low, as long as Roosevelt is Police Commissioner. You may rest assured of this fact. Any employee of the Police

Department who attempts any crookedness, or who is derelict in duty to the extent of a hairbreadth, will go sailing out, no matter what influence he may command."

The *Star's* attention to the story also reached onto its editorial page in the form of a prediction regarding Roosevelt, whether or not he took on the job. "Ten years from now, he will still be a young man for the Governor's chair, or a seat in the United States Senate, and there are experienced politicians who believe the Presidency itself lies in the path of the man."

On its editorial page the *New York Times* said, "If it shall turn out that Mr. Theodore Roosevelt will take the place of Police Commissioner, Mayor Strong will be entitled to both credit and congratulation, for Mr. Roosevelt represents very distinctly precisely the principle which Mayor Strong was elected to carry out—viz, business and not politics in city affairs."

As to Roosevelt, the newspaper noted "the principle which he has so successfully labored for in Washington is precisely the one that is required in the police department of New York. The essential vice of the department, to which all its thronging evils can be traced, has been the control of politicians. It has been the demoralizing influence of the politicians that has made corruption and favoritism possible, and honesty, discipline, responsibility, and efficiency difficult and largely impracticable."

Jacob Riis's *Sun* named Roosevelt a "power" whose appointment could hardly fail to improve New York's disgraceful law-enforcement situation. It then offered readers this on April 26.

On Mr. Theodore Roosevelt Moving from the United States Civil Service Commission to the New York Police Department

> Out of the fields Elysian
>   Out of the smile and kiss
> Of the pure ethereal angels
>   Into a job like this!
> Out of the soft sereneness
>   Of Civil Service peace,
> Into a coarse connection
>   With persons and police!
> Out of the chaste and classic
>   Realm of purity

> Into the low and common
>   Title of P.C.!
> Out of the heavenly highness
>   Out of the sweet and clean
> Into this thing, oh Teddy,
>   Teddy, what do you mean?

Despite rhymes, rumors, well-informed sources, and inside information, nothing official had been announced. On the same day on which the *Sun* waxed poetic the *Times* reporter at city hall filled eleven paragraphs with nothing more definitive to say than "it is generally credited that the plans of Mayor Strong are fairly well determined upon."

Four more days went by before anyone could report with certainty the character of the new board of commissioners. Mayor Strong revealed on May 1 that he had chosen Roosevelt and Colonel Frederick Dent Grant, a veteran Republican politician and oldest son of Ulysses S. Grant, to replace Murray and Kerwin. He also designated Andrew D. Parker, a Democrat and former assistant district attorney. Already appointed to the board was Avery D. Andrews, a Democrat who had replaced John J. Sheehan, a Tammany hack who had been thoroughly discredited during the Lexow Committee hearings.

In purging the board of Murray, Kerwin, and Sheehan Strong said, "These commissioners did not show any disposition to reorganize the force. That is why I am determined to get rid of them and find others who would. The Police Department is the only department that has been shown conclusively to be rotten. The City of New York has no use for anyone on the Board who is not ready to take a hand in its reorganization."

A month later TR stood ready and eager as the White House announced that President Cleveland had received the resignation of Theodore Roosevelt on April 30. Talking to reporters that evening, TR said, "Yes, it is true that I have resigned as Civil Service Commissioner. Mayor Strong has requested me to take the position of Police Commissioner, and I have accepted."

But all the ducks were not yet in a row. There still hung over the heads of everyone the fate of a measure pending in the state legislature in Albany to revamp the powers of the police board. Nothing could be considered official, Mayor Strong emphasized to reporters, until "the Bi-Partisan Bill shall be definitely settled." The keystone of this pending legislation was the granting to the mayor and his police commissioners the power to remove city officials from the previous administration whose terms had not expired. Exactly that authority had been granted to Strong, temporarily, in the form of the Power of Removal Act. Passed quickly in January, it had bestowed on Strong the ability to get rid of Murray, Kerwin, and Sheehan. But the law was to be in effect only for the first six months of Strong's administration. That deadline loomed only a month away.

When Strong indicated he would not use new powers of removal to assure a Republican patronage windfall, but would appoint men without considering party affiliations, the furious Republican boss in Albany, Tom Platt, counterattacked. The "Bi-Partisan Police Bill" would require that no more than two commissioners "belong to the same political party, nor be of the same political opinion on state and national interests." To take any action a majority vote would be required, that is, three "ayes" out of the four-man board. Furthermore, no one in the police department could be dismissed, suspended, removed, or fined without a majority of commissioners concurring. In effect, the legislation guaranteed perennial veto power to two Republicans on the board, no matter how long Strong's reform government remained in office.

Should the public grow weary of reform, as Dick Croker had forecast to Lincoln Steffens they would, any Tammany government in city hall would be bound by law to appoint two Republican police commissioners (or change the law, an unlikely proposition in the traditionally Republican stronghold that was Albany).

Despite being given a fig leaf by its being offered to the legislature by Senator Lexow, the bill had been denounced by Rev. Parkhurst and other reformers, including the Society for the Prevention of Crime. It attacked the legislation as a measure "which does not radically change the system that has produced our unspeakably corrupt police force and which does not reach the roots of evil."

Savvy enough a politician to appreciate that storm clouds surrounding the bipartisan police bill bore the seeds of lasting city hall-Albany enmity and heavy weather for him, Roosevelt told journalists, "I do not know what our powers will be, and so it is impossible to say what I think the board can accomplish."

Typically, he continued, "All I can say is that whatever ability I have I shall give to the work, and that as Police Commissioner I shall act solely with a view to the well being of the city and of the interests of the service, and shall take account only of the efficiency, honesty and records of the men. Neither in making appointments nor removals shall I pay any heed to the politicial or religious affiliations of anyone."

Anticipating struggles, he wrote to the man who had started all the furor. "I dread very much taking up the duties of police commissioner," he told Parkhurst, "though I have enough appreciation of the joy of battle to take some comfort out of the duties when they once begin."

They commenced at ten o'clock in the morning of May 6, 1895. In the company of Col. Grant and Andrew Parker, TR strode into the mayor's office at city hall, shook hands with Strong, took the oath of office, signed the official guest register and found a seat before Strong's desk to talk about the police department. Beginning a term of office that the law set at six years with an annual salary of five thousand dollars, he listened with satisfaction while the mayor described a police force that was to be administered with fairness to all and partisanship toward none.

The new board could count on hearty support of the mayor's office, Strong said. He would forcefully support reorganization of the department. Whatever powers the commissioners might have under the old law or any new statutes, the mayor expected his appointees to use them to the fullest extent in ridding the force of whatever irregularities the commissioners discovered. He said he expected them to restore efficiency, discipline, and high moral character, from 300 Mulberry Street to the most distant precinct station house.

With the formalities completed Roosevelt bade goodbye to Strong, strode from the office, passed down the marble corridor that ran east-west through the center of the ground floor, swung right through a graceful rotunda, and out the front door. Bounding down the steps, he turned right. Picking up his pace as he reached Broadway, he turned right again, then broke into a stride that was only a little short of becoming a flat-out dash, which left his fellow commissioners gasping for breath to keep up.

Proceeding in a straight but slightly northeasterly line up Broadway, they left behind the short blocks between the crosstown streets of lower Manhattan—Pearl, Worth, Canal, Grand, Broome; in all, sixteen intersections—until they reached Houston Street. Turning right for a last, tiny block, they came to Mulberry.

On the east side to the north between Houston and Bleeker Streets police headquarters appeared as a slightly tawdry-looking marble-fronted square, four-stories high, its forty-five windows shaded by awnings, save seven in the basement. Barred, they let little light into the jails behind and below them. Steep front steps led to an arched main entrance.

Lincoln Steffens could imagine no more dreary or depressing location in which to work. "Dew is a shower of jewels—in the country, and as it melts in the morning sun it sweetens the air. Not in a city," he wrote in his autobiography. Police headquarters was in a tenement neighborhood, which seemed to steam on the warm nights and sweat by day.

A damp, smelly chill greeted him when he came to work in the early mornings. The tenements stank, the alleys puffed forth the stenches of the night. Slatternly women hung out of the windows to breathe and to gossip or quarrel across the courts. Idle men and boys hung, half dressed, over the old iron fences, or lounged, recovering from the night, on the stoops of the houses that once had been the fine homes of the old families long since moved uptown.

In many ways the morning of Monday, May 6, 1895, was exactly like all such mornings Steffens and Jacob Riis had spent across the street from police headquarters. Should a shiny "Black Maria" pull to a halt before it bearing a load of dazed and probably clubbed prisoners, the reporters in the press shacks at 301 and 303, who could never mistake the rattling of a police wagon's wheels on cobblestone, would pour out and across Mulberry eager for a fresh headline for their next editions. But this day turned into one like no other. As Steffens slouched on the stoop Riis dashed outside. Shouting he had been on the phone to city hall, he blared excitedly that Theodore Roosevelt had been sworn in as police commissioner and was on his way to headquarters.

Half an hour later, TR and his winded companions appeared at the corner. Roosevelt broke into a run that Steffens recorded: "He came on ahead down the street; he yelled, 'Hello, Jake,' to Riis, and running up the stairs to the front door of Police Headquarters, he waved us reporters to follow. We did."

After slowing his pace for a moment while his fellow commissioners caught up, allowing Jake Riis to introduce Steffens, TR barged through the front door.

"Where are our offices?" he bellowed. "Where is the Board Room? What do we do first?"

Trailing behind were the others. Middle-aged and strongly resembling his father, Frederick D. Grant was born in St. Louis on May 30, 1850. At sixteen he followed his parent's footsteps to West Point, graduating with honors in 1871. As a horse soldier he served with the Fourth Cavalry and fought Indians in the West under General Phillip H. Sheridan, notable for his brilliant generalship in the Civil War, and his opinion, while he set out to tame the frontier after the war, that "the only good Indian is a dead Indian." After leaving the army in 1881 with rank of lieutenant colonel, Grant married the daughter of H. H. Honore, a Chicago millionaire. Defeated in a bid for election as Illinois Secretary of State in 1887, he was appointed minister to Austria-Hungary by President Harrison in 1889. When he returned to America he settled in New York, as had his father, to become active in Republican politics.

The Democratic commissioner who followed TR into Police Headquarters, Andrew D. Parker, had been in private law practice since serving as assistant district attorney in the first term of John H. Fellows. He left the post when Fellows was succeeded by De Lancey Nicoll, the Tammany prosecutor who had chosen to go after the Rev. Parkhurst rather than proceed against those whom Parkhurst had accused of wrongdoings. A protégé of Sheriff James O'Brien, whose recommendation landed him the commissionership, Andrew Parker had never been less than a loyal Tammany soldier.

Editorializing on the appointments, the *Times* said, "Nobody will question the excellence of the choice of Mr. Roosevelt. He is a Republican whose party fidelity has borne a good deal of strain, but he has shown his capacity for rising above partisanship in administering public trusts, and there is no doubt that he will perform his duty to the city without regard to party considerations. He believes in non-partisan municipal administration, and will doubtless do all he can to promote it."

Concerning Grant and Parker's appointments, the *Times* held the view that it was "difficult to regard them as having been made without regard to political considerations, but possibly the mayor contemplated a change in the law which would require the recognition of such considerations."

Awaiting the trio as they reached the second floor offices of the board of commissioners was their predecessor in office. Avery Andrews was also a graduate of the United States Military Academy, a distinguished lawyer, and a Democrat. He provided the answer to TR's question, "What do we do first?" As the senior commissioner in length of service, though only by a matter of weeks, he called the meeting to order and immediately nominated Roosevelt as President of the Board.

Exhibiting a spirit of nonpartisanship that reflected public opinion, the vote proved unanimously in favor. It entitled TR to be addressed as "President Roosevelt."

Taking up the reins of office, he turned to the business of committee assignments. To Parker went the tasks of reorganizing the detective bureau, as well as the police department's duties in supervising elections. Grant, the experienced military man, was assigned supplies and repairs. Attorney Andrews, in addition to being elected the board's treasurer, got the job of revising departmental rules and regulations.

The president of the board informed them that he would serve on each of the committees and coordinate overall administration. He then let it be known that he would be the board's spokesman in dealing with the press.

With the commissioners adjourned, TR drew Riis and Steffens aside. Rubbing his hands, he grinned and eagerly asked, "Now, then, what'll we do?"

The implication of the question's pronoun was not lost on either reporter. Steffens would write in his memoirs, "It was all breathless and sudden. It was just as if we three were the Police Board, T.R., Riis and I, and as we got T.R. calmed down and made him promise to go a bit slow, to consult with his colleagues, also, we went out into the hall, and there stood the other three commissioners together, waiting for us (Steffens and Riis) to go so that they could see T.R."

To Jacob Riis the words "what'll we do?" thrilled even more than the "I have come to help" written on TR's calling card five years earlier. Then, Theodore Roosevelt had been a member of the federal Civil Service Commission, hundreds of miles removed from a city that Riis burned to change for the better. Now, TR was back home.

And he was in charge of the one place where reform must go well if cleansing waters of change were to flow throughout the city.

Neither Riis nor the political figure he admired more than any other expected the work to go easily. Number 300 Mulberry Street embodied inhospitality. It remained the stomping grounds for Tom Byrnes, Clubber Williams (though he had left the day before on a vacation), their cronies on the force, and their political allies.

Police Headquarters was nothing less than enemy territory.

Chapter 5

A Set of Teeth

Theodore Roosevelt's first press release as president of the board stated: "The public may rest assured that so far as I am concerned, there will be no politics in the department, and I know that I voice the sentiment of my colleagues in that respect. We are all activated by the desire to so regulate this department that it will earn the respect and confidence of the community. Every man in the force will have to stand on his merits and all appointments will be made for merit only, and without regard to political or religious considerations."

Neither would gender be a factor in appointments. Readers of newspapers discovered this in May 10 headlines disclosing that the president of the police board had decided to save taxpayers twelve hundred dollars a year by replacing two gentlemen who had been employed as assistants to TR's predecessor with a "girl secretary." A family friend of the Roosevelts and protégé of TR's political buddy, Joe Murray, she was Minnie Gertrude Kelly. By all accounts her qualifications were unquestionable, though the reporter for the *World* may have been trying to suggest otherwise by describing her as young, small, and comely with raven-black hair. An unprecedented vision in a close-fitting gown, her arrival was deemed a "sensation" who "took the breath out of the old stagers in the Mulberry Street barracks."

While Miss Kelly's displacement of a pair of men suggested rapid progress in streamlining procedures of police headquarters, the new president of the board of commissioners bridled against the law's mandating administration of the police by a quartet of co-equals. When the governing apparatus was not only continued but mandated by enactment of the Pratt-Lexow Bi-Partisan Police Act to be evenly divided in complexion between the two political parties, he denounced the law as "foolish or vicious."

He told Riis, Steffens, and anyone else who cared to listen that the law modelled the government of the police department "somewhat on the lines of the Polish parliament."

To him the Bi-Partisan Law had been avowedly designed to make it difficult to get effective action. He complained "a four-headed board" already made it difficult to get a majority. And, "lest we should get such a majority, it gave each member power to veto the actions of his colleagues." Provisions of the law also hindered the mayor from removing a police commissioner should one become a stumbling block to action. Worse, in Roosevelt's view, the Lexow law granted to the chief of police, "our nominal subordinate," entirely independent action in "the most important matters" and made removal of the chief almost impossible. The only way would be dismissal on the grounds of proved corruption. In effect, the chief of police was "responsible to nobody."

Worried that these provisions so nettlesome in theory might soon become stymying in reality, he proposed a Police Reorganization Bill to give the police board true power and authority to reform the department. The measure would vest in the board the right to dismiss subordinates after a hearing, but without recourse to review or appeal, should the hearing determine those subordinates were "not possessed of the qualifications for the maintenance of the proper moral condition and discipline and the efficient conduct and administration" of the police department.

A resolution unanimously adopted by the police board on May 13 "earnestly" called the attention of the legislature "to the need that it (the Board) be given power for the purpose of present reorganization" to dismiss or discipline members of the force. "If this power be given to the board, we can guarantee a thorough reform of the force, and a clean and efficient police service; without this power, the board will do all it can to produce these results, but will necessarily be cramped and embarrassed by its action."

The proposal ran into a storm of opposition within the police force itself, quietly fanned by Chief of Police Tom Byrnes. An "anti-reform fund" materialized in all the precinct station houses. Each member of the force was expected to donate fifty dollars to help finance efforts to defeat the TR reorganization bill in Albany.

With the help of Tammany legislators, it was voted down.

A disappointed Roosevelt grumbled, "If the Reorganization Bill had only gone through, I would have had this force completely remodeled in six months."

A letter to his sister Anna was a blunt analysis of the task confronting him. "I have the most important, and the most corrupt department in New York on my hands. I shall speedily assail some of the ablest, shrewdest men in this city, who will be fighting for their lives, and I know well how hard the task ahead of me is." Despite this gloomy outlook, he could not resist finding a silver lining. In spite of nervous strain and worry, he said, "I am glad I undertook it; for it is man's work."

He saw the work as surgery, cutting out "the gangrene" of a system in which "venality and blackmail went hand in hand with the basest forms of low ward politics, and where the policeman, the ward politician, and the criminal alternately preyed on one another and helped one another prey on the general public." The symptoms of this sickness had been diagnosed by Rev. Parkhurst. Examination by the Lexow Committee had confirmed the diagnosis. The voters had called in a team of surgeons.

At two o'clock in the afternoon, May 8, 1895, the president of the police board in his first full day in office joined his fellow commissioners Grant and Andrews to begin applying the scalpel. Sitting as a court with Andrews presiding they listened to the particulars of seventy-four cases involving charges of police misconduct. They ranged from Patrolman William Williamson letting a prisoner named Murray, known as "a dangerous character," get away from him inside the Jefferson Market Court, to a charge by Jacob Maisel, a fish peddler, that Patrolman John J. Barnes and Andrew A. Trembig of the Union Market Police Station beat him and his wife because Maisel had not paid the dollar that was due that week for "protection."

In defending himself against loss of a prisoner Williamson claimed he could not watch the person in his custody and handle the paperwork the case required for an arraignment. The duty to watch prisoners in court, he insisted, belonged to the police department's court squad.

President Roosevelt suggested, "Either this officer or some other officer is guilty. But the methods in handling these prisoners in court may be defective." Allowing that "the system may be faulty," the board put Williamson's case off and ordered the officials of the court and members of the court squad to appear at a future hearing on the question.

Although everything he had learned about police protection rackets suggested there was truth in the fish dealer's story of being beaten for lack of payoff money, Roosevelt pointed out that no actual evidence had been produced to justify convicting the officers. Without corroboration, Maisel's charge could not stand.

Taking up a case brought by a supervising officer against Patrolman Thomas J. Sweeney for "leaving his post," the board listened to Sweeney explain that he had gone "just five feet" to fetch a cup of coffee for another officer.

Commissioner Grant turned his head to avoid being spotted laughing at such a fuss over a trivial offense. Forcing himself to maintain a straight face, Avery Andrews solemnly pronounced Sweeney guilty. He then lectured, "Carrying coffee has nothing to do with police work."

As the offending officer accepted the reprimand and returned to duty, presumably chastened, TR remained mute regarding the severity of Sweeney's misconduct, the board's finding, and the role of coffee in police work.

In this first day of trials the board meted out punishment in fifty-seven cases, from fines to suspensions. At the end of this initial experience of trying police officers, TR told reporters, "It is my first day, and, of course, I am unable to say much about the present system of conducting police trials, but I can state that I look upon the trials as of great importance."

Informing readers of the details of the trials the next morning, the *Times* offered the headline TRIED TO GET AT FACTS, with a straight-forward account of the proceedings and the dynamic president of the police board. Certainly, no commissioner prior to May 6, 1895, had matched him for energy and devotion to duty. Whereas his predecessors had been scarcely observed in Mulberry Street, President Roosevelt was an overweaning presence.

"I have never worked harder than during the last two weeks," he wrote to London where Anna was summering. "I am downtown at nine; and leave the office at six—once at eight. The actual work is hard; but far harder is the intense strain."

When the board met next on May 16 to conduct trials they began at nine in the morning with the docket listing eighty cases, many of them as petty as Patrolman Sweeney's brief desertion of his post in search of coffee. But allegations of dereliction of duty lodged against Patrolman Joseph Reitman of the Elizabeth Street Station were considerably more troubling.

Reitman stood accused by Roundsman McLaughlin of failing to patrol his post for nearly an hour on May second. As supervisor of Reitman's tour of duty, McLaughlin alleged that he had not observed Reitman on his beat between 10:35 and 11:17 P.M.

The patrolman answered that on the night in question he had had one hundred fifty doors to try and six cellars to investigate on his post. "There have been a number of burglaries in the precinct," he explained, "and the captain's orders were to pay special attention. There were two burglaries within a week."

On the night he received this order from his captain, he went on, he had seen "two suspicious-looking characters" and had stayed near Broadway to watch them. If this were true, Sweeney would appear to have been diligent in his duties to guard against burglars, although staying in one location kept him from his appointed patrol.

Roosevelt turned to McLaughlin. "What have you to say, Roundsman?"

The roundsman stuck to his charge that Reitman had been absent from his post at Elm and Howard Streets and deserved to be punished.

The patrolman shot to his feet. "Mr. Commissioner, can I ask the Roundsman a few questions?"

"You can," TR replied.

Reitman took out a sheet of paper with questions written on them. "Roundsman, did you ever go over my post?" he demanded.

"It was not necessary."

"Did you whistle in the center and on the extremes of my post?"

"No I did not."

"Do you know Rule 94 of the Manual?"

"I do. It requires the Roundsman to go over a man's post and whistle in the center and at each end."

"Mr. Commissioner," Reitman shouted at Roosevelt, "I ask that this case be dismissed on the grounds the Roundsman did not comply with Rule 94."

As Reitman began to read from the rule, Roosevelt cut him off. "Patrolman, that does not relieve *you* in the least."

Technicalities of the rule book, it seemed, would not be sufficient to get an errant policeman off the hook in a Roosevelt trial.

"You can make a charge against the Roundsman if you wish," Roosevelt said to Reitman.

"I do wish to, sir," the Patrolman answered, assuring that in due course the board of commissioners would be called upon to show that not going by the book in the police department henceforth would be as dangerous as failing to patrol or soliciting bribes.

Unfinished business came next, the case of Patrolman Williamson's escaped prisoner. Present to explain how such a thing could have happened were officials of the court, including the Roundsman whose squad policed the Jefferson Market Court. Thomas McGee insisted on placing the blame for the escape squarely upon Williamson. McGee's answers also suggested that questioning of police procedures in the courts, or anywhere else, should be strictly the province of Chief of Police Thomas Byrnes.

Roosevelt pounced. "Do you mean that the Commissioners have no right to find out for themselves who is responsible, or that patrolmen should not testify to what has been the usual practice in court?"

"The Commissioners have a right, certainly," McGee blurted.

What he had meant to say, he explained sheepishly, was that in disciplinary matters "Chief Byrnes is the man I look to."

What resulted from this questioning was recognition by the police board that the police department was in such disarray that disputes over lines of authority and disagreements over responsibilities between police squads had allowed a dangerous individual to escape and remain at large. Observed the reporter for the *New York Times* in his story the next day, "The disclosures during the trial will no doubt result in reorganization of the court squad."

An immediate effect was an order from an embarassed Chief Byrnes transferring McGee out of the court squad and back to precinct duty.

The day after the May 16 session the *World* offered readers a lively portrait of the Roosevelt who had emerged as a tenacious investigator:

"Sing, heavenly muse, the sad dejection of our poor policemen. We have a real police commissioner. His name is Theodore Roosevelt. His teeth are big and white, his eyes are small and piercing; his voice is rasping. When he asks a question, Mr. Roosevelt shoots at the poor trembling policeman as he would shoot a bullet at a coyote. He shows a set of teeth calculated to unnerve the bravest of the Finest. His teeth are very white and almost as big as a colt's. They are broad teeth, they form a perfectly straight line. The lower teeth look like a row of dominoes. They do not lap over or under each other, as most teeth do, but come together evenly. They seem to say, 'Tell the truth to your commissioner, or he'll bite your head off!'

"Generally speaking, this interesting Commissioner's face is red. He has lived a great deal out of doors, and that accounts for it. His hair is thick and short. Under his right ear he has a long scar. It is the opinion of all the policemen who have talked to him that he got that scar fighting an Indian out West. It is also their opinion that the Indian is dead.

"But Mr. Roosevelt's voice is the policeman's hardest trial. It is an exasperating voice, a sharp voice, a rasping voice. It is a voice that comes from the tips of the teeth and seems to say in its tones, 'What do you amount to, anyway?'

"One thing our noble force may make up its mind to at once—it must do as Roosevelt says, for it is not likely that it will succeed in beating him."

As useful as these trials were to Roosevelt and his three companions in stalking miscreants in uniform, the Williamsons, McGees, and Reitmans were small game. On their desks as they took office lay a list of twenty-six policemen who had been indicted for bribery in the previous year. Among them were Inspector William McLaughlin and six captains, including the star witness of the Lexow Committee hearings, Max Schmittberger.

Although McLaughlin's trial was only in jury selection in Brooklyn Supreme Court, Roosevelt let it be known that whatever the outcome of the proceedings, whether found guilty or aquitted under the law, McLaughlin would not be allowed to escape departmental discipline. Nor would any of those on the list.

"We want to get at these men who are under charges and try them," Roosevelt asserted, teeth bared.

Achieving that goal would not be easy. Taking a special interest in McLaughlin, TR deputized himself to investigate a report that irregularities surrounded McLaughlin's civil service examination for promotion to the rank of inspector. If this were to prove true, the McLaughlin case would doubly offend Theodore Roosevelt, the recent battler for the sanctity of civil service and now a fighter for efficiency, square deals, and morality in the New York City Police Department. Presenting himself at the rooms of the civil service board to examine McLaughlin's file, he learned the dossier had been sent to police headquarters. Suspecting chicanery, he demanded the chief clerk of the department "hunt up the papers" forthwith.

On May 20, the day of TR's revelation that McLaughlin's papers had gone missing, lawyers for McLaughlin argued in Brooklyn that their client could not possibly receive a fair trial in New York. Time and time again prospective jurors had been telling Justice Barrett of the Court of Oyer and Terminer that they felt such prejudice against the police department they could not possibly be open-minded regarding the defendant.

Would not chances of a fair hearing for Inspector McLaughlin be better, asked defense attorney Samuel French, if the trial's venue were switched? He proposed the more amenable, peaceable upstate country atmosphere of Saratoga, a resort famous for its waters and horse racing season.

That Monday, TR's third as president of the police board, proved to be a "busy one," reported the *New York Times* watchdog at 300 Mulberry Street. Earning a paragraph in the story dealing with the vanished McLaughlin papers was a brief visit to police headquarters by the individual whose sermonizing had triggered the chain of events that had put McLaughlin in the dock and Roosevelt on the police board. The object of the Rev. Charles Parkhurst's appearance seemed to be to see Commissioner Andrews. Finding him occupied with the meeting of the board, Parkhurst departed after twenty minutes, telling reporters his visit "was nothing of any consequence."

In the board room, however, matters unfolded of considerable consequence beyond the McLaughlin mystery. Presented to the board for immediate action were applications for retirement from the department in the names of Captain Joseph H. Eakins of the Mercer Street Station and Captain Thomas H. Ryan of High Bridge. Both boasted distinguished service records. Eakins had been on the force for nearly three decades (appointed March 1, 1866). Ryan had put on the blue uniform three years earlier. During his twelve years as commander of the Twenty-first precinct, more men from Ryan's precinct had been arrested, convicted, and hanged for their crimes than from any other in the city. Unfortunately, as the capstone of Ryan's and Eakins' careers, the Lexow Committee heard damning evidence of official corruption that made retirement with an ample pension far more appealing than any trial, especially one by Theodore Roosevelt.

The new police law also encouraged retirements. It mandated approval of applications from those who had been on the force for twenty-five years. It also required positive action in cases in which applicants were veterans of the Civil War. Dozens of high-ranking cops qualified regardless of whatever charges might be pending or contemplated.

Less than twenty-four hours after the police board referred the retirement applications of Eakins' and Ryan to the pension board for approving action, another longtime ranking officer appeared at Headquarters. He had not been seen around Mulberry Street since Theodore Roosevelt dashed up the front steps looking for his office and rolling up his sleeves.

Since May 6, Alexander S. Williams had been on a fifteen-day vacation. On May 24, reporters scrambled around him to ask if the Clubber might be thinking about following Eakins' and Ryan's example.

"Why should I retire? What for?" Williams demanded. "I'm a young man yet, and I never felt better in my life. What earthly reason is there for my filing such an application?"

In unmitigated bravado no man in the history of the police department, including the far-from-shrinking-violet Tom Byrnes, ever surpassed brash and brazen Alec Williams. Weeks after his admissions before the Lexow Committee he had stepped forward to offer his own plan for reorganizing the police force. Interviewed by a newspaper reporter on January 7, 1895, he posited that "the laws and the ordinances, not policemen," ought to be blamed for the abuses of the Police Department. As to rampant bribery, the failing lay in merchants of the city who were only too happy to push payoffs into naturally reluctant police hands.

"We are fast becoming a nation of bribe-givers and bribe-takers. Every man who is shaved in a barber's shop tips the barber. We call these gratuities 'tips.' But they are bribes," he said.

In discussing enforcement of the Excise Law governing the purveying of liquor he said the trouble was with the law and not the police. The way to put an end to saloons operating illegally on Sundays was to require the removal of all window shades and blinds from doors and windows, thereby making it impossible for the establishments to flaunt the law by blocking the view of the policeman walking his post. Even better, he went on, the Excise Law ought to be amended to *permit* Sunday liquor sales under certain restrictions and during specified hours.

The city's leading exponent of the law at the end of the police-man's club then caused eyebrows to arch by proposing legalizing disorderly houses and concentrating them in designated areas. "There are more houses of this character in this city at the present time than ever before in its history," he continued, "and many of them have crept into quiet and fashionable residential neighbor-hoods. They should be encouraged to congregate in certain lo-calities. The women who work in them should be given to under-stand that as long as they do not trespass upon forbidden ground they would not be molested by the police."

The interview offered a better explanation as to why he had permitted certain houses of prostitution to stay open in his Ten-derloin precinct than the answer he gave to Lexow Committee questioners. He said he had done so because they were fashionable and not because he stood to profit from bribery. In arguing for legalization of vice he now offered the provocative idea that the decriminalization would at the same time eliminate corruption of the police force, which originated from without, not within the de-partment.

Coming from the mouth of the living symbol of the corruption of the police, Williams' suggestions proved so sensational that they dominated the front page of the metropolitan news section of the *Times*, beginning with the observation, "Absurd as it may seem in the light of testimony he gave before the Lexow Committee . . ."

That Williams was able to conduct the interview as a free man and, in the *Times'* words, "sneer at the men who are endeavoring to obtain a better and purer government for this city" was because the statute of limitations covering the crimes about which he had been queried by the committee barred prosecution. Unlike Inspector McLaughlin and the other police officers on Theodore Roosevelt's list of indicted policemen, Williams did not have to worry about criminal charges being lodged against him.

However, as he came back from vacation, he did so with the certainty that the president of the police board had every intention of living up to his pledge that members of the force who had sullied the police department's reputation would be called upon to answer for their deeds to him, regardless of the statute of limitations or other legalities. Consequently, Williams returned from his vacation, not to a triumphal welcome back to Mulberry Street, but to a headquarters rife with rumors that he intended to follow the lead of Eakins and others by submitting a request for retirement.

Should he do so, the fifty-four-year-old cop who had become a legend in his own time would be entitled to an annual stipend from the city of one thousand seven hundred fifty dollars for the remainder of his life. It was a sum ample enough to keep him in comfort in his home in Cos Cob, Connecticut, and permit leisurely cruises on his yacht without ever having to worry about finances.

Across the street from police headquarters, the representatives of the city's newspapers watched, waited, and wagered. When Williams arrived at his usual hour on Friday, May 24, they dashed out and across the street to the steps of headquarters to pepper him with questions. Might this be the day Williams handed in his retirement papers? Was this to be his last day on the job? Were negotiations going on behind the scenes between the inspector and the president of the board?

Williams answered brusquely, "No," and bolted up the steps.

What happened a short while later was described by Williams' archenemy, Lincoln Steffens, in his memoir.

"TR threw up his second-story window, leaned out, and yelled his famous cowboy call, 'Hi yi yi.' He often summoned Riis and me thus. When we poked our heads out of my window across the street this time, he called me alone.

"'Not you, Jake. Steffens, come up here.'

"I hurried over to his office, and there in the hall stood Williams, who glared at me with eyes that looked like clubs. I passed on in to TR, who bade me sit down on a certain chair in the back of the room. Then he summoned Williams."

Minutes later, the inspector entered the board room. The door closed. After ten minutes, it swung open again and Williams made his way wordlessly to his office. Then Theodore Roosevelt emerged, a sheet of paper in hand. Crowded by the reporters, he adjusted his nose-glasses and read, "Inspector Williams has asked for retirement. The law is mandatory, and his request was unanimously granted by the Board."

He lowered the paper.

"Notice, I say he asked for a retirement, and that the law is mandatory."

As TR returned to the Board room, the journalists stampeded toward Williams' office.

"Inspector, you're a slick one," one of them said.

Williams let out a self-satisfied laugh, then replied with a smile. "I always was."

Lincoln Steffens noted for posterity that it was done almost without words. "Williams had been warned; the papers were all ready. He 'signed there,' rose, turned and looked at me, and disappeared."

FAREWELL TO WILLIAMS read the front-page headline of the *Times* the next morning. The lead of the story consisted of one sentence: "The public will know Alexander S. Williams no longer as a police officer."

Arthur Brisbane of the *World* wrote, "We have a real Police Commissioner. He makes our policemen feel as little froggies did when the stork came to rule them. His heart is full of reform, and a policeman . . . is no more to him than a plain, everyday human being."

These were hardly adjectives that Roosevelt's next target in his campaign to wring corruption out of the police department would have applied to himself. At no moment in his career as a policeman had Thomas Byrnes ever regarded himself as "plain" or "everyday." Neither had the scores of powerful men in both political parties whose favor he curried, as they did his. He had become accustomed to being introduced as "the personification of the Police Department."

Because of the revelations of the Rev. Parkhurst and the Lexow Committee, however, personifying the police had come to mean embodying a discredited and despised organization. Even though no one had been able to directly stain him personally, with the crimes unveiled in the repentant testimony of Max Schmittberger, and the frank admissions of police corruption by the madams of whorehouses and keepers of saloons, the sins of the department he headed inevitably came home to roost on Byrnes's doorstep.

Soon after being sworn in as police commissioner, TR had discovered the superintendent had no intention of assisting in the work of the new police board and its president. Byrnes's backing of the police reorganization measure further infuriated TR. He confided to old friend and ready advisor Henry Cabot Lodge, "I think I shall move against Byrnes at once. I thoroughly distrust him, and cannot do any thorough work while he remains."

Supremely confident of himself and his power at headquarters and Tammany Hall, Byrnes warned Roosevelt, "I will break you. You will yield. You are but human."

The contest of wills had been hanging unresolved over 300 Mulberry Street for weeks. Now, on May 24, flush with that day's victory over Inspector Williams, Roosevelt convened the board for its regular meeting and permitted the reading into the record of a letter from a citizen who signed himself Thomas MacGregor. It began with a reference to the McLaughlin trial, then underway in Brooklyn, and went on to ask, "Will the result of the McLaughlin trial cause Superintendent Byrnes to disconnect himself from the Police Department?"

Asserting "there is no question about McLaughlin's guilt," the letter contended that "fair-minded men who know anything about this city" believed McLaughlin was "not half as guilty as Byrnes."

It continued: "Byrnes confessed (to the Lexow Committee) that he was worth $200,000 or $300,000. He was not asked how much more than that amount. The fact is he is worth $1,500,000, and every dollar of it was wages of blackmail and corruption. He has any number of collectors in the department. McLaughlin being the chief one of them. But he (Byrnes) was cunning enough to feather his own nest in the meantime.

"The Police Department can never be improved with Byrnes at the head. It is getting worse every day, and no matter how hard you and your associates labor for its improvement it will be of no avail. The rank and file will never believe in Byrnes.

"Murderers and thugs continue to have their own way and bunko steerers and confidence men feel certain that they are safe in plying their business, knowing that Byrnes and McLaughlin have got a great share in the swag."

Recognizing a sensational new turn in the Roosevelt-Byrnes standoff, the city's newspapers blared the contents of the letter in their next editions. Having filed their stories, some in the press shack began to wonder about the timing of its release. What had prompted its writing? Who has Thomas MacGregor? Noting that he had not included his address, the curious denizens of 303 Mulberry Street scoured listings of city residents. They found no one named Thomas MacGregor.

Increasingly suspicious, the reporters reconstructed the manner in which the letter had come into their hands. Recalling that a copy had been made available by Commissioner Andrews to the reporter for *The Mail and Express,* they agreed that it had been logical to presume Andrews and the other commissioners had intended its publication in the press.

On Saturday, with the contents of the letter in print and no one able to locate its author, a reporter sought out Roosevelt and asked, "Do you know, Mr. Roosevelt, that the writer's name does not appear in the directory?"

"No, I do not know anything about him," TR replied.

"Was any investigation made of the charges before the letter was given out for publication?"

"No. It was looked upon as an anonymous communication and the publication of it was an accident. It was one of a lot of similar letters received every day, and it was ordered on file. I do not know how it came to be published."

TR hurried away and ducked into Parker's office. Presently, he reappeared to issue a statement bearing the names of all the commissioners. It said:

"The members of the Police Board, having had their attention called to various statements in the New York press, especially of this date, placing in their mouths statements derogatory to or reflecting upon Mr. Thomas Byrnes, Chief of Police, as having been made by individual members of the board to representatives of the press, do each unqualifiedly disavow and deny the making of any such statement or its authorization. Each of the Commissioners deeply regrets the unauthorized publication in the press of this date of an anonymous and slanderous communication filed at the board meeting of May 24, 1895. That communication was received simply because all communications to the board are received and placed on file."

With masterful understatement the reporter for the *Times* noted for the record that after releasing the statement the commissioners "were not inclined to discuss the matter any further." Ignoring this understandable reluctance, the journalists pressed the man believed to have given out the letter.

Avery Andrews said he did not recall having done so.

The *Mail and Express* reporter refreshed Andrews' memory, pointing out that he had observed the letter as it was handed by the chief clerk of the police board to President Roosevelt, who read it, and then handed it to Commissioner Parker, who in turn gave it to Andrews, who also read it.

"Then," the reporter said to Andrews, "I asked you if I could use it, and you said I could. Don't you remember that?"

Commissioner Andrews replied that he did not. Roosevelt then interjected that he did not recall ever having read the letter.

Expecting to elicit nothing further from the evidently embarrassed commissioners, the press corps made their way to the office of Chief Byrnes in search of a comment.

Brushing his luxuriant mustache with a thumb, he appeared calm and even amused as he told them, "I have nothing to say in the matter. The commissioners are apparently doing all the talking. All I ask is fair treatment, which I think I have the right to expect after over thirty years' service in the department. If I am not entitled to respect, the position I occupy certainly is, and while I occupy it I shall expect manly treatment."

Whatever the source of the letter may have been, whether genuinely from a concerned citizen or a contrivance planned to humiliate Byrnes and goad him into quitting, and however it came into the hands of a reporter, the matter left the commissioners looking either incompetent or guilty of a malevolent plot that was beneath officials from whom the people of New York rightly expected higher standards than those of the department they were expected to correct. Then, having been caught in either ineptitude or a dirty trick, they compounded an already tawdry situation with what journalists a century hence surely would term "a coverup."

Regardless of what happened, whether release of the letter was a mistake or intentional, that such a badly handled episode involved Theodore Roosevelt, paradigm of uprightness in public service, remained as astounding and disappointing one hundred years afterward as it had that Saturday in May of 1895.

Sunday papers brimmed with speculation that Byrnes was on his way out. The *Times* led with, "Unless there is a sudden change of front at police headquarters, an impartial authority says, Chief of Police Byrnes will vacate his office before the end of the present week. He will retire on his own motion with all the honors of war." Allowing that the paper might be wrong, it added, "If this programme is not carried out, it will be because the Chief of Police will have reconsidered his present intention, owing to something said or done by the Police Board in the meantime."

In their warren of offices in the building opposite police headquarters, the men who had covered the crime beat for years and had never experienced a day when Byrnes was not the major figure on the force argued the pros and cons of his departure without reaching a consensus. Jacob Riis and Lincoln Steffens held opposite views on the man and the fate he deserved. Steffens had never liked Byrnes and had resented him since Steffens' first day on the job when he felt Byrnes had threatened to withhold news from him if he did not go along.

Steffens also recalled with disgust instances he interpreted as attempts by Byrnes to seduce him into providing Byrnes and the police favorable coverage. When invited to Byrnes's office for informal talks in which the chief of police regaled him and other reporters with detective yarns in which Tom Byrnes was the hero, Steffens dismissed what he heard as bragging. Then, Steffens related in writing his own life's story, he discovered that much of Byrnes's story-telling had been outright plagiarism.

"I had found out where he hid the detective storybooks he was reading, and borrowing them when he was not looking, I read and recognized in them the source of some of his best narratives. Thus I discovered that instead of detectives' posing for and inspiring the writers of detective fiction, it was the authors who inspired the detectives."

Steffens saw in Byrnes a master at sleight-of-hand. "It was his pose to remain in the background, receiving communications through others—detectives or attorneys—and working in the dark, suddenly hand out his results."

Indeed, Steffens had experienced the Thomas Byrnes "magic" himself. After drawing his salary one Saturday afternoon shortly after he took up his posting at police headquarters, he took his wife to dinner. But when he was about to pay the waiter, he discovered the pay envelope containing his money was gone. He had had his pocket picked. Reporting the theft directly to Byrnes by phone, he answered the detective's rapid string of questions. How much cash was in the envelope? How was the envelope addressed? What lines of cars had Steffens used since collecting his pay?

"All right, I'll have it for you Monday morning," Byrnes said, at the same time reassuring and confident.

Soon after reporting to work on Monday, Steffens was called to Byrnes's office and handed the envelope. It contained his pay, down to the penny.

"How did he do it?" Steffens asked the veterans of the press shack as they played poker and waited for their next story.

Jake Riis answered, "He knew what pickpockets were working the carlines you rode and he told the detectives who were working them to tell the crooks they had robbed a friend of the chief's of so much money in such and such an envelope. The word was put out that Byrnes wanted that dip back by Monday morning, and so, of course, it came back Monday morning."

Should Byrnes put in for retirement voluntarily, or find himself forced into doing so, Jacob Riis would not count himself among those like Steffens who would shout "Hurrah." To the *Sun*'s man in Mulberry Street Byrnes was a "big policeman" the like of which would not soon be found. Conceding that Byrnes might have to go because he was chained to the meanness and smallness that had been revealed by Parkhurst and the witnesses before the Lexow Committee, Riis continued to believe Byrnes was cast in a different mould.

Certainly he was unscrupulous. Yes, he had the failings of his trade. "He was a Czar, with all an autocrat's irresponsible powers, and he exercised them as he saw fit," Riis said. "But he made the detective service great."

While others called Byrnes a great faker, in Jake Riis's book he was simply a great actor, and without being that no man could be a great detective.

"He did ride a high horse when the fit was on him and he thought it served his purpose." But he made life in a mean street picturesque, and for that something was due him. "Police service looks to results first," Riis said. "There was that in Byrnes."

While the men in the press shack, the police board, and the city hung on tenterhooks concerning Tom Byrnes's fate, a case in which Byrnes had demonstrated his abilities as a leader of cops was reaching its climax in the State Court of Appeals in Albany. The judges were being asked to stay the execution of the death penalty upon Dr. Robert W. Buchanan.

Scottish-born and qualified in medicine at the University of Edinburgh, Buchanan had settled in New York with his wife and set up practice in 1886. While the office flourished, the marriage did not, for Buchanan harbored a zest for the seamier side of life. He discovered it in New York's brothels in general and in the charms of a particular bordello proprietress, Anna Sutherland. In 1890 he divorced his wife and married Anna, who humored him by signing a last will and testament in his favor. Two years later, as Buchanan readied himself for a sentimental and solitary journey back to Edinburgh for a visit, Anna fell gravely ill. After she died of a cerebral hemmorhage on April 23, the doctor collected five hundred thousand dollars. A month later he remarried his first wife.

Reviewing these facts, a police reporter for the New York *World,* Ike White, smelled something fishy. Digging in Buchanan's past, he found reason to believe the doctor had brought about Anna's demise by administering some type of poison in the form of eyedrops, possibly morphine. He published an account of his investigation in the *World.*

Chief of Detectives Byrnes immediately ordered Detective Arthur A. Carey to place Buchanan under surveillance. But Carey was ordered not to be too secretive about following Buchanan. Byrnes desired the doctor to know he was being watched. The chief of detectives wished Buchanan to wonder and worry. While Byrnes's psychological third degree was being practiced, Anna's body was exhumed and autopsied. The results showed she had been given a large dose of morphine. Byrnes told Carey to bring Buchanan in.

In a long trial that became a milestone in criminal forensic pathology, but which left the jurors in doubt, Buchanan might have gotten off. However, he insisted on taking the stand. Defending himself against a battering cross-examination by the prosecution, based on evidence gathered by Byrnes's detectives, he spoke in a whining and superior manner and became so entangled in numerous contradictions that no one believed him. On April 25, 1893, the jury found him guilty.

Granted a reprieve from the death penalty by Governor Levi P. Morton pending an appeal to the state's highest tribunal, Buchanan on May 26, 1895, occupied a cell in Sing Sing while Ike White and the other crime reporters at 303 Mulberry Street kept an ear cocked toward Albany—even as they trained their eyes on the comings and goings across the street for any clue as to the fate of the tenacious sleuth who had risen from running the detective bureau to chief of police.

They also debated the issue of who might succeed Byrnes if Roosevelt turned out to be the victor in the arm-wrestling going on at number 300 Mulberry Street. Many argued that the leading contender to fill Byrnes's shoes ought to be inspector Peter Conlin. Born in 1841, he fought in the Civil War as a member of the Irish Brigade of the Sixty-Ninth Regiment at the Battle of Fair Oaks, Gaines's Mill, Williamsburg, White Oak Swamp, and Malvern Hill, where he had been wounded severely enough to compel retirement from the army in the rank of captain. He joined the police department in 1869 and rose steadily through the ranks to become Inspector Conlin on August 9, 1889, the same date Alexander Williams received his inspectorship. Now, Williams was gone.

Weighing in on who ought to replace Byrnes was the Rev. Dr. Charles Parkhurst, though without providing a specific name. The reformer preferred to describe the traits he looked for in an "ideal" chief of police. "He must first be a man of immense force of character —a Napoleonic sort of man, in fact—so that his slightest order will compel obedience on the part of his subordinates. That should be the warp of his character," he told a reporter.

But there had to be more. "In the second place, he will have to be a man of great natural executive ability, so that he will be the practical enacting clause of every statute which it is his duty to enforce without fear, favor or affection. This should be the woof of his character."

Yet even this exceptionally fine fabric was insufficient for the windy clergyman. In addition to a Napoleon with outstanding executive abilities, Parkhurst's perfect chief of police must be dignified; fair; impartial; courteous in bearing; well imbued "with the learning which nourishes a man, and not that which dries him up;" a man of affairs, accustomed to moving about in the world and familiar with persons and events; non-patronizing; clear-headed; courageous; and—need it be said?—honest.

Could such a paragon be found? asked a reporter.

Parkhurst could have said, "Yes." Instead, he answered with another gust of wind. "I believe that when the superincumbent corruption which is weighing down on the force has been lifted off, we shall find plenty of executive ability and honesty, which has been hidden in the ranks of Sergeant and Roundsman."

Perhaps so, but the Bi-Partisan Police Law required that a chief of police be promoted from the rank of deputy chief or from the list of inspectors and captains. It also mandated that a majority of the four Commissioners agree on the selection.

As the guessing game continued, Chief Byrnes spent all of Sunday, May 26, at Police Headquarters, while none of the Commissioners put in an appearance. "Everyone whose duties take him to Police Headquarters is awaiting the course of events with as much patience as possible," noted the *Times* on Monday. "The certainty that the end of the week at most will settle the question of Mr. Byrnes's retirement on honorable terms is regarded with satisfaction by those officers who feel that the present strain could not be kept up much longer without serious detriment to the best interest of the force."

For a moment the tension of not knowing the fate of Byrnes was relieved by the breaking of suspense over the future of Dr. Buchanan. The Court of Appeals announced from Albany on Monday that the convicted wife-murderer must pay the supreme penalty sometime during the week of July 1. (Buchanan did so in Sing Sing Prison's electric chair on the second.) But the newspapermen of Mulberry Street hoped the Buchanan case would be old news. The headline for evening papers such as Jake Riis's *Sun* and the *Post* of Lincoln Steffens, as well as the next morning's publications, would depend on what occurred during the day between Tom Byrnes and TR.

Everybody understood that this contest of wills was strictly between them. The entire Police Board would have to vote. But TR would be the one whose leadership Grant, Andrews, and Parker would seek and follow. Whatever the outcome—Byrnes retiring on his own or being shoved out the door, or a continuation of the struggle with disastrous results for the force—the end would be decided between the proud fifty-four-year-old detective, a son of Irish immigrants with more than thirty-two years on the police force who said "youse" when berating his inspectors, and the thirty-seven-year-old descendent of the Dutch settlers of New York who had not set foot in headquarters before May 6, and whose flawless command of the language graced succeeding volumes of *The Winning of the West*.

Roosevelt arrived in Mulberry Street at nine o'clock and went directly to the police board room. Ordinarily the commissioners would convene in executive session at ten. The hour came and went, followed by a series of closed-door meetings, including one in late morning between Byrnes and Commissioner Parker. At its conclusion Byrnes entered his own office and closed the door.

The Board then went into executive session, closing their door behind them at noon.

When it swung open more than an hour later Parker gestured to the reporters crowded into the corridor to come in. Roosevelt and the others were seated around a confiscated gambling table that served as their conference table and a symbol of the crime and corruption they were pledged to fight. Whatever actions were about to be revealed, whatever negotiations that may have taken place between Byrnes and the board, it was evident as the room fell silently expectant that Parker, a Tammany man, had played a key role. This impression took on added credence a moment later, for it was Commissioner Parker, not the president of the board, who spoke.

As Parker began, the room suddenly began to go dim. Through the windows commissioners and reporters watched in amazement as what the next day's *Times* would describe as a "thick darkness at noon spread over the city with such density that it seemed the prelude to some great convulsion of nature."

Glowering black clouds and swirling, thick yellow fog cast the rooms of police headquarters into nearly total darkness. They turned Mulberry Street instantly into night and threw upon the streets of lower Manhattan with its proud new skyscraping towers the unreal perspective of a moonless twilight without any of the softness.

"So grim and terrible was the aspect which the murky sky lent to the things of earth," reported an awed *Times* scribe with tongue in cheek, "that the chattering of the men of business was imperatively silenced, while they waited with fear and awe for the culmination of the calamitous portent of the heavens."

The skis poured down nothing more disastrous than rain. Torrents slashed against windows as Commissioner Parker said, "Some time after the appointment of this board, and, consequently, after I came into office, the Chief of Police, probably because of former official acquaintance, told me privately if at any time the interest of the force in which he had served for almost a lifetime, and in which he had risen from the lowest to the highest rank, should in the opinion of the Board of Police, be served better by his retirement than by his continued presence upon it, he would feel it his duty not to embarrass the board by his continued presence, but to hand them his application for retirement."

After a few more words deploring speculation in the press that had preceded the present moment, Parker called upon Chief Clerk Kipp to read Byrnes's application for retirement on a pension of three thousand dollars a year. The board voted unanimously to accept it.

In doing so they laid to rest any possibility that Byrnes would be compelled to face a departmental trial for any of the crimes alleged against him. The assumption was that this was the deal which Byrnes had demanded and TR accepted. The official version would be that Byrnes had departed voluntarily. But everyone in the storm-battered room understood otherwise.

In assaying the action of the board against the spectacular effect of the weather at that moment of highest drama and almost unbearable suspense, the lettered occupants of the police board conference room, which certainly included Theodore Roosevelt, might well have thought of Thomas Byrnes in terms of a line of Shakespeare's *Richard III:*

> For God's sake, let us sit upon the ground
> And tell sad stories of the death of kings;
> How some have been depos'd . . .

The board summoned Byrnes and the man they would presently designate to succeed him as acting chief, Peter Conlin. The inspector presented himself in uniform. Byrnes walked into the room in civilian clothes, head held high. Moments later he appeared in the detective bureau and found it jammed with men with grimly set jaws and tear-streaked faces. After shaking hands and saying his goodbyes, Byrnes left police headquarters as a private citizen for the first time in more than three decades.

Then he headed for Red Bank, New Jersey, and the idyllic banks of the Shrewsbury River. Awaiting him was a rambling brownstone house that not only Jacob Riis's "other half," but the overwelming majority of New Yorkers, believed had been built with ill-gotten funds that had flowed to him solely because of his policeman's uniform.

Of his going the Rev. Dr. Parkhurst said, "Our labors will not cease. We shall continue persistently to watch police work and the work of suppressing crime. It is good work and gratifying, especially with the encouragement of past victories."

Standing beside him inside 300 Mulberry Street was Theodore Roosevelt. "The doctor has never seen what Police Headquarters looked like," he said to reporters. "I imagine it was a great source of satisfaction to him to go through the offices and see new officials in the places of the men whom he had been fighting for years."

Jacob Riis wrote of this passing of an era in Mulberry Street, "Untrammeled, Byrnes might have been a mighty engine for good." But Byrnes was "the very opposite of Roosevelt, without moral purpose or the comprehension of it." Therefore Thomas Byrnes had to go.

"There was not one of us all who had known him long who did not regret it," Riis said, "for Byrnes stood for the old days that were bad."

Lincoln Steffens had not known Byrnes long. He did not regret his going. Neither did he grasp what Byrnes's departure meant to others. When a friend he had made while covering Wall Street looked terribly afraid said, "What will happen to us now I dread to think," Steffens was amazed.

In the days following Byrnes's retirement, he noticed that thieves walked past police headquarters and seemed even more frightened than the honest men. One sat on the steps with his head in his hands, his elbows on his knees.

Steffens inquired of the Headquarters' doorman, a fellow named Tom, who the man on the stoop was.

"Oh, just an old dip that the old man was good to sometimes," Tom replied. "Thinks the world is coming to an end."

It did not.

"When Superintendent Byrnes retired that day and walked without good-by to any of us out of his office forever," Steffens recalled in his book, "men stopped and stood to watch him go, silent, respectful, sad, and the next day the world went on as usual."

Chapter 6

Midnight Rambles

At nine o'clock on the morning of May 29 the acting chief of police addressed roll call in the detective bureau. At the age of fifty-four Peter Conlin was of medium height and slight build with light blue eyes, a sallow complexion, and a personal style marked by politeness and a suave demeanor. Educated in public schools, he had enjoyed the extracultural benefit of having been taught the value of speaking well in public by his half-brother, well-known actor William Florence. Therefore, his remarks to his attentive men contained none of the "dees, dem, doze and youse" of his unlettered predecessor.

Assuring the detectives in general terms that each member of the bureau would have an equal chance for promotion and merit, and that good work would be rewarded, Conlin warned that bad conduct and half-hearted discharge of duty would reap reprimand and remand to street patrolling. These words drew no particular response from the assembled sleuths. His next did. He announced that the departmental policy of using the time-immemorial institution of detective work, the informant—in police and underworld parlance "stool pigeons"—was under review by the commissioners and might be banned. As their new, if temporary, chief left the room, the astonished plainclothesmen shook their heads and murmured to one another in disbelief.

Moving to his own office, Conlin greeted a room filled with anxious acting inspectors and captains. These men bore the day-to-day responsibility of supervising a rank and file that had named itself "the Finest" but which the public viewed with disdain and distrust. They also constituted the segment of the department that had been hit hardest by the scandal unmasked by the Parkhurst crusade and the Lexow Committee. As their new chief addressed them, the top ranks of the department to which they belonged had been depleted by dismissals, retirements, or suspensions of three inspectors and three captains. In fact, only one of Byrnes's inspectors survived the purge; the posts of the three displaced officers had been assumed by "acting" inspectors.

The force that they and the captains commanded also had been left seriously undermanned. Rolls of sergeant and roundsman stood three hundred fewer than authorized strength.

While the numbers in the police force had been dented by the scandal, Conlin reminded the commanders, there was no diminution in the number of lawbreakers. The gambling houses, policy shops, and disorderly resorts that had existed when Parkhurst went out looking for them had not been shut down. He warned the men in his office that highest priority must be given to the suppression of these establishments. That responsibility rested on the shoulders of captains of precincts. The acting inspectors were to be held strictly accountable for the conditions of the precincts in the districts under their command.

Turning to the problem of saloons and other establishments that operated illegally on Sunday by serving alcoholic beverages, he declared he would not tolerate laxity in enforcing the letter of the law. Enacted in 1857, the Sunday Excise statute banned most business activities on the Christian Sabbath, especially the sale of liquor. It had been inscribed in law books in response to extreme pressure from rural regions of the state having a large number of voters who supported the national temperance movement.

The essence of this drive to rid the nation of "demon rum" could be found in the position of the Rev. Charles Parkhurst's Presbyterian Church, set forth in the following manifesto on the subject of selling and consuming liquor:

"We regard the traffic as an evil which can never be removed without political action and we regard its entire prohibition as the most pressing political question of the times; and it, therefore, becomes our duty as Christian citizens, in the careful and prayerful use of the ballot, to meet the question directly."

The call to abstainers to flock to the polls if they did not get action sent chills down the spines of politicians everywhere.

A Christian cleric's righteous opposition to strong drink, therefore, had been as much a part of Dr. Parkhurst's frenzied declaration of war as the duty he felt as a citizen to speak out against official corruption. His denunciations added to pressures from the big bloc of temperance voters to assure reaffirmation of New York's Sunday Excise Law by the State Legislature in 1892.

But in the city of New York with its enormous population of wage-earners whom Jake Riis called "the other half," living in Lower East Side tenements and putting in six days of toiling in sweatshops, Sunday was more than a day for church-going. After fifty-seven hours of work, it was a cherished and much-needed day of respite and refreshment. This break from labor was not their sole reason for seeking thirst quenchers on the Lord's day, however. Most of them boasted an Old World heritage in which wine and beer were afforded an honored position. This was especially true for the people of Little Italy and the better-off residents of the uptown enclave known as Germantown. Added to these masses of Sabbath imbibers were the upper class "swells" of Theodore Roosevelt's social set, for whom a Sunday brunch at a posh Fifth Avenue hotel would be incomplete without a glass of champagne.

As Acting Chief of Police Conlin's primary command, deputies and his small band of detectives returned to their duties after his combination peptalk and warning lecture, they had on their hands a city whose crime rate had not been affected by turmoil and shake-ups in Mulberry Street. With unwavering regularity the population of law-abiding residents suffered at the hands of the lawless.

In the first five months of 1895 the police were called upon to investigate no less than eighty murders. Ten in the month of May ranged from the homicide of Emily Hall on the thirteenth, in which the prime suspect was the Rev. J. Bell, to the gunning down by D. F. Hannigan of S. H. Mann in revenge for the "betrayal" of Hannigan's sister. Since Mayor Strong had taken office, the police had looked into circumstances surrounding half a dozen deaths by poisoning, lest one of them be the result of murder. Scores of robberies had been noted on police blotters, including the embarrassing case of Cohn's Shop at 8 Delancey Street, in which Police Detectives Jacobs and MacManus had been charged with "aiding and abetting." Assaults and affrays involving weapons required police interventions, including one by Eddie Clarke, who shot Andrew Berkenbow in Orange Church three days after Thomas Byrnes handed in his badge and three days before Peter Conlin moved into the office of chief of police.

In the nearby room allotted to the president of the police board, TR wasted no time ruminating on the ouster of Tom Byrnes. He was glad the man was gone, not out of personal animosity but because Byrnes had stood in his way in fulfilling the dual role TR envisioned for himself in the police department. First came the actual administration of the organization. The second task was to use his position to help in making the city a better place in which to live and work for those to whom the conditions of life and labor were the hardest.

He saw the two duties as being closely connected, for one thing never to be forgotten in striving to better the conditions of the New York police force was the connection between a general standard of morals in the city at large and the morals and behavior of the police. This concern for propriety among the cops expressed itself in the employment of a substantial number of informants by the detective bureau. What troubled some citizens about these so-called "stool pigeons" was that they were paid for their information from the public purse. Two principles lay at the crux of the issue—whether the people received their money's worth, and was the practice moral? While keeping an open mind on the subject TR welcomed the review of the policy that Conlin had made public, however unintentionally.

When the acting chief of police revealed the review of the policy of using stool pigeons, what might have been a quiet and internal survey of the pros and cons of the issue immediately became grist for the mills of the city's papers. "Would criminals return?" asked a *Times* headline, rhetorically, on May 29. In the accompanying story the writer noted that against the moral issue was "the acknowledged success with which the stool-pigeon system has had in ridding New York City of gangs of organized criminals; the fear which all criminals have of going back to old haunts in New York City after the commission of a serious crime; the data which have been collected by this method of the characters, the habits, pursuits, occupations, and pleasures of criminals before they have committed the crimes which made them notorious, and the possession of which made their subsequent capture a much easier matter than it would otherwise have been."

The *Times* article then reported Commissioner Andrew Parker's opposition to abandoning the stool-pigeon system. "The present system is a common sense one," he said. "I have no sympathy with mawkishness in catching criminals. If a man committed no crime, or does not intend to commit any, he has no fear of stool pigeons or detectives, or any of the machinery for detection of crime. There is an old saying that it is always the wounded bird that flutters, and it is the criminal pure and simple who fears the methods which result in putting him behind prison bars."

Ultimately, the study of the value of the informant system and an examination of the morality of it slipped lower and lower on TR's agenda, then vanished entirely. Stool pigeons continued to be a mainstay of police work, although a century later that breed of individual was afforded by law enforcement a far more dignified classification, "C.I.," meaning "Confidential Informant." Untold numbers of them were assured of their safety in the federal government's Witness Protection Program.

Regarding TR's short-lived flirtation with kicking stool pigeons out of the New York Police Department's arsenal against crime, one can only speculate whether someone, perhaps Jake Riis or Lincoln Steffens, might have whispered into Roosevelt's ear a reminder that Captain Max Schmittberger had been a stool pigeon and that without Max's turning informant, men of the caliber of Thomas Byrnes and Alexander Williams would still be running the show in Mulberry Street.

Observing the man who was in charge at headquarters, TR's colleague, Commissioner Avery Andrews, found himself impressed with President Roosevelt's effective command of the proceedings of the police board. He liked TR's disposition to expedite the meetings as much as possible. "He made up his own mind quickly, and, while allowing reasonable discussion, was impatient at delay or any irrelevant comment. At one meeting which had been unavoidably delayed several hours beyond the usual time, Roosevelt rushed through several matters brought up by the Chief Clerk with the exclamation, 'That goes,' to which we all agreed. Then, taking up a large bundle of papers, he said, 'These all relate to civil service matters. With the Board's permission, I will decide them all. Even if I decide some of them wrong, that will be better than taking up the Board's time with them.'"

In Andrews TR believed he had found a steady ally. Despite their belonging to opposing political parties, and deep differences over national politics, they agreed that politics must have no role in their work as commissioners. For his part, Andrews was content to go along with TR's frequent appropriation of authority that ought to have been shared with the other commissioners. The same was true of TR's fellow Republican on the police board. In TR's eyes, as well as most other observers of the Board, Fred Grant was "a good fellow, but dull and easily imposed upon," traits that seemed surprising in the son of the flinty, bullheaded, "unconditional surrender" general who had commanded the Army of the Potomac and drove it to victory in the Civil War.

Only Democrat Andrew Parker resented Roosevelt's ways and means, hating the way TR took command from the first day. He kept saying "I" and "my policy," instead of "we" and "our." Domination of the police board by Roosevelt was also duly noted by the *Times*. "Commissioner Roosevelt puts the stamp of approval or disapproval firmly on every action of the Board," it reported. Should there be any argument, "he usually wins."

In fact, TR believed there ought to be only one person in charge. An organization with four heads was anathema. He held the view that executive power could never be effectively employed by a committee. Authority divided added up to no authority. There had to be one leader who "boldly faces the life of strife, resolute to do duty well and manfully, resolute to uphold righteousness by deed and by word, resolute to be both honest and brave, to serve high ideals, yet to use practical methods." If that spelled bending the board to his will, bullying a pair of police department heroes into quitting, and ruffling the feathers of a wounded Andrew Parker, so be it.

He also had no difficulty in handling a potentially dangerous situation that arose to challenge legally constituted authority two weeks after the departure of Byrnes. The question was whether the people of sections of Westchester County that had been recently annexed by New York City would accept the new reality. The territory included Throgg's Neck, Unionport, Bronxdale, William's Bridge, Olinville, Baychester, East Chester, Barton, Wakefield, and a patch of ground on which stood Morris Park Race Track. Concerned that there might be trouble instigated by officials who had been legislated out of office, Roosevelt sent letters to them, delivered on June 6 by Acting Inspector James McCullagh and Captain Richard Allaire at the head of a force of fifty city policemen and a mounted squad. The recipients of the letters decided to take the fight to the courts rather than into the streets.

Inevitably as TR strove to put his mark on the department,

comparisons were made with the way Thomas Byrnes had run things, especially by members of the force who felt indebted to Byrnes for their careers. In the course of many years at the head of the detective bureau and then as chief of police he had favored loyal allies with the most desirable assignments in terms of potential enrichment, but also because of the prestige accruing to a post.

In the latter category was the detective office that protected the Wall Street financial district. A Tom Byrnes creation, it had been set up in 1880 when Byrnes became an inspector in the detective bureau. Located in a small room on the second floor of an old marble building at the corner of Wall and Broad Streets, its two detectives, John J. Dunn and George Radford, were tasked by Byrnes with expelling "crooks" from the area and seeing that they did not return.

The methods employed were pure Byrnes. Dunn and Radford were ordered to arrest any "suspicious individual" found in the district and haul him into the detective bureau office to explain his presence. If he could not he was slapped into a jail cell for the night, then released with a warning not show his face in the Wall Street area again. Word soon spread through the underworld of Byrnes's *cordon sanitaire*. It encompassed the territory from John Street to the Produce Exchange and from Broadway to Pearl Street.

To be certain the Wall Street branch of the detective bureau was carrying out the orders, Byrnes traveled downtown every day for a not-so-discreet observation, walking around to be certain "the lads were covering the field properly." Working in pairs, they looked out for anyone or anything out of the ordinary. Should they spot an individual who "didn't look right," they followed him even into elevators.

When the crime rate plummeted Byrnes boasted, "Not even so much as a ten cent piece was lost in Wall Street through thievery by outsiders. Whatever stealing had been done has been accomplished by the employees of the financial institutions. From time to time a peddler has sneaked off with a hat or coat, but that's the extent of the thievery."

With Byrnes gone the detectives in whom he had placed his trust for so long pondered events unfolding uptown under the new police board and its no-nonsense boss, added up their years of service on the force, and began putting in retirement papers. In the final week of May only Johnny Dunn was left of the original Wall Street detectives. At sixty-three he was one of the oldest men on the force. In fact, he was older than the New York Police Department. He had become a "municipal" in 1854, three years before the creation of the Metropolitan Police District. Like all other "municipals," he had resigned, then applied for a job with the new force. Hired as a patrolman, he was the first officer to walk a beat in the Seventeenth Precinct located on the Lower East Side, at First Avenue and Fifth Street. He rose to detective in 1872 and was promoted to detective sergeant in 1882. One of Tom Byrnes's most trusted men, he intended to hand in his request to collect a pension by the end of the last week in May, 1895. Eager to shed all vestiges of Byrnes, TR welcomed the news.

On Wednesday evening of "Wall Street Johnny" Dunn's last week on the force the president of the police board dressed up in evening wear to attend the final dinner of the winter season of the Republican Club as the guest of honor. It was by far the biggest audience of the year. Fifty members had to be turned away at the door for lack of room. Master of ceremonies was Elihu Root. A close friend and advisor to TR, and a major Republican power, he was a corporate lawyer and former United States attorney for the southern district of New York, appointed by President Chester A. Arthur. He would leave the Republican Club that night and go on to become United States Secretary of State (1905–1909) in the administration of President Theodore Roosevelt, U.S. Senator from New York (1909–1915), President of the Carnegie Endowment for International Peace (1910–1925), recipient of the Nobel peace prize in 1912 (TR would get it in 1906), and an architect of the World Court. Introducing Roosevelt to the packed-in Republicans on the evening of May 29, 1895, Root could not resist a joke. "Theodore Roosevelt," he said with courtly bow in the direction of the guest of honor, "is distinguished in his field for his retiring disposition."

The Republicans enjoyed a good laugh.

TR told them that the work of reforming the police department was "half done, because it was well begun." The Republicans heartily agreed, giving their speaker a rousing ovation.

Five nights later TR spoke again, though not as the main attraction. His audience was the Good Government Club. They gathered two-hundred strong for a meal and speeches at Jaeger's restaurant at Fifty-ninth and Madison. The guests of honor were Assemblyman Howard Payson and Alderman Benjamin E. Hall. But it was TR who garnered the headline in the next morning's *New York Times:*

NO POLITICS FOR POLICE
Theodore Roosevelt Tells What Honest
Reform Accomplishes

TR's topic was billed as "How to Aid Police Reform." His answer was an appeal for support of nonpartisanship in police affairs. "It would be ruin to the cause of municipal government if the Police Board were to divide on party lines. It has been said that non-partisanship and civil service in the force would be impracticable. We will show all men to the contrary," he said.

Then he launched a slashing attack upon legislation under which he and his fellow commissioners had been compelled to oper-ate, the hated Bi-Partisan Law. "We were left worse off," he said angrily. "Now we are working with the law worse for us than for the boards that preceded us. They failed to give us the law they were in honor bound to give us—the law to reorganize the force."

At this point the plural pronoun turned singular. "I wish to make every honest and decent member of the force feel that he has in me a firm friend and that I shall wage a merciless war on corrup-tion. There is no connection between virtue and inefficiency. I will guarantee that the force is at this moment as well able to handle the foes of peace as it ever was."

Concluding with a pledge of "honesty, decency, courage and com-mon sense," he received cheers.

Following him to the rostrum was Dr. Parkhurst, overflowing with gratitude for the hospitality Roosevelt had afforded him in welcoming him and showing him around police headquarters during his recent visit. "We have four Commissioners," he declared, "who have no earthly ambition but to do their duty."

Confident in the state of the reformation underway at 300 Mul-berry Street, the minister who had started it all left the city in the morning for a summer vacation in Switzerland and Russia.

Having made considerable progress in cleaning out a bevvy of tainted inspectors and captains, the police board at TR's urging turned to the next vexsome level. On June 5 the *New York Times* reported, "The Commissioners have been examining records of the

Sergeants, and making other investigations, which have resulted in their coming to the conclusions that there are in the department a number of incompetent and undesirable officers. There are many superior officers who, according to the ideas of the Commissioners, must be dismissed before there can be actual reform in the department."

Meanwhile, the board proceeded with trials of members of the force in the rank of patrolman. Charles E. Sherwood, Charles Baxter, and John Tyrell of the West Twentieth Street Station had to answer for failing to discover the burglary of several pounds of lead from the Erie Storage Warehouse and West Twenty-fourth. Samuel Magrane of the West Thirtieth Street Station was arraigned on charges of failing to arrest the culprits who had burglarized the Brill Brothers' furniture store on Fourteenth Street on the morning of May 21. Magrane suggested that because Brill Brothers made capital out of robberies by advertising the fact and collecting insurance, the broken window and thefts in question might well have been the result of an inside job. The board apparently took the same view, letting Magrane off. Patrolman John Neill did not fare as well. The board convicted him of beating up prisoner John Madden. They also found fault in Patrolman John McGrath of the West Thirtieth Street Station, who had been caught romancing a woman in a doorway when he ought to have been patrolling. He had brandished a club to threaten the nightwatchman who caught him. The charge of verbal abuse was also brought by John W. Morgan, proprietor of a hotel on Charlton Street, against Charles Street Precinct Patrolmen Alexander Kirk and James McCabe. Patrolman Michael J. Griffin of the city hall precinct had to answer the allegation by Frank Faber that he had called Faber a "loafer" and barred him from entering Part I of the Superior Court. Griffin escaped reprimand by proving that Faber habitually used courtrooms to sleep in. The policeman's case was considerably bolstered by the fact that half a dozen lawyers showed up for Griffin's tial to testify on his behalf. The clincher for Griffin, however, was a deputy of Judge Edgar Ransom who averred that Faber was a nuisance and an affront to the dignity of courts of law.

As these trials continued, Jacob Riis and Lincoln Steffens let TR know that they disapproved of the process. For the veteran of the police beat, Riis, the disapproval was largely sentiment for the accused, many of whom were old friends. Steffens nurtured an instinctive opposition to punishment meted out under the guise of "discipline" when what was sought was "revenge." But Steffens did concede in his book that he, too, lusted for revenge in the case of Clubber Williams. He also thought the trials by the police board "were long, the law technical and unsure."

Roosevelt sought to show that Steffens was misguided. One day he poked his head out his office window and yelled to him across the street, "Hey, there, come up here."

When Steffens arrived in Roosevelt's outer office he found it crowded with "all sorts of respectable people, evidently business-men, lawyers, doctors, women, and two priests."

Waving his hand at the assemblage, TR said, "I just want you to see the kind of people that are coming here to intercede for proven crooks. Come on, come into my office and listen to the reasons they give for letting bribers, clubbers, and crime-protectors stay on the force and go on grafting on the public."

Most miscreants paid a price. Some got off. How Roosevelt dis-tinguished between the cases puzzled Steffens, Riis, and many others, not the least of whom were members of the force. One old sergeant took Steffens aside one day and, looking very perplexed, said, "What gets me, what I can't unpuzzle is why he'll listen to Tim Sullivan (a politician) and throw down the Mayor himself and laugh a Platt Republican leader out of his office; and then turn right around and tell Charlie Murphy (a Tammany leader) to sing his song to the high marines in the harbor, and do a favor for Lem Quigg up the river."

Steffens was as puzzled as the old sergeant. (Steffens said "Old Sergeant" was the wisest rank on the police force.) Long after these trials ended, Steffens admitted in his memoir that he never did figure out what "got" TR and what did not when he was deciding a case. Part of the reasons seems to have been that TR could be as sentimental as Jake Riis, who recorded for posterity one instance in which TR's good nature was taken advantage of. The cop called to account for his many peccadilloes was expected to be kicked off the force. But when the man showed up for trial before TR he brought with him eleven children. The doomed patrolman introduced each by name, then with a catch in this throat and a sob, told Roosevelt of the recent death of his wife.

TR peered through his pince-nez spectacles at the tots and gasped,

"What, no mother? All these children? Go, then, and don't go wrong again."

The policeman led the children out and presently returned them to their real parents, neighbors who lived in the basement of the policeman's tenement.

As the trials continued, TR noted with satisfaction on Saturday, June 8, that the trial of Inspector William McLaughlin had ended at eight o'clock that morning with McLaughlin convicted of extortion. He was conveyed across the Brooklyn Bridge to jail in the Tombs. Arriving at the city prison, the disgraced former inspector found himself, because of overcrowded conditions in the lockup, sharing a narrow cell on "Murderer's Row" with one Mike Considine, who had killed John J. Mahoney on Broadway in January.

As McLaughlin must have appreciated, the cell had quite a recent history. It had been occupied by Thomas Pallister, a cop-killer who had gunned down Policeman Kane of the Broadway Squad in 1892. Sent from the Tombs to Sing Sing Prison, Pallister broke out, only to be drowned in the Hudson River with fellow convict and escapee George Roehl.

While McLaughlin paced his small cell Roosevelt called in reporters to inform them that a departmental trial of the former chief deputy to Thomas Byrnes would have been held even if the Brooklyn jury had acquitted McLaughlin. And, he added, a trial by the police board of McLaughlin was still in the cards, despite the fact that once certification of his conviction reached the office of the district attorney, McLaughlin would be automatically removed from the police force.

As newspapers recorded the loss of "one of the most expert thief and criminal takers in the history of the department," McLaughlin's lawyer, Emanuel Friend, let it be know that he felt confident that McLaughlin's conviction would be overturned on appeal.

But the story that galvanized reporters on the police beat, astonished their editors, and left their readers breathless with amazement that second weekend of June 1895 was not the fate of McLaughlin but an extraordinary thing done early in the morning of Friday, June 7, by Theodore Roosevelt.

At 2:00 A.M. the president of the police board had stepped out of the Union League Club on Fifth Avenue into a warm night. Yet he had on an evening coat with the collar pulled up and a soft hat with its wide brim drawn low over his eyes. He stood for a few moments on the steps, his head turning side to side as if he were looking for someone. Presently, as a figure in rather shabby attire and wearing green-tinted eyeglasses turned the corner, Roosevelt dashed to greet him. When they walked east on Forty-second Street a more shady-looking duet of mysterious characters had never attracted the attentions of Tom Byrnes's eagle-eyed sleuths in the detective bureau.

They proceeded unimpeded by any policeman of any rank to Third Avenue, first stop on a route that had been laid out by TR's companion, Jake Riis. It would take them along First, Second, and Third Avenues, from Forty-second Street to Bellevue Hospital at First and Twenty-sixth. This was much of the territory that had been the stomping, clubbing, and testing ground of Alexander Williams before the Clubber moved up to the tastier pickings of the Tenderloin.

The hour and their endurance permitting, Riis suggested, TR and he might then venture farther downtown to the area of Hester and Eldridge Streets in an area of the city that once had been the center of the city's nightlife—the Bowery. But the area had been surpassed by the theaters, restaurants, and other thrills, legal and otherwise, of Broadway. A popular song written in 1892 by Percy Gaunt (music) and Charles H. Hoyt (lyrics) told of a rube who went looking for a good night out on the big town, wound up fleeced and went home singing, "The Bowery, the Bowery; I don't go there anymore."

Strolling down Third Avenue to Forty-first Street, Roosevelt and Riis spotted two policeman engaged in what appeared to be an interesting chat. It was so compelling that they paid no attention as the two men passed them. Riis had no trouble recognizing one of them, Patrolman Mahoney, whose post covered the blocks of Third Avenue between Forty-second and Thirty-sixth. The second man was assigned to Forty-first Street. Giving both men the benefit of the doubt—they might have been discussing official business, after all—Roosevelt strode on, intending to come back. But when he turned round to do so he saw both policemen had gone. He looked for Mahoney five more times, unavailingly.

Between these fruitless checkups on Mahoney's whereabouts, the president of the police board and his knowing guide covered other posts in the immediate vicinity. They found a patrolman enjoying an early breakfast in front of a coffee shop on Twenty-ninth

Street. Moving to a beat encompassing Third Avenue between Twenty-seventh and Thirtieth, they found no one on duty. Nor was a cop to be noticed during two revisits to that area.

In the midst of their search for whoever had the responsibility for that neighborhood they were startled by the appearance of the owner of a Third Avenue coffee shop banging a stick on the sidewalk.

"Where in thunder does that copper sleep?" he shouted. "He orter'd tole me when he changed, so's a fellow could find him when he's wanted."

TR inquired into the merchant's need for help. The man said he thought there was a problem with an electric light in his cafe and wanted a policeman to help him. The rapping of the stick had brought no response from the wandering cop.

Five posts were investigated in Second Avenue. One patrolman was found talking at length to a citizen. Another was discovered in the shelter of a doorway. One was witnessed sitting asleep on a butter-tub in the middle of the sidewalk, his snoring loud enough to be heard across the street. They met Patrolman Elbert Robertson seated in a doorway. Another was all but lost to view in the swirl of a woman's skirts. During all this time no supervisor in the form of a roundsman or a sergeant crossed their path. Only one cop was observed carrying out his duty.

At four o'clock Roosevelt barged into the police station from which all these men were assigned and asked the sergeant at the desk the whereabouts of the roundsman. When he said he did not know, Roosevelt asked to see one of the other sergeants. He was told the precinct had three; the one to whom Roosevelt was speaking, one who had the night off, and the other on reserve and asleep in another room.

"Wake him up," TR demanded. "Let him see if he can find the Roundsman and Patrolman Mahoney."

Unsatisfied, he stormed out of the station on yet another hunt for Mahoney. This time he found him, along with two other men and Roundsman Patrick White, in front of a saloon at Forty-second and Third.

"What are you doing here?" TR demanded.

Not recognizing his interrogator, Mahoney snapped, "Why, I'm standing, of course."

TR asked White his post number.

"Post seventeen," White said.

Recognizing a lie, the seething president of the board of police commissioners returned to the station house and ordered the sergeant to instruct Mahoney and White, along with every other slacker listed on the duty roster to report to his office in Mulberry Street at 9:30 that morning. He then inspected the station house itself, declared it dirty, ordered a cleanup, and headed downtown to the Bowery.

Four policemen were found, none doing his duty. All were ordered to report for trial. The Eldridge Street Station House passed muster.

With six names and badge numbers recorded in a notebook TR arrived at police headquarters at 7:15. The incriminated cops trailed in at 9:30. They all got warnings.

When the reporters of the city's newspapers showed up at the desks in the building opposite headquarters and learned from Jake Riis what had transpired while they slept, they thundered across Mulberry to try to blunt the edges of the clear scoop scored by the old hand from the *Sun*. A delighted Theodore Roosevelt beamed a toothy grin as they wedged themselves into his office.

"I have had the men before me and severely reprimanded them, especially the Roundsman," he said. "Whether I will have charges made or not, I have not decided. I certainly shall have charges preferred and deal severely with the next Roundsman or Patrolman I find guilty of any similar shortcomings."

The next editions of the papers enjoyed a field day, flinging headlines at their readers:

ROOSEVELT AS ROUNDSMAN

POLICE CAUGHT NAPPING

President Theodore Roosevelt Makes
an Early Morning Tour

He Makes the Night Hideous
for Sleepy Patrolmen

One reporter with a high opinion of himself as poet gave his readers this:

> At midnight, on his guardless beat,
>   The cop was dreaming of the hour
> When all his foes in full retreat
>   Should wonder at his power;
> An hour passed on, the cop awoke,
>   That bright dream was his last;
> "He comes! He comes! Look out! Look out!"
> He woke to learn that he was caught
> At doing what he hadn't ought;
>   He wondered what had passed.
> As lightings from the thunder cloud,
> He heard, as with a trumpet loud.
>   T. Roosevelt makes remarks
>   As follows:
> "What are you here for, anyway?
> What do you do to earn your pay?
> What is your name and number? Say?"

Word of Roosevelt's wanderings around the city in the wee small hours sped throughout the uniformed force like wildfire. One fraternal warning showed up on the wall of the men's room in the Thirteenth Precinct Station in the form of a crudely drawn cartoon of TR on the prowl. The work was unsigned by the artist, which was unfortunate, because after looking at it during a surprise visit to the station on June 14, TR found it amusing and, surely, would have been "dee-lighted" if he could have met the creator.

This second venture onto the streets was not in the company of Jake Riis. Apparently desirous of avoiding appearing to be playing favorites, TR walked the dim sidewalks and alleys of the area around Union Market with Richard Harding Davis, the roving correspondent of *Harper's Monthly,* and TR's amiable and admiring fellow commissioner, Avery Andrews. They found almost all patrol posts properly manned. The lone miscreant, Patrolman William E. Rath, apparently had not gotten the word. TR found him enjoying himself at a Third Avenue oyster bar.

"Why aren't you on your post, officer?" TR demanded.

Rath swallowed an oyster, then responded with a question of his own that the newspaper *Excise Herald* felt in its subsequent reporting of the encounter required some editing. It deleted an expletive. "What the _____ is it to you?"

At that moment a man behind the counter, evidently the proprietor and not a diligent reader of the newspapers, chimed in. "You gotta good nerve," he bellowed at Roosevelt, "comin' in here and interferin' with an officer."

"I'm Commissioner Roosevelt."

Reaching for a bottle of vinegar, Rath scoffed. "Yes, you are. You're Grover Cleveland an' Mayor Strong all in a bunch, you are. Move on now, or . . ."

As the counter man took a closer look at the red-faced man with the pince-nez spectacles, he whispered in horror, "Shut up, Bill, it's His Nibs, sure, don't you spot the glasses?"

"Go to your post," TR ordered. "At once."

The *Excise Herald* noted the end of the little drama with the following, written as if it were a stage direction:

(EXIT *patrolman, running.*)

Quite a lot of people who were out in the post-midnight hours of that Friday/Saturday night had no trouble spotting the president of the police board. As TR, Andrews and Davis paused in their meanderings for a steak dinner at Mike Lyon's all-night eatery on the Bowery, several nightowls from the journalistic trade noticed them. They peppered TR with questions, forcing him into holding a press conference while his steak grew cold.

From Mike Lyon's they crossed town to Inspector Williams' former haunts, the Tenderloin, and reaped a harvest of delinquent policemen. TR jotted down their names and numbers in a pocket notebook. Later in the day as he gave the list to Chief Conlin, he said somberly, "This time there will be no mercy." At the trials he acted not as judge but as the complainant.

Riis wrote that because of these excursions into the realm of the police force in the hours when the city slept, "the police force woke up." Avid newspapermen began calling the meandering police commissioner "Haroun-El-Roosevelt," after the caliph in "Tales of Arabian Nights."

The *New York Recorder* described him as "the new cop in town." From distant Chicago an admiring *Times-Herald* judged him "the biggest man in New York." The editorial writer for Jacob Riis's

Evening Sun took the view that, "No matter what the police estimate the duties of a commissioner may be, the fact is that, that officer, particularly if he is President of the Board, has no business to remain inactive or indifferent if he suspects any member of the force, from the Chief of Police down to the plain patrolman, of neglecting or shirking his duties."

The ever-adoring *Washington Star,* which had already speculated upon the former member of the Civil Service Commission as a future resident at 1600 Pennsylvania Avenue's imposing white mansion, suggested to any New York cop who might happen to be a reader of the *Star* that he watch out for trouble "whenever teeth and spectacles came out of the darkness." In the same spirit a cartoonist drew a policeman with a look of horror on his face as he gazed upon a sign in the shape of eyeglasses advertising the firm of Blink and Squint, Opticians, and below it the shingle of a dentist's office in the form of large, bared, grinning teeth.

Just how ubiquitous the Roosevelt teeth had become as an easy caricature of himself TR discovered one day at the very doorstep of police headquarters. A peddler with a sure instinct for the marketplace showed up hawking sets of celluloid dentures and toy police whistles. The peddler quickly sold out. TR found them to be "very pretty."

The object of all this press exaltation and entrepreneurial imagination called his inspection tours "midnight rambles" and allowed that they were "great fun." But they served another purpose besides catching slacking cops, for Roosevelt saw in the explorations of the city in the dead of night an opportunity to have a look at the lowest of New York City's social strata, the one Jacob Riis called "the other half." The rambles were not always undertaken solely to wake up the police, Riis recalled in *Theodore Roosevelt, the Citizen.* "Roosevelt wanted to know the city by night, and the true inwardness of some of the problems he was struggling with . . . for the President of the Police Board was by that fact a member of the Health Board also. One might hear of overcrowding in tenements for years and not grasp the subject as he could by a single midnight inspection."

Nor could a man of Roosevelt's rather comfortable financial situation comprehend the difficulties thousands of people faced in earning a living until he saw them up close. On one of the midnight rambles with Riis they paused to purchase peanuts from a pushcart purveyor of fruits and nuts. It was long past midnight. With the streets deserted it did not seem to Roosevelt that the peddler could sell enough merchandise to pay for even the fuel for his torch that threw a meager light on the dark street. He inquired how the peanut man made any money.

With a forlorn shrug the vendor said in broken English, "What I maka on de peanut I losa on de dam' banana."

TR wrote to Anna, "The work brings me in contact with every class of people in New York, and I get a glimpse of the real life of the swarming millions."

Regardless of such all-night meanderings or how late TR may have remained at his office in Mulberry Street, the denizens of the press shack across the street learned they could count on him charging down Mulberry from Bleeker Street the following morning so as to arrive at his desk no later than nine o'clock. Shunning a waiting elevator, he scaled the stairs to his second floor room overlooking the street and the stoop and windows of the press offices opposite. Next came a flurry of paperwork with decisions addressed to Minnie Kelly as to which document went into a bin for action, the files, or the wastebasket. A good deal of what he regarded as useless material simply landed crumpled on the floor.

If trials were on the day's docket he approached them with as much caution regarding the charges against officers as zeal to root out the bad apples. He found great difficulty in getting at the facts in the more complicated cases. He appreciated the importance of backing up a superior officer who brought a charge. But he could not dismiss the possibility that the superior officer was consciously or unconsciously biased against the subordinate. Wariness was also required in cases brought by private individuals. He found it necessary to be always on guard. Often an accusation would be brought against a policeman because he had incurred someone's animosity by doing his duty.

Occasionally, an officer had made a mistake, as in a case of a man being arrested for engaging in the numbers racket known as "policy." The event was so vivid in Roosevelt's memory that he felt impelled to recount it thirteen years later in his autobiography. In terms of TR's colorful way of describing the human condition, few, if any, passages in the memoir match this.

"The officer in question was a huge pithecoid lout of a creature, with a wooden face and a receding forehead, and his accuser was a little grig of a red-headed man, obviously respectable, and almost incoherent with rage. The anger of the little red-headed man was but natural, for he had just come out from a night in the station-house. He had been arrested late in the evening on suspicion that he was a policy-player, because of the rows of figures on a piece of paper which he had held in his hand, and because at the time of his arrest he had just stepped into the entrance of the hall of a tenement-house in order to read by lamplight. The paper was produced in evidence. There were three rows of figures all right, but, as the accuser explained, hopping up and down with rage and excitement, they were all the numbers of hymns. He was the superintendent of a small Sunday-school. He had written down the hymns for several future services, one under the other, and so on the way home was stopping to look at them, under convenient lampposts, and finally by the light of the lamp in the tenement-house hallway; and it was this conduct which struck the sagacious man in uniform as 'suspicious.'"

Writing to his sister, he told Bamie that days in Mulberry Street were a continuous struggle with "vile crime and hideous vice."

At week's end he caught a train (often the last one) that carried him to Oyster Bay, pedaled a bicycle to Sagamore Hill and lost himself in the embraces of Edith and their children, who cleansed him of the foulness he had dealt with at Headquarters as thoroughly as a scrubbing in a high-sided, narrow tin bathtub.

Bright and early Monday he returned to Mulberry Street, the place that could never be the same, in the opinion of the *Washington Star* author who looked back at TR's first four months in office and afforded readers the following in an August issue:

Since Teddy Came to Town

A lot of things are different from what they were of yore;
The man who pays the taxes now and then may take the floor,
And talk to a policeman without meeting with a frown
Which freezes him completely, since Teddy came to town.
The elevated railway men have studied all they know
What train you ought to take to get you where you want to go;
No more they'll trample on your neck when they have thrown you
   down;
They call you "Sir," and say "Good day," since Teddy came to town.
There isn't any telling where the thing is going to stop;
At present it seems likely the regenerated cop
Will grow himself a pair of wings and wear a shining crown,
And play a harp upon his beat, if Teddy stays in town.

Chapter 7

Honesty and Efficiency

The month of June 1895 started quietly. The body of men who called themselves "the Finest" did not march en masse up Broadway. Believing that the department had become the laughingstock of the city, Roosevelt persuaded the commissioners to ban the force's yearly parade.

On the tenth he summoned the top echelons of the department to his second floor office and declared war on anyone who dared to sell strong drink on a Sunday. He demanded rigid enforcement of the Sunday Excise Law. Whether they believed in the statute or not they were to see that the men carried out the orders "to the letter."

TR was neither a prohibitionist nor a puritan. His job was to enforce the laws, no matter how unpopular. He said, "I do not deal with public sentiment." For part of the public the decree was welcome news, for the tremors shaking the foundations of the police department were an extension of an upheaval of the social reforms demanded by a brand of American Protestantism embodied by Rev. Charles Parkhurst's fiery sermon. When he titled it "Ye Are the Salt of the Earth," he called Christians to rally round his battle flag. "This is a corrupt world," he said in February 1892 to the parishoners in his church and to those of like mind beyond its gothic walls, "and Christianity is the antiseptic that is to be rubbed into it."

The preacher of the Madison Avenue Presbyterian Church was but one of an army of moral reformers on the march across America in the 1880s and 1890s. One group founded in England in 1878 and transplanted in America even called itself the Salvation Army. Having reached New York City, the men and women in its blue and red uniforms called upon Christians to reach out to save lost individuals and thereby bring about redemption of society as a whole. This meant one sinner at a time.

Their preachings found common cause with others. It was the message of Dr. Felix Adler's Ethical Culture Movement. Founded in New York in 1876, its purpose was "to assert the supreme importance of the ethical factor in all relations of life." So, too, preached Christian Endeavor, founded in 1881 by Dr. Francis E. Clark of Maine to promote Christian morality among the young.

All these groups evangelized on behalf of a Protestant-based morality that melded into the Social Gospel Movement. Its goal was the elimination of drinking, prostitution, gambling, and other vices that flourished in the cities of America and threatened to corrupt youth, and did corrupt the politicians who controlled the very system established to root out such evils—the police.

It had been the allure of "the social evil" to the young that Rev. Parkhurst had gone after through the Crime Prevention Society before exasperation with the disinterested and thwarting efforts of politicians and police drove him into denouncing them from his pulpit.

One reformer asked, "Who would ever have prophesied a century ago that today, like hardware and groceries, the daughters of the people would be bought and sold? But to such a day as this our greed for money has brought us." Another said, "It is therefore the duty of the police to enforce all measures necessary to stamp out this evil and the plain duty of all those in authority to give means necessary to effort such an action."

That same fervor to stamp out prostitution was expected in the matter of intoxicants. Strong drinks and alcoholism were viewed as vices undercutting the moral underpinnings of America and a direct challenge to the Christian conscience. If laws were inadequate to stem the problem, then new ones must be enacted. In the legislative halls of Albany, New York, the response had been the Sunday Excise Law, forbidding sale and consumption of alcohol on "the Christian Sabbath" and Christian holidays.

To assure the attention of politicians the reformers made it clear that they stood prepared to express themselves on election day as readily as they spoke out in churches. To drive the point home even harder they formed a variety of groups whose goal was upright governance. In New York and elsewhere they and other like-minded reformers started Good Government Clubs. Philadelphians created the Citizen's Municipal Association. Baltimore had its Reform League. Chicago saw formation of the Civic Federation. Los Angeles got a Committee of Safety, its name echoing the days of an earlier American Revolution. Their common objective was bringing police forces into line with public demands that social evils be expunged—immediately and thoroughly—not tolerated, as Inspector Williams had done, because they were fashionable.

All these objectives of the Social Gospel Movement conformed to Theodore Roosevelt's personal code of morality, based on the religious convictions he carried throughout his life. "The true Christian is the true citizen, lofty of purpose, resolute in endeavor, ready for a hero's deeds," he would say in an address to the Young Men's Christian Association in New York City on his last night in office as Governor of New York. It was a belief he had embraced early in life, taught by his father and underscored by his own experiences with evil in government and without.

Had TR not shared the high purposes of those in the Social Gospel movement, it seems unlikely that Jacob Riis could have succeeded in enlisting "the Christian Endeavorers and Methodist ministers to the support of Roosevelt," as Riis proudly claimed to have done in *The Making of an American* and again in *Theodore Roosevelt, the Citizen*.

Time and again Roosevelt spoke and wrote on the subject of high ideals. But he went on to stress that no amount of idealism could reach desired results unless the idealist was also a hardheaded pragmatist "capable of achievement in practical fashion." In 1895 few figures in the public arena had demonstrated such a blending of the idealist's goals with measurable results as had Theodore Roosevelt.

As the idealists looked to the Christian gospel to guide them in their reforming zeal, practically-minded individuals such as Roosevelt appreciated that the refashioning of a police department could not be achieved by looking up the right instructive chapter and verse in the New Testament. The reformers of policing looked, instead, to the organizational charts of military organizations. The analogy was an appropriate one, for an army and a police department had the same objectives; the maintenance of peace and security and, if needed, their restoration by force. That a police department could be set up and operated on a military model had been shown in the experience of England. In 1822 Sir Robert Peel had borrowed liberally from the army in creating London's Metropolitan Police, famed the world over in 1895 as Scotland Yard. Even its uniform and beehive helmet had been borrowed from Queen Victoria's soldiers. The only thing England's "Bobbies" lacked that the army enjoyed was permission to carry guns.

Patterning cops on soldiers made perfect sense to TR. He saw a need for instituting in the governing of the police "many of the principles . . . which obtain in the army." As his thinking reflected a martial bent, so did his language. The purpose of the police was to "make war against crime" and to do so with "fighting efficiency," he often said.

Consequently, when Commissioner Avery Andrews laid before him a plan for reorganizing the police along military lines, TR was "dee-lighted" and enthusiastic. Presented with a design for a new uniform that would dress the members of the force in a military fashion, he liked what he saw—a double-breasted army-type coat, leggings, and a helmet that resembled an upside-down bucket.

Next, he took another page from the soldier's and sailor's manual—recognition of merit. He announced that in making promotions the police board would take into account not only a man's general record, his faithfulness, industry, and vigilance, "but also his personal prowess as shown in any special feat of daring, whether in the arresting of criminals or in the saving of a life, for the police service is military in character, and we wish to encourage the military virtues."

In assessing a present or potential member of the force he looked for men "of strong physique and resolute temper, sober, self-respecting, self-reliant, with a strong wish to improve themselves." A man's religion could have no part in the process of selection, though conveying this reality proved to be somewhat of a challenge in dealing with two clergymen who came to see him concerning members of their flocks who wished to join the force.

The first to call was a Roman Catholic priest who ran a "temperance lyceum" and wished to find out if men who attended it would be disqualified from police service. Roosevelt told the priest he was looking for just that sort of sober men. In time he counted upwards of thirty members of the force from the priest's adherents to temperance.

But it was not a question of views on drinking that troubled a Methodist minister who came to see him. The clergyman worried that several of his congregants who wished to become policemen might be required to buy their way into the department or need political "pull." TR layed the fears to rest. Later, he noted "a dozen or fifteen members of that little Methodist congregation" had achieved their goal without paying a penny or calling upon someone with influence. Both practices had been relegated to the pages of history in Mulberry Street.

Eager to maintain good relations with the religious leaders of the city, the president of the police board frequently spoke to various church groups. One of those he visited early in his term was the Young Men's Institute, a local branch of the Young Men's Christian Association, located in the Bowery. After his remarks he was asked by his host, Cleveland H. Dodge, to meet a young man who had recently become a neighborhood hero. He had rescued some women and children from a fire.

TR exclaimed that he would be delighted to meet him. Dodge took him to a corner of the room where Roosevelt saw "a powerful fellow, with good-humored, intelligent face." Dodge introduced the youth as Otto Raphael. Whatever surprise Roosevelt might have experienced at finding a Jew at a Christian meeting, he did not record. But Raphael certainly left a good impression.

After asking him about his education, TR invited him to "try the examination" for the force. Taking up the suggestion, Raphael passed, received an appointment and, in Roosevelt's words in his autobiography, "made an admirable officer." TR learned later that Raphael's parents had emigrated from Russia and Otto had several brothers and sisters, born in New York. His pay as police officer allowed him to put them through school. He also paid the passage to the United States for two relatives who had had to remain in Russia.

Unquestionably, TR had been affected by Raphael's bravery in rescuing people from a blazing building. Courage was exactly what he sought in members of the force, whether they were newly appointed or already on the rolls. Courage ranked with honesty and efficiency on the Roosevelt list of desirable traits. He found he did not have to look far to find it.

"We did not have to work a revolution in the force as to courage in the way that we had to work a revolution in honesty," he wrote. "They had always been brave in dealing with riotous and violent criminals."

A month after taking office Roosevelt seized an opportunity to demonstrate to the public and the police that a man could not only do his job but do it in an extraordinarily admirable manner. His example was Policeman Michael Nolan of the One-hundred-fourth Street Station. On May 4 while patrolling a stretch of the Harlem River Nolan had heard frantic cries for help from a child in the water. Plunging in, he swam to the drowning boy and dragged him ashore. This was precisely the conduct that TR admired and wished to spotlight. But the rescue of little Edward Christal provided Roosevelt with more than the pleasure of rewarding a brave man with a medal and a certificate of appreciation. He found in the dramatic circumstances an opportunity to point out a disturbing fact about the police force.

While reviewing the Nolan case he learned of another rescue from a city river. In this instance Policeman Cox of the Leonard Street Station had jumped into the Hudson River at Canal Street in an effort to fish out a woman who had attempted suicide. Unfortunately, Cox's heroism had been necessitated by the fact that the first policeman on the scene did not know how to swim.

Relating this event to those gathered in the police board room for the award to Nolan on June 5, 1895, TR said, "I think that all policemen who patrol the river front should be able to swim. In this warm weather many people go down to the river to get cool. It would be a great advantage to have policemen on duty who know how to swim."

Turning to the chief clerk, he directed that a list be drawn up of every officer on active duty on the force who had a record of lifesaving so that those men could be immediately assigned to waterfront duty. Swim-training for the entire force would then be presented for the board's consideration for the first time in the history of a police force surrounded by water.

Noting the shift of winds at Headquarters in the direction of courage, competence, honesty, and efficiency, Jacob Riis wrote, "For the first time every man had a show on his merits. Amazing as it was, 'pull' was dead. Politics or religion cut no figure. No one asked about them." But should a policeman, "pursuing a burglar through the night, dive running into the Park Avenue railroad tunnel, risking a horrible death to catch his man, he was promptly promoted." He also noted with satisfaction that if a policeman ruined his uniform in the line of duty, it would be replaced at no cost to him—a reversal of previous policy.

A few weeks after Policeman Nolan had been honored and rewarded with promotion for giving everything he had to his job, a young cop who had been on the force only a few months caught Roosevelt's attention in dramatic fashion. His name was Edward J. Bourke.

Daring to believe that the new commissioner with the funny glasses and the large teeth meant what he said about making the police force a proud organization again by enforcing laws without favor, the fledgling officer decided to enforce the statute that required saloons to be closed on the Christian Sabbath. The one he chose to shutter on Sunday, June 23, 1895, was Pat Callahan's on Chatham Square.

History does not record whether Bourke knew anything about Callahan, other than the fact that he owned a saloon operating in violation of the law. Had the policeman asked anyone in the area for particulars about Pat he would have learned that Callahan was a former Assemblyman with historic and strong ties to Tammany. Everyone called him "King." And everybody had heard him brag on the day he opened his saloon that its doors would never be found closed. To back up the boast, the story went, he tossed the keys to the place into the river.

Suddenly that Sunday in June, a cop was tapping Pat Callahan on the shoulder and telling the King he was under arrest for violating the Sunday closing law and ordering the saloon closed. Callahan responded by suggesting he was being kidded. Bourke shook his head solemnly and repeated his order that Pat was to close up shop and come along peaceably to the Eighth Precinct Station. Callahan punched Bourke, knocking him to the sawdust floor. Springing up, Bourke replied by swinging at Callahan with an object at the end of which there was supposed to be more law than in any order of the Supreme Court.

"Now, Pat was a man of strength as well as power, and all his gang was there," Lincoln Steffens recorded for posterity. "He fought, the gang fought, there was a boozy, bloody battle, but the young cop with his night stick laid out enough men to hold off the rest."

Bourke conveyed Callahan to the station. Handed a summons, Callahan was ordered to appear in Tombs Police Court for arraignment and a hearing on whether he would have to go on trial. As arresting officer, Bourke also had to present himself. When he arrived on the appointed day he discovered a court overflowing with politicians.

Also in the room was Lincoln Steffens of the *Post*. Looking round, he recognized a congressman, a state senator, and many of the biggest names in city politics. Sensing that a scenario was about to unfold that would result in Callahan walking away and Bourke pilloried, Steffens dashed up to Mulberry Street to alert Roosevelt.

Blurting at the startled president of the policy board, "Pat Callahan is a sacred person in the underworld, a symbol," he told TR he would be courting disaster for police reform if he did not rally to Bourke's rescue at once.

Roosevelt rushed the few blocks to the courthouse, barging in with teeth bared for a fight, only to discover that somehow word that he was on the way had preceded him. Wanting no part of a showdown with the embodiment of "reform," Callahan's political pals had scurried out. Minutes later, a shocked Callahan found himself remanded to trial.

TR grabbed the rookie cop's hand. "Bourke, you have done well, you have shown great gallantry," he boomed. "The Board is behind you."

Although he was too green under regulations to be promoted, the commissioners understood that if they reneged on President Roosevelt's pledge they might doom any likelihood of other cops daring to do their duty, thereby spelling the end to any hope of changing the way business was done, not only in the department but throughout city government. They voted to elevate Bourke to roundsman. Eventually he earned the rank of captain and two-and-a-half pages of glowing tribute and gratitude in TR's memoirs.

Such daring and personal prowess as Bourke's received recognition in two ways. A man in the ranks was awarded a medal or a certificate. He also received a guarantee that the citation would be weighed heavily in his favor if and when the man came up for promotion.

Should an act of bravery or other outstanding demonstration be recorded by one of the higher ranks, however, recognition was harder to come by. TR assumed that anyone who had reached the higher echelons of the department already had received sufficient reward.

One policeman who did not fit snugly into TR's categories of reward or punishment was Captain Max Schmittberger, whose testimony before the Lexow Committee had precipitated the events that propelled Theodore Roosevelt into a second floor office of police headquarters. Public opinion cried for the confessed collector of the police graft system to be punished severely.

"The belief in the existence of good men and bad men and that the guilty should suffer is deeply implanted in all men, and the star Lexow witness was a villain in two ways, in two worlds," wrote Steffens. "The good were against him for his grafting, the underworld for squealing."

A man of innate generosity toward the human spirit, Steffens wondered, "Cannot an honest man do dishonest things and remain honest? Isn't a strong man, however bad, socially better than a weak man, however good?"

To those caught up in the righteousness of the Social Gospel Movement, such as Parkhurst, the answer, should they even stop to ponder such a question, was "No." But Steffens did not detect in Roosevelt the adamant approach to human failings so apparent in the Parkhursts of the city and nation. In Roosevelt he sensed a chance to "save" Schmittberger. And Lincoln Steffens desperately wished to do precisely that.

Since the recitation of the sins of the police in the Tweed Courthouse, Schmittberger had had a rough time. In January he had been threatened with indictment because "he had not told all he knew." He had failed to report a five hundred dollar bribe from an agent of the steamship firm Compagnie General Transatlantique. A threat of a criminal prosecution had been a ruse to compell him to provide even more information about venal cops. The tattle-tale officer had also been removed from his command and transferred to a distant precinct. The cops' phrase for such a posting was "going to Goatville."

Steffens conceded that Schmittberger had been "strong as a crook." He had been bold in collecting blackmail and honest in distributing graft to Williams and others. His confession before the Lexow Committee had been "complete, detailed and picturesque." Yet within the cocoon of corruption, Steffens believed, beat the heart of a basically decent human being. If Christians such as Rev. Parkhurst and others in the reform army were truly believers, then, surely, they had to embrace Christ's doctrine of salvation through repentence.

Appealing to Parkhurst to enlist in the redemption of Max Schmittberger, he argued, "We, the reformers, cannot afford to penalize a policeman for coming over to our side, exposing organized evil and for confessing his sins and reforming."

Parkhurst shook his head. He thought. The moral warrior felt revulsion against all that Schmittberger had done. But Parkhurst preached Christ's word of forgiveness. The gospel won out. Yes, he said, he would back Steffens.

Now came the hard part. Persuading Theodore Roosevelt. To do so Steffens argued that by bringing Max Schmittberger back from Goatville and placing him in charge of "a bad, fat, grafty precinct," TR would find that Schmittberger would "clean it up, make the police under him enforce the law."

Roosevelt banged a fist on his desk. "No, no, no."

Did not Steffens appreciate that he was deep in a struggle within the department, trying to command or persuade the men to believe in him and in reform? How could he possibly look with favor upon a corrupt cop? Never mind that Schmittberger claimed to have turned over a new leaf. No.

Steffens pleaded. In rehabilitating this fallen policeman the police board would show that it would favor the police officers who were on the side of right and reform. "The police and Tammany and the vice men and women know that Schmittberger is against them now and for us," he said. "That's why they want him out. But as Dr. Parkhurst asks, why do *we* want him out?"

Roosevelt relented. But he wanted no part of it personally. "Go to Parker," he said. "I am not cunning enough to deal with that sort of—espionage. Parker loves it. Let him try out your honest crook. I'll abide by his decision."

Although Steffens would have preferred to strike the deal with TR, he appreciated Roosevelt's position. Andrew Parker was exactly the type to grasp the subtleties of the rationale for bringing back Schmittberger. Steffens had met characters like Parker in literature and in history but never before in life. He saw Parker as one of those men "that liked to sit back and pull wires just to see the puppets jump." Roosevelt was never such a person and never could be.

In approaching Parker, Steffens proved equally wiley. He explained his plan, then noted Roosevelt's reservations about it. "I wish you would try it out," he implored, convinced that Parker would do so simply because Roosevelt was against it.

Parker smiled slyly at Steffens. "You know how to get me, don't you? Well, we'll see."

A few days later Schmittberger was transferred to another precinct. Within a week he closed down two pool rooms, hangouts for a criminal element. Impressed with these results but wary about Schmittberger's "new leaf," Parker decided to test him. He arranged the arrests of a gang of "wire-tappers" who picked off the results of horse races and held up the news of the wins until their confederates could place bets. Parker let the gang know that they could continue their shady operation if they paid off Schmittberger. He even provided them money. It was marked. If it turned up in Schmittberger's possession it would prove that he had taken a bribe.

A few days after setting the scheme in motion, Parker sent for Steffens. "Remember those wire-tappers that were going to bribe Schmittberger?" he asked. "Well, they're in the hospital. They tell me that they had hardly got started talking business when Schmittberger leaped on them, knocked them down and kicked them bodily out of the police station, across the sidewalk and into the street."

Steffens asked, "And what did Schmittberger say?"

"Not a word. He hasn't reported the case. He called an ambulance and forgot it. I think that, if you'll warn him to wear gloves on his fists, we can use him to clean up all the bad precincts in town."

Told what had happened, Roosevelt shouted, "Atta boy."

At Headquarters, Schmittberger received a new name: "The Broom." However, one aspect of his character troubled Steffens. The Broom seemed too quick to resort to his fists or his club against ordinary citizens. Once he shouted to a group of "Reds" who carried placards proclaiming their constitutional right to march, "To hell with the Constitution." He also showed what to Steffens was an unappealing propensity for violence against strikers, groups with whom Steffens sympathized.

Deeply worried and desiring to teach Schmittberger a lesson in humanity, Steffens arranged through Parker to have the Broom transferred to the Lower East Side's Jewish ghetto.

Schmittberger protested he knew nothing about Jews.

Steffens lectured. Jews were poor. Immigrants. Friendless people who never got a square deal. Yes, they could be difficult, quarrelsome, aggressive, sharp in their dealings, and insistent upon their rights. No matter. They had to fight, not only for their life, but for a living wage. "Be patient with them. Be considerate. Be fair. When they come to you, listen to them and try to settle their quarrels without a fight or an arrest."

When Steffens visited the precinct one morning he found Schmittberger had convened a court of complaints. He heard not only of financial disputes but contentions of an ecclesiastical nature, quarrels over art and culture, husbands versus wives, wives against husbands, bosses against workers and vice versa, even children with complaints about their parents.

"My ex-collector of bribes was a success," Steffens wrote proudly in his memoirs. "He could learn; he had learned as much from us reformers as he had from the old grafters."

Despite numerous passages of the New Testament in which Christ said "Go and sin no more" and taught that all of heaven rejoined when one lamb that had been lost returned to the fold, Rev. Parkhurst found Schmittberger's conversion astonishing.

The formerly dubious TR dee-lightfully took to calling Schmittberger "my big stick."

For the president of the board of police commissioners and his three associates reform meant more than dealing with the men of the force. They discovered that the structure of a department with an annual operating budget of six million dollars needed revamping. While Parker supervised the policing and Colonel Grant managed the tangible assets, Avery Andrews took charge of bringing order out of the chaos of the department's business affairs. Sealed bids were demanded for the first time in the history of police department procurement. Politically-connected monopolies of departmental business were broken up. Stringent controls were imposed on accounts. In every sense the headquarters bureaucracy was expected to become as professional as the men in the station houses and walking patrol.

The reformers under President Roosevelt also required all those in police blue to pledge their loyalty to only two groups: the public and the force. Accordingly, the board ordered everyone on the force to quit political clubs. The edict issued by Roosevelt said, "No person in the police force shall be permitted to contribute, directly or indirectly, to any political fund, or to join, or be, or become, a member of any political club or association."

The command fell hard on a clubhouse called the Pequod, a favorite trysting place of the man the *Times* called "the late and unlamented Commissioner John C. Sheehan," whom Mayor Strong had targeted as the first person to be purged from the police. The Pequod had also welcomed Inspector William McLaughlin to membership. Captain Bill Devery also belonged, as did a long list of lower-ranking policemen whom the *Times* delighted in listing by name in its story on the edict, which struck at the heart of political bossing in the police department.

No endeavor was undertaken with more zest on Roosevelt's part than a frontal assault on "the bosses." They had always been his enemies, as a group and as individuals, and would remain so throughout his life. Writing "Machine Politics in New York City" for *The Century* in 1896, his second year as police commissioner, he said, "In a society properly constituted for true democratic government—in a society such as that seen in many of our country towns, for example— machine rule is impossible. But in New York, as well as in most of our other great cities, the conditions favor the growth of ring or boss rule." He went on to describe a boss as a politician "with a genuine talent for intrigue and organization. He owes much of his power to the rewards he is able to dispense." A boss was always a man who gained his power by secret and corrupt means. Their work was done behind closed doors and consisted chiefly "in the use of that greed which gives in order that in return it may receive."

As TR strove to reform the police, the two political parties were headed by men who were either a boss or a leader, depending upon one's own political affiliation. The Democratic boss was Richard Croker. The Republicans followed Thomas Platt. Neither winced if addressed as "Boss."

Friends saw Platt as energetic, industrious, tenacious, and unyielding. Enemies said he was a grinding, persistent machine. Roosevelt knew him as friend and enemy. As a fellow Republican he had opposed Platt at times in the legislature. One observer saw Platt's political style as feline while Roosevelt's was that of a full grown bull moose. TR had found Platt to be "always kind and friendly" personally, but he saw in him a lack of "any tastes at all except for politics, and on rare occasions for a very dry theology wholly divorced from moral implications."

On visits to New York City the Republican boss had occupied a seat in a pew of Rev. Parkhurst's church—that is, until the minister rose in the pulpit on that fateful February Sunday to declare Thomas Platt worse than five Dick Crokers.

Whereas results-minded Roosevelt might hold his nose and look to Platt for support from time to time in Platt's powerbase, the state legislature, TR knew exactly where he stood with Dick Croker, the unquestioned boss of Tammany Hall. They could only be antagonists. He could expect Croker to fight him at every step.

Roosevelt had studied his primer in political bossism at the knee of Joe Murray as a fledgling candidate for office. He had earned a degree in the subject as an assemblyman and Republican leader in Albany. Jacob Riis gleaned the facts of life as a newspaperman. But Lincoln Steffens had attempted a crash course in the subject from a man who was a master.

Shortly after going to work for E. L. Godkin's *Post* he had trekked up to Fourteenth Street and barged into Tammany Hall looking for Boss Croker. Although the political insiders of the city knew that Croker rarely put in an appearance there, the novice newsman did not. By chance he found Croker in.

Steffens saw in the legendary ruler of the Democratic machine a sweet-faced man. Hat, hair, and neat suit were iron gray. The eyes were kind as Steffens blurted, "Mr. Croker, the *Post* wants to know . . ."

"Yes, I know that the *Post* wants to know, the *Post* needs to know," Croker interjected sourly, "but Larry Godkin would not learn anything from Dick Croker. He sends you up here to get me to say something to quote and roast. Isn't that so? If I said something—no matter what—wouldn't he jump on me and it? He would pick it up and pound me with it. And so you know that it would be foolish for me to say a word for publication."

Steffens promised "man to man" that not a word between them would see print.

Croker agreed to the terms. "What do you want to ask me?"

"Well, about this boss-ship. Why must there be a boss when we've got a mayor and—a council and—"

"That's why," Croker broke in. "It's because there's a mayor *and* a council *and* judges *and*—a hundred other men to deal with. A government is nothing but a business, and you can't do business with a lot of officials who check and cross one another and who come and go, there this year, out the next. A businessman wants to do business with one man, and one who is always there to remember and carry out the business."

"They don't have graft in business," said the former Wall Street reporter. "How can you stand for graft in politics?"

Croker suggested Steffens was talking about "dirty graft, like the police graft."

"Yes, that's what I meant," Steffens said.

Now, from a master of the subject, Steffens learned about political corruption.

"Police graft is dirty graft," Croker said. "We have to stand for it. If we get big graft, and the cops and the smallfry politicians know it, we can't decently kick at their petty stuff. Can we now? We can't be hypocrites, like the reformers who sometimes seem to me not to know that they live on graft. This I tell you, boy, and don't you ever forget it: I have never touched a cent of the dirty police graft myself."

"But you do make money out of politics."

"Like a businessman in business," Croker answered, "as hard as nails." And according to Steffens' account of the conversation, "I work for my own pocket all the time."

Ever after, Steffens would spin for a new reporter the tale of his extraordinary chat with Boss Croker and tell the listener with a kind of admiring tone in his voice, "Croker's a crook, but he's a great crook."

Therein lay the difference between Croker and Roosevelt and why they could never be less than mortal foes in a war for the soul of a city, one that would be decided in Mulberry Street.

Opening another front in the contest, Roosevelt announced that police department reform would encompass the election process itself. The law required the police board to appoint poll watchers, two each from the parties garnering the most votes in the previous election. This usually meant Democrats and Republicans. Traditionally those appointed were chosen by the respective bosses. Henceforth, TR told the press, "only men of good character would be appointed Inspectors of Election, poll clerks and ballot clerks," and all would have to pass muster with the board, meaning himself.

However he might be viewed by New Yorkers as summer came in, whether loved, hated, admired, despised, respected, derided, the most feared or the greatest man in the city, TR made good copy for the newspapers and a crowd-pleasing public speaker. Requests for him to fill the latter role poured in.

On July 16 he traveled to 134 East 115th Street to make his first major address as president of the police board. Much on the minds of the German-American citizens who had invited him to the auditorium of the Good Government Club was his edict to police to enforce the law against selling alcoholic beverages on Sundays. His message was simple and blunt. "It is the plain duty of a public officer to stand steadfastly for the honest enforcement of the law."

The German-Americans gave him polite applause.

Picturing Roosevelt as a Puritan Dutchman, newspapers referred to his enforcement edict as "Teddy's Folly." But the *Commercial Advertiser* saw in TR's courage and conviction a man marked for bigger things, perhaps an office in city hall, the Governor's mansion, or the White House. The Rev. A. C. Dixon agreed, stepping forward on July 21 to declare Roosevelt unquestionably suited to become President of the United States.

Two days later, after another midnight ramble in which he found his policemen carrying out their duties, Roosevelt looked forward to Sunday, July 28, becoming "the dryest New York ever recorded."

Unfortunately, a sharp-eyed downtown saloonkeeper found a loophole in the law. For some reason, the hours between midnight Sunday and 1:00 A.M. Monday did not fall within the span of the law's effect. Word of the discovery swept the city. At the stroke of midnight, the beer, whiskey, and other intoxicants flowed freely. The next afternoon Jacob Riis's *Evening Sun* headlined that Roosevelt was beaten, overlooking the fact that for the twenty-four hours prior to midnight Sunday saloons and other bistros had not dared to risk arrests by serving intoxicants.

One individual who was not pleased with the closings did not limit himself to verbally abusing Roosevelt. He mailed his protest in the form of a letter-bomb. It went off harmlessly on Wednesday, August 5, as it was being handled in the post office. Informed of the event, TR called it "a cheap thing" and went back to work. On the evening of the seventh he took his place on the stage of Carnegie Hall to engage in a discussion of the issue of the Sunday law with State Senator "Big Tim" O'Sullivan, one of Tammany's stalwarts and pride of the city's beer-fancying Irish population. The forum was the Catholic Total Abstinence Union's annual convention. When the audience sang "While We Are Marching for Temperance" with all the vigor and enthusiasm of Civil War Yankees who sang the tune when it was titled "Marching Through Georgia," Big Tim waited in silence. When he rose to speak it was to decry the "Puritan's gloomy Sunday" and champion the right of the orderly citizen "to drink in moderation." The abstinent Catholics roundly booed him.

Referring to O'Sullivan in tones of one who felt sorrow for a misguided child, TR drew a burst of encouragement from one enthusiastic teetotaler. He cried, "Rub it in to him, Teddy," and drew a thunderous ovation from seven-thousand fellow Catholics.

Roosevelt went on to express his hope that he would soon see "the time when a man shall be ashamed to take any enjoyment on Sunday which shall rob those who should be dearest to him, and are dependent on him, of the money he has earned during the week; when a man will be ashamed to take a selfish enjoyment, and not to find some kind of pleasure which he can share with his wife and children."

The speech got a five-minute ovation. Even Mayor Strong leapt to his feet in approbation. Big Tim sat silently.

Henry Cabot Lodge penned to his friend and protégé, "You are rushing so rapidly to the front that the day is not far distant when you will come into a larger kingdom."

When the next Sunday came and went into the history books as the driest on record in New York City the correspondent of the *London Times* signalled his readers, "There has not been a more complete triumph of law in the municipal history of New York."

The verdict was to prove premature.

New York City policeman walks his beat in the 1890s. (New York Public Library)

Police headquarters on Mulberry Street. (New York Public Library)

As president of the Board of Commissioners, Theodore Roosevelt carried out his reforms from a second-floor front office at headquarters on 300 Mulberry Street. (Theodore Roosevelt Collection, Harvard College Library)

(a)

(b)

(c)

TR's allies in reform: (a)
Jacob A. Riis of the *Sun*;
(b) Lincoln Steffens of the
Post; and (c) Rev. Charles
H. Parkhurst. (New York
Public Library)

TR called the four-man Police Board "the Polish parliament" because most decisions required unanimity of the four. When the Tammany man, Commissioner Andrew Parker (on TR's right), blocked several TR initiatives, the Board became deadlocked. In 1896, an investigation by the *New York Times* (below) revealed a conspiracy between Tammany Hall boss Richard Croker and Republican boss Thomas Platt to get rid of Roosevelt so that the old days of graft could return. (Theodore Roosevelt Collection, Harvard College Library)

THE REPUBLICAN PLOT TO OUST ROOSEVELT

Political Cowards and Assassins Would Strike Him
Down for His Honesty and Courage.

LEGISLATE HIM OUT—RESTORE THE SIDE-DOOR SUNDAY

That is Platt's Scheme in Order to Recapture the Lost City Vote and Hood-
wink the Cold Water Men of Herkimer.

A POLICY OF CONTEMPTIBLE COWARDICE AND HYPOCRISY

Mayor Strong's Vacillating Views and Caution Appearing First a Friend
of Liquor Men and Again for Restriction.

His Attitude Toward the President of the Police Board Varying and Puzzling—Will the Prominent Citizens Who Uphold the Commissioner for Enforcing the Laws Help Repel
His Assailants?

The Platt politicians of this State have determined to remove Theodore Roosevelt, President of the Police Board in this city, from office. They intend—if they can—to legislate him out of the board as a punishment, mainly, for his persistent, untiring, and courageous efforts to enforce laws framed by Republicans.

excise question by the police force. There is no doubt of this in the mind of any rational resident of New-York.

MAYOR'S VACILLATING VIEWS.

Col. Strong Appears Friendly to Both
the Liquor and Temperance Men.

The politicians and the public know where

(a)

(b)

TR's version of "Good Cop, Bad Cop":
The Bad: (a) Chief Thomas Byrnes and (b) Inspector Alex (Clubber) Williams.
The Good: (c) Captain Max Schmittberger, later in his career on his horse in
rank of inspector; (d) patrolman Otto Raphael, a heroic Jewish youth whom TR
personally recruited for the force; and (e) patrolman Edward Bourke, promoted
by TR for his daring arrest of a notorious saloon keeper with political "pull."

(c)

(d)

(e)

After TR began his drive against saloons illegally selling liquor on Sundays, he became a target for political cartoonists.

"Chamber of Horrors." A cartoon by C. G. Bush in the *New York Herald* showed prominent figures in the police department. TR is at far left.

Chapter 8

"I deal with the law."

On an evening in 1894, bathed in footlights of the Bowery's London Theatre, Miss Lottie Gibson introduced a jaunty song that would outlive Lottie, her audience, and the two men who wrote it. She sang

> East Side, West Side, all around the town,
> The tots sang "Ring-a-rosie," "London bridge is falling down";
> Boys and girls together, me and Mamie Rorke,
> Tripped the light fantastic on the sidewalks of New York.

Arguably the best-known musical valentine to any city, the tune for "Sidewalks of New York" was first whistled by hopeful songwriter Charles Lawlor in a hat shop where he and his partner, lyricist James W. Blake, worked while waiting for their big break in the musical mecca of America, Tin Pan Alley. The collaboration made them rich enough to quit their mundane employment. It also persuaded the people of the decade known as the Gay Nineties, and every generation since, that New York City must be a swell place for indulging oneself in unbridled fun.

That indulgence invariably involved consuming alcoholic beverages, for New York City had always been a hard-drinking town. And the pleasure-seekers of Miss Lottie Gibson's day faced choices that ran the gamut of taste and purse.

A well-heeled gentleman and his lady's night on the town might include the floorshow at the Casino on Broadway at Thirty-eighth Street, famous for its Floradora Sextette, six stunningly beautiful young women upon whom adoring millionaires lavished champagne, flowers, furs, and jewels just for the thrill of being seen with them. The most famous of these charmers was Lillian Russell, who had affairs with industrialist Jesse Lewisohn and, the king of the big spenders, Diamond Jim Brady. It was of the portly Jim that George Rector, owner of the lobster palace that bore his name, said, "Mr. Brady is the best twenty-five customers we ever had." Should a lesser luminary with far fewer coins in his wallet desire to go for broke and emulate Diamond Jim and Miss Russell, he and his lady would stay at the Waldorf and strut the hotel's Peacock Alley, have drinks at the Hoffman House, take in a show at one of a dozen theaters studding the Tenderloin like Brady's diamond stickpins, and top off their evening dining at Delmonico's. Other choices for the genuine and would-be "swells" included Tony Pastor's in Greenwich Village, German cuisine at Luchow's on Fourteenth Street, and Louis Sherry's in the former Goelet mansion at Fifth Avenue and Thirty-seventh Street.

Although Brady and men who longed to be like him escorted their companions in private carriages or hansom cabs, most New Yorkers stepping out for an evening settled for making use of public transportation in the form of street cars. Motivated by a complex network of cables just beneath the street, the Broadway trolleys appeared to twenty-four-year-old Stephen Crane to be "long yellow monsters which prowl intently up and down, up and down, in a mystic search."

Born in Newark, New Jersey, in 1871, Crane had attended Lafayette College and Syracuse University before moving to New York to pursue a career in writing. While reporting for the *Herald* and the *Tribune,* he had written and published at his own expense and under a pseudonym *Maggie: A Girl of the Streets* in 1893. While Theodore Roosevelt was taking over the helm of the New York City police department, Crane was on the verge of becoming one of the most famous authors in the country with a novel about the Civil War, *The Red Badge of Courage,* published in 1895.

As a newspaperman observing New York at night in the 1890s, he wrote, "The cable cars come down Broadway . . . a diagonal path through the Tenderloin . . . the place of theaters, and of the restaurants where gayer New York dines, for in evening dress the average man feels that he has gone up three pegs in the social scale, and there is considerable evening dress about a Broadway car in the evening. A car with its electric lamp resembles a brilliantly-lighted salon. . . ." Later, he continued, various inebriate persons might emerge from darker regions of Sixth Avenue and tell of the fun they think they had, while strolling policemen "test the locks of the great dark-fronted stores." Presently, in the grey of the morning the same cable cars traveled the same route "bearing janitors, porters, all that class which carries the keys to set alive the great down-town."

For these people, the city's working folks, a night on the town meant the saloons of their own neighborhoods. "Just mention saloon," one New Yorker opined, "and my cares fade away." Through the years had sprouted such watering holes as Harry Hill's in West Houston Street. East of Broadway, it boasted a huge red and blue lantern above the door and a signboard welcoming passers-by to come in and enjoy:

> Punches and juleps, cobblers and mashes.
> To make the tongue waggle with wit's merry flashes.

American Mabille stood at Bleeker and Broadway, owned and operated by Theodore Allen, known as "The Allen" to customers, friends, and family. Three of his brothers, Wesley, Martin, and William were professional burglars. The fourth, Johnny, ran a gambling den. The Allen's resort offered the bar on the ground floor and a dance hall in the basement in which naughty women cavorted in the kind of tights that had shocked the Rev. Charles Parkhurst. Not far away, The Allen had thriving competitors, the Black and Tan on Bleeker Street, and Billy McGlory's Armory Hall at 158 Hester Street in the heart of the old Five Points.

A reporter described McGlory as "a typical New York saloon keeper—nothing more, nothing less. A medium-sized man, he is neither fleshy nor spare; he has black hair and mustache, and a piercing black eye. He shakes hands around as if we were obedient subjects come to pay homage to a king."

Saloon keeper Mike Kerrigan, also known as Johnny Dobbs, had been cut from the same coarse fabric. Apprenticed as a young man to a gang of river bandits, he matured to flourish as bank robber and fence, earning more than two million dollars in stolen money. Johnny Dobbs's combination saloon and gambling joint had been set up in Mulberry Street only half a block from police headquarters. Asked why crooks dared arrest to flock through its never-closed doors, he said, "The nearer the church the closer to God."

By one count in 1895 the city of New York had 15,000 such places, offering thirst quenchers in keeping with the ethnicity and classes of their neighborhoods. They ranged from the wines of Little Italy, hearty beers of Germantown, whiskeys of the Bowery, Sixth Avenue, and the waterfronts, to the champagnes of Diamond Jim's and Inspector Alec Williams's Tenderloin.

In all of these locales where one could enhance the tripping of the light fantastic with intoxicants, the booze flowed day and night, but especially on Saturday evenings. How ridiculous, how outrageous, thought the drinkers of New York, that so much fun was expected to have stopped by 12:01 A.M. Sunday simply because a law written in Albany had decreed so.

"To hell with the law," said saloon keepers and customers alike, who wanted to drink past midnight and all day Sunday. But in that defiance had been planted seeds of the bitter fruit that Theodore Roosevelt had inherited, for in that willingness to shun the law, corrupt and avaricious men in police uniform, encouraged by their political bosses, had found rewarding advantage.

As TR described the situation in an essay in the *Atlantic Monthly*, published in September 1897, a few months after TR had left office, "In New York the saloon keepers have always stood high among professional politicians. Nearly two thirds of the political leaders of Tammany Hall have, at one time or another, been in the liquor business. The saloon is the natural club and meeting place for the ward heelers and leaders, and the barroom politician is one of the most common and best recognized factors in local political government."

A politically-connected saloon keeper, therefore, was able to employ his "pull" to see to it that it was a competitor who felt the brunt of police enforcement of the Sunday closing law.

"The powerful and influential saloon keeper was glad to see his neighbors closed, for it gave him business," Roosevelt wrote. "On the other hand, a corrupt police captain, or the corrupt politician who controlled him, could always extort money from a saloon keeper by threatening to close him and let his neighbor remain open. Gradually, the greed of corrupt police officials and of corrupt politicians grew by what it fed on, until they began to blackmail all but the most influential liquor sellers; and as liquor sellers were numerous, and the profits of the liquor business great, the amount collected was enormous."

TR's personal attitude toward drinking was simple. Whether a man imbibed was that man's business, so long as he did not put his family in jeopardy. He believed that liquor worked more ruin on the poor than any other cause. But he did not believe in prohibition. He had opposed a state law banning alcoholic drinks while serving in the legislature. He understood the difference between a man drinking whiskey alone in a saloon and light wines and beer in respectable restaurants or at the family table. In the Sunday closing law he found an intolerable situation that pleased the temperance people who had demanded enactment of the law, and pleased those who saw profit in enforcing it "with such laxity as to please the intemperate."

On assuming the presidency of the police board he found that the Sunday liquor law was by no means a dead letter in the city. No less than eight thousand arrests for its violation had been recorded the previous year. Police enforcement of the Excise Law was very much alive. But he found that it had been executed against those who either had no political pull, or who refused to pay the police so as to keep their doors open.

Consequently, he had summoned the commanders of the force to his office on Monday, June 10, 1895, to spell out for them the new policy of the police department in these words: "I want all of you to understand that your personal feelings on the Sunday opening question, or any other phase of the law, have nothing to do with the enforcement of the law. While the law is on the statute book, it must be enforced without question."

By summer's end the saloon keepers of New York calculated a loss of twenty thousand dollars each per weekend. The Wine, Beer and Liquor Sellers Association complained that one-quarter of its membership was nearing bankruptcy. Residents of Manhattan who had the wherewithall streamed across the two rivers of their island to the open bars of Brooklyn, still an autonomous city, and New Jersey. But what working-class patron of a *trattoria* in Little Italy or a *biergarten* of Germantown could afford that luxury of time and money?

Feeling the pinch and desiring to express its ire against the man who had put teeth in the closing law, an organization calling itself the United Societies for Liberal Sunday Laws declared plans for a protest parade through Germantown for Wednesday, September 25. The mood of the march was to be funereal, the death and burial of the Old World tradition of harmless sabbath imbibing known as "Continental Sunday." Purple bunting and black crepe were distributed for hanging from windows and draping on lamp posts. To be certain Roosevelt found out about the event, the group sent an envelope to him at Mulberry Street, enclosing an invitation to come uptown to review the mournful procession.

TR accepted in typical fashion, alerting no one in advance, simply arriving at Eighty-sixth Street and ascending to the reviewing platform and standing beside such Germantown luminaries as Oswald Ottendorfer, editor of the city's German-language newspaper, *Staats Zeitung,* and the leader of Tammany Democrats, State Senator David Hill. The parade proved anything but grim.

Leading off, a dozen men on bicycles sported outlandish chin whiskers and blue noses, symbolizing the upstate hayseeds who had forced the hated law onto the books. A coffin labeled "Teddyism" rolled past. TR bared his teeth in an approving grin. Numerous banners floated before his pince-nez. They protested "Roosevelt's Russian Rule" and "Roosevelt's Razzle Dazzle Reform Racket." One said, "Good Morning, Have You Seen Roosevelt's Name In Print?" "Send the Police Czar To Russia" and "Tain't Sunday" were toted by men in *lederhosen* and waving bottles of Rhine wine. A float offered a woman representing the Statute of Liberty but in a black dress and mourning veil. Another presented a tableau of fancily dressed swells called "The Millionaires' Club" gulping down champagne. One of the figures was made up with large teeth and eye glasses in the Roosevelt fashion.

Animated, laughing, pointing and applauding, TR watched more than twenty thousand citizens, most in traditional German attire and hats, flow past. When one of them shouted, incredulously, *"Wo ist der Roosevelt?"* TR nearly tumbled from the stand as he eagerly bent forward to boom, *"Hier bin ich!"*

When the parade ended after more than two hours he left the platform to applause and cheers and carried with him to Mulberry Street two of the taunting banners as souvenirs for his office wall: "Roosevelt's Razzle Dazzle Reform Racket" and "Send the Police Czar to Russia." But he told his astonished yet admiring hosts as he departed, "A hundred parades can't swerve us from doing our duty."

Neither could those who profited from Sunday liquor sales be swayed from doing what they saw as their duty and their right. Some saloon keepers came up with ingenious methods by which they hoped to sidestep the law and the long arm of "Teddy Roseyfelt's" enforcers in police blue, or the devilishly deceptive mufti of the plainclothesman. Most prevalent among their ruses was pulling down window shades, locking the front door and leaving side and rear entrances open. Some let the customers know that thirsting regulars would gain admittance if they uttered a proper password. Others sought to assure their usual Sabbath profits by selling a drink on Saturday and handing the customer a receipt entitling him to come in and consume it on Sunday, thereby averting an exchange of cash on the Sabbath.

Another scheme assured an ample supply of intoxicants to patrons for Sunday consumption at home. When a customer came in on Saturday evening he was importuned to buy a case of beer to take with him for the next day. To make this offer even more enticing, the twenty-four-bottle cases were offered at the same price found in the grocery stores, one dollar per case. If the customer did not plunk down a buck to lug home the booze he was not-so-politely informed that he would no longer be regarded as a patron of the house. A contrary customer was told he no longer "stands in with Tim." The patron usually heeded the threat and took home a case, whether he could afford it or not.

One saloon keeper confessed to a reporter on October 6, "We are getting desperate. We can't make our expenses without our Sunday profits. If we can only make $25 on Sunday we can see it through all right. But without that we will have to close, and rather than do that we'll risk the fine and imprisonment."

Cops also ran a risk. Some who attempted to enforce the law were greeted with violence. Attempting to enter Daniel O'Rourke's saloon on Park Row, Policeman Tom Gamson of the Elizabeth Street Station was stopped by Nathan Callahan, a lookout, and knocked to the ground. Policeman Alexander Schueing of the Sixty-seventh Street Police Station was detailed to don civilian clothing in order to watch Molooney's Saloon at Fifty-ninth and Second in early-morning hours. He succeeded in gaining entrance and found liquor for sale. He arrested the bartender, William Rafferty, but when he attempted to remove Rafferty he discovered the man who had the key to the locked door had disappeared. Schueing remained a prisoner until the uniformed officer assigned to that area sent an alarm to the stationhouse that Schueing was missing, bringing other officers racing to the rescue. When Officer John Hefferman followed half a dozen men into the side door of Dowling Brothers' saloon at Twenty-seventh Street and Second Avenue he was spotted as being "suspicious" and surrounded by irate drinkers. Pounding on the front window, Hefferman managed to alert a passerby to run to the stationhouse to summon help. A squad led by Captain Ed Smith thundered to his assistance.

While inspecting saloons in most areas of the city to see if they were in compliance was a random, hit-or-miss enterprise, the watering holes of the Tenderloin were assigned one policeman per saloon. Compliance was uniformly observed.

As the crackdown appeared to be having an effect, ministers took to their pulpits to preach on behalf of continued and increased diligence. Typical of the sermonizing was that of the Rev. Dr. Charles Eaton of the Universalist Church of the Divine Paternity. "There has been no more important issue raised than the one which confronts the citizens of New York today," he told congregants at Fifth Avenue and Forty-fifth Street. "The real question forced upon us does not relate to the value of special laws, but to the authority of all law. The decision to be made in private and at the ballot box is not as to the desirability of the law providing for a weekly day of rest, or for the regulation of the liquor traffic, but as to our obedience of legally constituted authorities and the legislation of accredited representatives."

This was precisely TR's reasoning.

While Rev. Eaton preached to his flock police were finding few saloons daring to take risks. Only twenty-eight arrests were reported to police headquarters that day. But in the sprawling city across the East River from Manhattan no one was arrested. Although Brooklyn saloons were subject to the same law as those within Theodore Roosevelt's jurisdiction, Brooklyn saloons were wide open for business because the Brooklyn police had no orders from their commissioner to enforce the law. The only arrests reported were for drunkenness, a total of forty-eight. By far the busiest saloons were to be found in the shadow of the Brooklyn Bridge. They were thronged with people who strolled across the span from "dry" Manhattan.

Reporting to the police board on October 9, Acting Chief of Police Peter Conlin told the commissioners "there is practically full and complete compliance" on the part of all licensed liquor dealers in the city. He noted that in the previous four months 3,036 arrests had been made for violation of the Sunday liquor law. "However, the thoroughness of the work of the police is not to be judged by the number of arrests made for its violation," he continued proudly, "but rather by the uniform manner in which it is now observed, and by the evidence on all sides, even to the most casual observer, that the saloons of this city are effectually closed on Sundays and during prohibited hours."

Although Conlin's report on the impact of the enforcement of the closing law was newsworthy in itself, the fact that Conlin made a report to the police board was significant. It was the first time in the history of the New York Police Department that the chief of police had presented his bosses a formal accounting of his stewardship. That Conlin desired to drop the word "Acting" from his title and be appointed chief in his own right may have contributed to this willingness to create a precedent. Whatever the motivation, his act would be required of all his successors.

No one in the police board room doubted Conlin's competence as a police officer. But they may not have expected him to demonstrate the capacity for politics that he went on to reveal in his report. He included an impassioned plea for passage by the state legislature of the Roosevelt police reorganization bill. He blamed Albany's truculence in not affording the police board a free hand in reforming the department for the continued presence in the force of "a not inconsiderable number of men who are, for a variety of reasons, rather a detriment than an assistance in the work of reform." In effect he said that unless the hands of the commissioners were untied by Albany lawmakers efforts at reforming the police department would be nullified.

Political point-making aside, Conlin presented a heartening account of successes in arrests on charges of keeping disorderly houses, running gambling parlors, and policy-making. To achieve these triumphs, he noted, it had been necessary for him to shift around many men who had their usefulness impaired by being kept in one command too long.

At the completion of Conlin's report the commissioners went into executive session to deal with cases of improper conduct by several members of the force. One was that of Thomas McGee, who had been removed from the Jefferson Market Court squad over the issue of the prisoner who had escaped while arresting officer Williamson was doing paperwork for the arraignment. In being reassigned McGee had been made a roundsman by an embarrassed Chief Thomas Byrnes, pending action by the police board. Taking up the case for final disposition, the board, with TR presiding, took only a few seconds to fine McGee one month's pay and reduce him in rank to patrolman.

As the commissioners meted out punishment and pondered the future of Acting Chief Conlin on that sparkling Wednesday, October 9, two weeks after TR's triumph at the Germantown parade, more than a year had flown by since he had passed up the chance to run for mayor, clearing the way for the election of Strong on a wave of reform sentiment. Now another election loomed, this one for state offices. As usual, campaigns for the governorship and the legislature would pit upstate Republican strengths against the Democratic stronghold of New York City where turnout could spell the difference in determining the character of the state government for the next four years. By all estimates the overriding and determining issue in the city would be the record of a year of "reform" and its personification, Theodore Roosevelt.

Nervous Republicans in their convention at Saratoga voted in public for a lukewarm endorsement of the Excise Law. Privately, they approached TR to implore him to relax his all out campaign to enforce it.

The lifetime advocate of morality and principle as the guiding lights of public men snapped, "The implication is that for the sake of the Republican party, a party of which I am a very earnest member, I should violate my oath of office and connive at lawbreaking."

He wrote Henry Cabot Lodge, "I shall not alter my course one handsbreadth, even though Tammany carries the city by 50,000." He brushed aside a suggestion from Mayor Strong that he "let up" on the saloons. When old friend and ally Lemuel Quigg accused him of ingratitude, TR retorted, "He is a goose."

Resigned to being the dominant issue in the city, he flung himself into the campaign as if he were a candidate for office himself, firing the opening shot on October 10 before an audience of two thousand in Columbus Hall. Under auspices of the Young Men's and Women's Societies of the Church of St. Paul the meeting was a celebration of the birthday of a revered fighter for temperance, Father Theobold Mathew. An Irish social worker who had been called "the apostle of temperance," Mathew had been a Capuchin priest working in behalf of the welfare and education of the poor of his native land. In 1838 he took a pledge of total abstinence and thereafter devoted himself to the cause of temperance in Ireland,

England, and North America until his death at the age of sixty-six in 1856.

Preceeding Roosevelt to the rostrum, Father George McDermott turned to TR and said, "Father Mathew, too, was cried down and called a bigot and fanatic when he commenced his great work, but three months afterward 25,000 persons signed the pledge."

Several minutes of cheers and applause delayed TR from beginning his remarks. When the tumult waned, he wasted no time in getting to the point. "The essential lawlessness of many of the men in the liquor trade, and many, if not most, of their political supporters is shown by the attitude in the present city campaign of both classes. Not only are they carrying on a campaign in favor of a change of the law in reference to Sunday closing which, of course, they have a right to do, but they are attacking the board of which I have the honor to be a member, in every way, simply because it has enforced the law."

Referring to the previous evening's Tammany Hall convention, he said, "They did not content themselves with demanding that the saloon keepers should be given a privilege denied other trades, and should be allowed to keep open on Sunday, they further denounced us because we have declined to give saloon keepers who violate the law an immunity which is vouchsafed no other lawbreaker. They denounced us for having honestly enforced other laws. On behalf of the saloon keeper who violates the law, they clamor for the dishonest enforcement of the law."

Noting that the chairman of the Tammany convention praised the Tammany platform as "without taint of bigotry and without taint of 'Rooseveltism,'" TR responded, "By freedom from bigotry he apparently means that he and his colleagues have drawn a platform which no self-respecting priest or minister can support. In this respect I grant that he had been entirely successful. As for what he means by 'Rooseveltism,' I can only guess." If the term meant "impartial and resolute enforcement of the law," he said as he grinned, "I have nothing to complain of."

He went on to defend the use of plainclothesmen in policing the saloons, but he decried characterization of the detectives as "spies." Suggesting that his opponents chose the word because it was "offensive," he said, "In catching lawbreakers who are trying to evade the law or violate the law, there are times and ways in which we have to use men not in uniform. Of course, what really makes them angry is that we use effective instead of ineffective methods. We expect their indignation and are complimented by it; for it is a tribute to the effectiveness of our work. Remember that nobody has to fear a detective unless he is a lawbreaker. If the saloon keeper observes the law he is not in danger."

He then cited figures showing that since the police began enforcing the closing law, arrests for felonies and drunkenness on Sundays had been reduced by forty percent.

While Tammany disapproved of the results, the annual session of the Long Island Baptist Association welcomed them. Meeting in Brooklyn, the group passed a resolution calling upon the mayor and police commissioner of the city across the great bridge from New York to emulate President Roosevelt and "enforce the Excise Law in this city."

Ten days after his rousing speech to followers of Father Mathew, TR addressed the congregation of the Cornell Memorial Church. Striking the same themes, he acknowledged the presence of Mayor Strong on the same platform. "When the mayor appointed me," he said, "he told me to administer the law without regard to politics, and I have tried to do so."

While the president of the police board found himself the centerpiece of the election contest there was a second President Roosevelt on the hustings in mid-October 1895. TR's uncle Robert was president of the Democratic Club of New York City. At its annual dinner he said the gathering was a sort of "celebration of the victory of the Democratic Party this Fall, which it is about to win."

Meanwhile, those who had been pleasantly surprised when TR had accepted an invitation to review the protest parade in Germantown in September announced plans for a new demonstration. But in calling for the gathering at Tompkins Square Park and a march to a rally at Cooper Union on Thursday, October 31, the Campaign Committee of the United Societies for Liberal Sunday Laws omitted any reference to Theodore Roosevelt being welcome.

Whether TR noticed the announcement of the plans in newspapers of October 22 is not known. However, there is no question of his taking note of another event reported in the papers that day. Magistrate John O. Mott presiding at the Tombs Police Court had issued an order that relegated to history one of the prides and joys of the former chief of police, Thomas Byrnes, and an important tactic in the police department's war against criminals.

On Sunday Magistrate Mott had found before him in court the person of Henry Murphy, an individual well-known to the police as a habitual criminal. Mott inquired of Detective O'Connell of the Wall Street police station house what Murphy had done to warrant being arrested.

O'Connell replied that Murphy had been spotted in the vicinity of Pine and Williams Streets, his intentions unknown but suspicious, given his history. He had been picked up for that alone.

"It's an outrage, your Honor," Murphy cried. "I wasn't doing nothing at all, but just walking down the street, when O'Connell comes up and grabs me. It ain't right. That fellow's Captain had ordered him and all the rest of the detectives to arrest me on sight. And I never done nothing. I'm as innocent as your Honor, and I'll swear it—"

Mott cut him off. Would O'Connell please explain?

The detective answered that Murphy's offense had been in his crossing the "dead line" of Liberty Street. This was a boundary of Tom Byrnes's famous and dreaded *cordon sanitaire*.

Mott pointed out that he had heard of a "dead line" but had never actually found its authorization in any statute. "The law knows no district in which habitual criminals or suspected men are forbidden to go," he said. "The police have the power to arrest known thieves on suspicion when the occasion warrants, but they cannot establish boundaries within which their power is greater than in another. I have read of the 'dead line' in the newspapers and have heard it talked of, as has nearly everyone else, but so far as my rulings in court go, none exists. It may be of practical benefit to some to have all criminals forbidden to enter any special neighborhood and so influenced that they would obey. It would be of still greater benefit if the thieves could be prevented, altogether, from stealing. But as far as the law goes, the thief has as much right to walk south of Liberty Street as he has to travel north of it."

Henry Murphy walked out of court a free man.

Acting Police Chief Conlin put the best face possible on the embarrassment. "There never was any 'dead line,'" he told reporters who had surged across Mulberry Street, knowing very well that Byrnes had ordered one drawn. "My orders to my men were to arrest every habitual criminal when found in any neighborhood that made it probable that he was there for the purpose of robbery. If they (detectives) have, among themselves, established Liberty Street as a line which thieves cannot cross, they have transgressed my orders," Conlin insisted.

The *New York Times* headline on Tuesday declared "Thieves Can Now Visit the Wall Street District at Will." Its reporter in Mulberry Street stuck his tongue in cheek and wrote, "Bankers and brokers in the purlieus of Wall Street will be interested in knowing that the 'dead line' in which they placed so much confidence exists no more, and that they are now as liable to invasion by a gang of thieves as in the old days were the ordinary mortals who did business north of Liberty Street. Acting Chief Conlin says the line never existed. However that may be, it doesn't exist now."

On Wednesday, October 23, Roosevelt left dead lines and the proper police handling of habitual criminals temporarily behind to journey to Boston to speak to the Republican Club of Massachusetts. The Bay State Republicans had invited him to give an address not only on his work in reforming the police and his general views on good government but on "national issues."

Regarding the former, TR pledged honest and fair enforcement of laws. Good government in New York City would be assured by strict police supervision of the polls and diligent guarding of ballot boxes in the forthcoming elections. As to national issues, he called for annexation of Hawaii and admitted, proudly, that he was a "jingo," if jingoism meant "a policy in pursuit of which Americans will with resolution and common sense insist upon our rights being respected by foreign powers."

Back in the city on Thursday, he caught up with work at his desk in Mulberry Street and then joined Commissioners Parker and Andrews at the St. Denis Hotel for the third annual banquet of the City Vigilance League. The president of the League, the Rev. Parkhurst, served as their host and master of ceremonies. When TR spoke he repeated the themes of earlier speeches, citing the need for the police to remain unconcerned with politics.

Facetiously, he asked, "What difference does it make to a policeman whether the prisoner whom he arrests is a high-tariff or low-tariff man? Why should the policeman saving a drowning man stop to inquire for what Presidential candidate he voted last election?" Turning serious, he went on, "All we have employed to enforce the law is common sense. This does not require party allegiance. Heretofore, the Police Department has been the head of New York politics, and it is the one department of all which should be eliminated from politics, and we have eliminated it." He promised "hum drum honesty and the laws of morality" as his only guides. "Conscience without common sense," he said, "is a balloon."

No wine, beer, or other intoxicant was served at the banquet.

The next evening, Friday, October 25, he addressed a meeting of the Friends of Honest Government at the Grand Central Palace. He sat beside Commissioner Parker again, but it was Roosevelt's remarks that garnered the attention of reporters. In a slashing attack upon Tammany on the issue of the Sunday closing law, he noted, "Tammany Hall kept one-half the saloons open by its 'intelligent and discriminate' enforcement of the Excise Law" while it oppressed the keepers of the small saloons who had no political influence.

"We have got things pretty tight right now," he continued, "but we will put on an extra turn of the screw. The greatest benefit to the people, I am convinced, is the enforcement of the laws, without fear or favor. We have counted the cost, and we won't turn back. We will enforce the laws without regard to what the consequences may be to ourselves."

With a final swipe at Tammany, he concluded, "There is not a city on earth that deserves an honest government more than New York, and no city in the Union lacks that kind of government more than our city. The bitter cry against dishonest municipal government has gone up all our lives. The Republican Party is not entirely without blame in this state of affairs, but it is due in far greater measure to Tammany Hall. In the present political situation Tammany Hall is not for personal liberty because it likes it, for it has been the greatest tyrant we have had to endure. Year after year it has extended its system of blackmail. It began with petty larceny and advanced with rapid strides to the most prodigious system of plunder ever known in civilized times. Its stench in the nostrils of decent men is not confined to the Union alone, but goes all the world over."

As election day approached it seemed that Roosevelt was everywhere, talking. On October 27 he denounced Tammany Hall to the Presbyterian Union of New York, crowded into the banquet hall of the Brunswick Hotel. He vowed that he would "not lighten so much as the weight of my little finger the pressure now bearing on the saloon keepers, but will rather give the screw half a turn more."

Tuesday, October 30, saw him at a mass meeting in Chickering Hall, sharing billing with Seth Law and Felix Adler of the Ethical

Culturists while driving home the same message of not letting up in carrying out the letter of the law.

On the last day of the month, the Friday before election day, he vowed at a hearing of the board of alderman, "Whatever the law is, the Board of Police will endeavor to enforce it to the best of its ability." And he again defended the use of plainclothesmen in going after illegal saloons. Asked to reveal his personal views on the Sunday closing law, he said he had an opinion but declined to give the alderman the benefit of it.

Privately, as he indicated in a letter to Sagamore Hill, he felt the law was too strict. "But I have no honorable alternative," he said, "save to enforce it."

The message in all his speeches in the heat of the campaign was, "I deal with the law." If the public did not care for the law, the public had the right and the duty to change it, but no one had the right to ask him as police commissioner to ignore it.

In a burst of speech-making to West Side groups on the evening of Sunday, November 1, he contradicted Uncle Robert by forecasting victory for the forces of reform over Tammany Hall when the voters trekked to the polls on Tuesday.

Uncle Robert proved the better seer. Although Republicans carried upstate New York, Tammany Hall swept the city. German-Americans who usually voted Republican and had liked TR's pluck in showing up at their parade in September went eighty percent for the Democrats. Political pundits at city hall and in Park Row attributed the Republican disaster in the city to Roosevelt.

Undaunted, he summoned Conlin, inspectors, and captains to his office and informed them, "The Board will not tolerate the slightest relaxation of the enforcement of the laws, and notably the Excise Law." The board would hold to "most rigid accountability any man in his precinct if any such relaxation occurs."

He then called in reporters. Noting that law and order had been maintained throughout the city on election day, he boasted that strict enforcement of the law requiring saloons to be closed on election day had been the reason. The saloons had been closed, he said with pride, adding, "This had never been the case before on election day."

With the disappointing election behind him the president of the police board's next public address came a week later. He and his colleagues were guests of honor at the dinner of the Methodist Social Union at the St. Denis Hotel, though Grant was unable to attend. Feeling less constrained than he had been in his appearance before the board of alderman, he discussed the vexing Sunday closing law in terms of how it might be changed. Perhaps unknowingly, he borrowed one idea that had been put forward by Inspector Alexander Williams. "In the first place," TR said, "make the saloon keepers keep their blinds open during the time they are supposed not to be doing business. In the next place, make them allow the right of entry to a policeman at any time to a place where liquor might be sold or where he has reason to believe it is sold. Third, a single conviction for selling liquor shall, ipso facto, work a revocation of license and prevent its renewal the following year."

Recognizing "the election went the other way," he said the police board intended, "not by words but by deeds, to make good our guarantee that no matter which way the election went, the result would not make us let up one hair's breadth." He promised that "if the Legislature puts the provisions I have asked into the law, where now we scourge with whips, then we shall scourge with scorpions."

While the President of the police board expressed confidence that his work at reform would proceed, 300 Mulberry Street, Park Row's newspapers, and city hall were caught in a swirl of rumors that Theodore Roosevelt was on his way out of office. So widespread were the whispers that they became a news story. The *Times* printed the following in its edition of November 11.

RUMORS ABOUT MR. ROOSEVELT

All sorts of rumors about the politicians in the Republican ranks being anxious to get Commissioner Roosevelt out of office have been started since the election. One story yesterday was that Mayor Strong was plotting to get him out.

The story probably grew out of a remark by the mayor at a banquet in which Strong intended a jest. "I thought I would have a pretty easy time," he had said, "until the Police Board came along and tried to make a Puritan out a Dutchman."

Asked about the rumors, Strong said, "Mr. Roosevelt is going to stay. He is going to stay just as long as he wants to."

When reporters stampeded across Mulberry Street looking for a comment from TR, fully expecting to hear a colorful retort, they learned from Miss Kelly that TR had left police headquarters at two o'clock and that he had announced his intention to take a long-needed rest at Sagamore Hill.

Chapter 9

Unbought, Unawed, Unknown to Fear

Two and a half centuries before Theodore Roosevelt arrived in Mulberry Street, the Indian chief Sagamore Mohannis had signed away his tribe's rights to hilly woodlands on the north shore of Long Island. During his junior year at Harvard when he was still contemplating a career as a natural scientist, TR had compiled and published a small pamphlet on the region's winged wildlife, "Notes on Some of the Birds of Oyster Bay." Following his graduation and his engagement to marry Alice Hathway Lee, he selected a spot at the top of the hill and set out to build their home. The plot was separated from all other houses by fields and belts of woodland, and overlooked Oyster Bay and Long Island Sound. He then created an interior plan with a large parlor, plenty of bedrooms, a dining room ample enough for a public man to entertain, grand fireplaces, and a library. The architects Lamb and Rich were engaged to execute it and to design the exterior.

They gave their illustrious client an abode in keeping with both his character and his era. No better description has been written than that by TR's contemporary and admiring biographer, Hermann Hagedorn, in *The Roosevelt Family of Sagamore Hill*. "So the architects gave him on the outside what self-respecting men of substance of the late 1880s valued more than beauty, and what architects were summoned to express: solidity, first of all; dignity, hospitality, comfort, the social stability of the owner, and permanence." Foundations were twenty inches thick. Joists, rafters, and roof boards were solid enough to withstand the gales that swept across Long Island. Abundant windows let in the air. Should the eight fireplaces prove inadequate against the winter's cold, the cellar held a pair of hot-air furnaces.

TR had two favorite places, the library and a piazza. The former overflowed with volumes on every subject that interested him, and shelves bearing books on Edith's taste, for his wife was as avid a reader as he. In the library he could roam the world or go back in history, searching for meaning from both the journeys. From the piazza he enjoyed watching the sun go down beyond the long reaches of land and water and the lights of tall Fall River boats as they steamed by. Revealing the naturalist in him, he wrote, "We love all the seasons; the snows and bare woods of winter; the rush of growing things and the blossom-spray of spring; the yellow grain, the ripening fruits and tasseled corn, and the deep, leafy shades that are heralded by 'the green dance of summer;' and the sharp fall winds that tear the brilliant banners with which the trees greet the dying of the year."

Contemplating "outdoors and indoors" in his autobiography, he wrote that among the men he had known "the love of books and the love of the outdoors . . . have usually gone hand in hand."

In December 1895 the bookish, roomy house was filled with the sounds of five children. Alice Lee was the oldest, born to Alice Hathaway Lee Roosevelt, who died before they could move into Sagamore Hill. The four born to Edith Carow Roosevelt were Theodore, Kermit, Ethel, and Archibald (Quentin would be born in 1897). As frequent guest, Hermann Hagedorn was often witness to a domestic tableau in which the table talk was over the children's heads but never the sparkle of it. He recalled in his biography, "Their father bubbled with ideas, many of them challenging; he had a remarkable vocabulary, moreover, and delighted in using it to castigate enemies or to characterize some 'amiable old fuddy-duddy with sweetbreads for brains,' who had crossed his path; he had a quality of wit which inspired wit in others."

Most guests at Sagamore Hill rose to the challenge. Among them were TR's political allies and mentors, Joe Murray, Jake Hess, Lemuel Quigg, and Henry Cabot Lodge. Roosevelt relatives also filled the rooms of the house, including TR's sisters, Uncle Robert, and numerous cousins, nieces, and nephews. Among them to keep company with TR's children was a shy and ungainly niece, Eleanor Roosevelt, age eleven. Edith wrote of her, "Poor little soul, she is very plain. Her mouth and teeth seem to have no future . . . but the ugly duckling may turn out to be a swan." A thirteen-year-old cousin also called from time to time in the company of his formidable mother Anna—Franklin Delano Roosevelt.

Also counted frequently as a guest at Sagamore Hill were TR's "kitchen police board," Jacob Riis and Lincoln Steffens.

"Sagamore Hill is the family sanctuary," Riis wrote in *Theodore Roosevelt, the Citizen.* "I never go away from Sagamore Hill without a feeling that if I lived there I would never leave it. On a breezy hilltop overlooking field and forest and Sound, with the Connecticut shore on the northern horizon, its situation is altogether taking. The house is comfortable, filled with reminders of the stirring life its owner has led in camp and on the hunting trail, and with a broad piazza on the side that catches the cool winds of summer. It is the people themselves who put the stamp upon it—the life they live there together."

Hermann Hagedorn also found fascination in the artifacts of the place. "The house itself exuded romance," he wrote. There were game heads on the walls. Framed original illustrations of TR's hunting books. A rug of beaver skins taken near TR's ranchhouse on the Little Missouri in Dakota. A hide painted by an Indian artist gave the Sioux version of the defeat and demise of George Armstrong Custer at the Battle of the Little Big Horn in 1876. A rifle had belonged to the time TR met Captain Seth Bullock in Deadwood. Not a trophy hung on the wall or lay underfoot without a story to be told about it.

"Father, mother, children," Hagedorn wrote, "it was a very happy family."

Yet Sagamore Hill was as much Edith's home as TR's. It was she who handled the finances. Managing money was not one of TR's strengths. He told a friend, "Every morning Edie puts twenty dollars in my pockets, and, to save my life, I never can tell her afterward what I did with it." While he filled days dealing with intrigues in Mulberry Street she cared for the children and ran the house. Hagedorn's portrait is that of a chestnut-haired woman of delicate beauty, gentle spirit, charm, wit, and a gift for "laconic utterance and evocative listening" that provided "a perfect foil for her militant, occasionally dogmatic and over-forceful husband."

Because of newspaper coverage of TR's activities Edith knew exactly what was going on when he was not at Sagamore Hill. "The papers are full of his doings," she said in a letter to TR's sister Anna.

That she experienced no reticence in expressing her opinion on his activities was evident in a remark TR made to a clergyman in Oyster Bay: "Mrs. Roosevelt doesn't like me to get into public rows. She says I am not at my best in them."

Just such a row occurred eleven days after the rumors that Mayor Strong was on the verge of replacing Roosevelt. Calling in reporters, TR railed against a story going round that since he had taken office crime had shown a steady increase. "It is not true," he growled. "The fact is that there has been a remarkable falling off in the number of felonies committed, and the arrests have increased." Waving a sheet of paper containing a comparison of June, July, August, September, and October of the previous year with those months since he assumed office, he continued, "In five months of 1894 the total number of arrests was 42,000, while in the five months of the present year the arrests numbered over 51,000."

He pointed to a "gratifying increase" of arrests for felonious assaults (350 in 1894, 472 in 1895). Homicide arrests had gone up from fifty-nine to sixty-nine.

"This must be taken as conclusive evidence of the efficiency of the police force when it is remembered that during the five months referred to there was an average patrol force of 2,635 in 1895, as against 2,816 in 1894," he went on. "The records show that the force of 1894 made an average of 15.11 arrests each, and the force of 1895 during the same period an average of 19.60."

As the reporters scribbled notes, he rattled off even more statistics.

"This is sufficient answer to the stories that are in circulation that crime is on the increase," he concluded.

One of the reasons that the stories gained circulation lay in a change of the command structure that had been imposed in an attempt to get at the problem of corruption. Soon after the new police board assumed power it had directed Chief Thomas Byrnes to abolish the position of "ward detective." These men had enjoyed great influence in the precincts because they had performed the task of collecting bribes and blackmail money and distributing it to deserving officers. But they also had the official duty to report crimes promptly to police headquarters. Since they had gone out of existence, the flow of data into Mulberry Street had slowed considerably. Frequently, reports of crimes arrived so late that by the time the detective bureau dispatched an investigator the criminals had several hours' start on their escape. In the murder of one John Krauel four hours went by before a detective was sent, permitting the suspected murderer to flee. Several robberies also went unsolved as a result of slow reporting. Recognizing the problem, the police board admitted its mistake and announced that the ward system would be revived.

Another reaction to public outrage at the revelations of the Lexow Committee had been revulsion against use of nightsticks. Horrifying tales had been told by innocent citizens who had been clubbed. Consequently, carrying of nightsticks had been banned by Chief Byrnes. But the new police board had reversed the order. Noting the receipt of a letter from a citizen protesting the reinstatement of the policeman's club, TR answered publicly at a meeting of the board. "The nightsticks are in and they will stay. They ought never to have been taken away," he said. He warned any policemen who did not "use them right" would be held to a strict accountability. If found guilty of abuse they would be dismissed.

Nothing about the remaking of the force was trivial. One of the requirements was a neat appearance, especially of those who were assigned to police headquarters. To ensure that the men complied, Acting Inspector Moses Cortright ordered Sergeant Ned Brown of his staff to conduct inspections. They began in mid-October. One by one the men reported to headquarters in neat, well cared-for trousers. In noticing this sartorial splendor, Sergeant Brown, who had been on the force many years and understood cops, grew suspicious. When the next man showed up with spotless trousers Brown secretly put a mark on the back of one of the legs. The trousers appeared the next day on a different cop. TR was content to leave the investigation of this case of official bamboozlery in the hands of the eagle-eyed Sergeant Brown.

Among weightier matters on the agenda of the police board in the autumn of 1895 was creation of a police district in the newly annexed Westchester. The commissioners voted to designate it the Thirty-eighth Precinct. Under command of Captain Henry Frers, it would be located in Westchester Village. A force of sixty-five men was authorized to cover the communities of City Island, Wakefield and Williams Bridge, as well. In taking the action TR did not have to issue a blunt warning against noncompliance as he had had to do when the region was first absorbed into the city.

In the day to day flow of decisions and actions taken by Roosevelt in the waning months of 1895 it is impossible to imagine any event as pleasing to him personally, or more illuminating of the manner in which he ran the police department, than a ceremony held at headquarters on Saturday, December first. Before him stood twenty-two men being promoted to acting roundsmen. In his midnight rambles TR had come to appreciate that no rank of the force was more important, for it was roundsmen who shouldered the responsibility for seeing that patrolmen carried out their tasks. Had each roundsman assigned to the streets that TR investigated been doing his duty the president of the board would have discovered no slackers.

Each of the men who were being promoted would take the place of a roundsman who had been found derelict and reduced in rank. "In one precinct, the Twenty-sixth," Roosevelt told them, "we reduced all the Roundsmen because they were not attending to their duties. We shall judge you by the discipline of the men under you. We expect you to keep the men up to the mark. I am disappointed in the way the men patrol. They don't patrol. They lounge, loiter, and talk with each other."

Five minutes was enough for one officer to talk to another or a citizen, he said, leaving unsaid the possibility that they might find themselves observed and timed by himself in the wee hours of a morning when one might expect a police commissioner to be home and in bed.

Lest any of the new supervisors think one of them might have risen to his new position through political influence, Roosevelt asserted, "Every one of you owes his place to nothing but his record. In three or four cases friends have appealed in your behalf. They have hampered your chances. There is one man among you who would have been promoted some time ago, but for his friends, who sent letters here constantly."

Their orders were simple. Duty. Carry it out diligently. Honesty. "We will turn out any man if we have proof of his dishonesty." He went on, "Look out for your men, for if they show a marked lack of discipline, the whole outfit will be reduced. If I find many burglaries, I will not only put on trial the officer on whose beat the burglary occurred, but the Roundsman as well."

Each must possess courage. Here, TR offered with unabashed pride an example of courage among the men standing before him, Edward J. Bourke. For his exemplary handling of the arrest of Big

Tim Callahan for ignoring the Sunday closing law he found himself excused from the probationary period for a patrolman and elevated to acting roundsman, with a jump in pay from one thousand dollars to one thousand five hundred dollars a year.

"He rendered a service by disregarding the pull of a man, and showing the citizens that a lawbreaker has no influence with the police force, no matter how high he stands, politically or socially," TR said proudly. But he added, sternly, "It behooves Officer Bourke, who has only been a short time on the force, to be specially careful, and show that he deserves promotion."

There could be no "pull" in the form of Theodore Roosevelt's personal interest in an individual, either.

He concluded with a warning. "All of you have one month to prove your fitness for the place you have been detailed to. It remains with yourself to make it permanent. I want to caution you that any man found wanting will be remanded to patrol duty."

While this combination pep talk, hearty pat on the back, and lecture on the pitfalls ahead proceeded in TR's office, the man who stood at the head of the force, Peter Conlin, remained in the category of "Acting" himself. Here the board found itself on the horns of a dilemma of its own making. In its insistence on merit as a condition of promotion throughout the force they had placed themselves in the awkward position of wanting to move Conlin into the position of chief of police permanently while remaining true to the principle that positions be filled only after an applicant had passed an examination. What if someone of equal merit applied for the job of chief and outperformed Conlin in the examination?

The question was tackled by the board of commissioners in an executive session in Andrew Parker's office on November 30. Each of them pledged secrecy regarding the discussion, but that did not keep the press from publishing authoritative articles on how the board might open the position of chief of police to qualified applicants yet assure that Conlin came out the winner. The *Times* wrote, "One way in which they could do this, even after the officers concerned have undergone a competitive examination, would be for the board which decided the percentages of marks to be given for each subject to give the officers who had been on probation for seven months a larger percentage for the successful period of probation which they have already undergone." That is, give Conlin extra credit for having served as acting chief.

The secret meeting of the board lasted far into the evening. At its conclusion Parker told reporters the board had agreed not to discuss the matter publicly. Andrews and Grant were also mum. Asked if he had anything to say on the issue, TR, the man a member of the state assembly had described in 1881 as possessing "a wealth of mouth," replied, "No, sir; not a word."

Newspapermen were surprised by this tight-lipped Roosevelt. From his first day on the job he demonstrated a keen sense of the value of the press by appointing himself spokesman for the police board. In doing so he had assured himself abundant news coverage. But he discovered that he had unsheathed a double-edged sword. Like all intimate relationships, his dealings with the city's newspapers became one of love and hate, of need and revulsion.

He described his feelings in "Administering the New York Police Force." Published in *Atlantic Monthly* a few months after leaving Mulberry Street in 1897, it said, "Of all the forces that tend for evil in a great city like New York, probably none are so potent as the sensational papers. Until one has had experience with them it is difficult to realize the reckless indifference to truth or decency displayed by papers such as the two that have the largest circulation in New York City. (*World* and *Tribune*). Scandal forms the breath of the nostrils of such papers, and they are quite as ready to create it as to describe it. To sustain law and order is humdrum, and does not readily lend itself to flaunting woodcuts; but if the editor will stoop, and make his subordinates stoop, to raking the gutters of human depravity, to upholding the wrong-doers, and furiously assailing what is upright and honest, he can make money, just as other types of pander make it. The man who is to do honorable work in any form of civic politics must make up his mind (if he is a man of properly robust character he will make it up without difficulty) to treat the assaults of papers like these with absolute indifference, and to go his way unheeded. Indeed he will have to make up his mind to be criticized, sometimes justly, and more often unjustly, even by decent people; and he must not be so thin-skinned as to mind such criticism overmuch."

Years later, after leaving the White House, he wrote for a number of publications, including the Kansas City *Star*. In that undertaking he wrote an editorial attacking the brand of newspapering that vexed him throughout his public life. He wrote in 1912, "Yellow journalism deifies the cult of the mendacious, the sensational, and the inane, and, throughout its wide but vapid field, does as much to vulgarize and degrade the popular taste, to weaken the popular character, and to dull the edge of the popular conscience, as any influence under which the country can suffer. These men sneer at the very idea of paying heed to the dictates of a sound morality; as one of their number had cynically put it, they are concerned merely with selling the public whatever the public will buy—a theory of conduct which would justify the existence of every keeper of an opium den, of every foul creature who ministers to the vices of mankind."

A good deal of the Roosevelt antipathy toward newspapers stemmed from his years on the Civil Service Commission. He had found many of the editors and publishers who preached in favor of Civil Service Reform to be hypocrites. They "favored all good, and many goody-goody, measures as long as they did not cut deep into social wrong," he wrote in his memoirs, "and above all, they opposed every non-milk-and-wafer effort, however sane, to change our social and economic system in such a fashion as to substitute the ideal of justice towards all for the ideal of kindly charity from the favored few to the possibly grateful many."

In this category TR relegated Lincoln Steffens' boss, the editor of the *Evening Post*. He regarded E. L. Godkin as archetype of the unpractical idealist who thought New York City could be governed as he ruled the subscribers of his newspaper, by admirably written editorials and semisatirical essays.

The feeling of animosity was mutual and long-standing. When Roosevelt had refused to back James G. Blaine for President in 1884, saying that Republicans ought to look for a good Democrat, Godkin had excoriated him in the *Post*. TR shot back a letter to the editor, describing Godkin as suffering from "moral myopia, complicated with intellectual strabismus." Larry Godkin was not amused. Nor did he forget.

But it was the *World* that nettled TR most. One of its early headlines had described Roosevelt's goal as police commissioner as "publicity, publicity, publicity." For himself, of course. The *World* would remain a harsh critic.

Yet Arthur Brisbane, the *World* reporter who provided readers with the vivid description of TR's teeth as he grilled miscreant coppers in police board trials in an "exasperating voice, a sharp voice, a rasping voice," was one of the press shack's most ardent admirers of

TR. Another was Joseph B. Bishop, who shared the *Post* office at 303 Mulberry with Lincoln Steffens. He believed that TR "is talking to a purpose. He wishes the public to know what the Police Board is doing so that it will have popular support."

For reporters the politician who had been said to have a wealth of mouth was a welcome commodity. He made good copy. In the history of the relations between the New York press and the city's politicians, those in office who exhibited similar traits invariably charmed and won over reporters, if not their editors. After TR came other colorful New York characters. Mayor James J. "Gentleman Jimmy" Walker held sway in the 1920s. Fiorello "the Little Flower" LaGuardia and his police commissioner, Lewis J. "Muss up the gangsters" Valentine dominated the 1930s and the years of World War II. Mayor Edward I "How'm I doin'?" Koch in the 1980s also bore the affectionate sobriquette "Crazy Eddie."

A phenomenon of Theodore Roosevelt's treatment by the lords of the press was the emphatically enthusiastic treatment he got the farther away the newspaper. He had made news aplenty in the nation's capital as Civil Service Commissioner and carried that attention with him back to New York. The Philadelphia and Chicago newspapers found him irresistible. And while New York City's Park Row barons exhibited considerable nervousness over Roosevelt and spread the story that he was on his way out in November 1895, the London *Times* printed the following without feeling a need to provide readers with the subject's first name:

Roosevelt

> The hour has found its man—a rock
> Uprisen in the seething tide.
> The wild wave's dash, the tempest's shock
> Fall harmless on his mailed side.
> Unbought, unawed, unknown to fear,
> In vain the snarling tiger's paw
> Essays to smite, while loud and clear
> Rings out his war-cry, "Law is law."
>
> O mighty man of valor, set
> Thy standard on a loftier height;
> And louder, higher, clearer yet,
> Peal out the watchword, "Right is right."

Regarding how the press saw Roosevelt, worshipful Jacob Riis wrote, "As the days passed in Mulberry Street, Roosevelt seemed to me more and more like a touchstone by rubbing against which the true metal of all about him was brought out: every rascal became his implacable enemy; the honest, his followers to a man."

Lincoln Steffens viewed TR as something of a bull in a china shop. As a result, he ran over fellow commissioners, especially Andrew Parker. Steffens found nothing sinister in this, merely a kind of blind enthusiasm. He wrote, "He had been asked to take the police job, he had been urged to clean out the department, and considering it with his friends, had been thinking of it as his job, his alone, forgetting that it was a board, and so, when the others were appointed, he kept forgetting them. He was so intent upon the task that he did not think of his associates or anything else."

Believing this, Steffens was astonished when Andrew Parker told him that Theodore Roosevelt viewed the police department as a rung on a ladder to something higher. Still rather naive and unsophisticated politically, Steffens passed along Parker's view to Jacob Riis.

"Of course," the wizened veteran of the press shack said. "Teddy is bound for the presidency."

A dubious Steffens said, "Let's ask him."

"Come on," Riis said, springing up from his desk to lead Steffens on a dash across Mulberry Street and up to TR's office. Bursting in, he blurted to Roosevelt, "Settle a dispute between Steffens and me, TR. Are you working to become President of the United States?"

Roosevelt leapt to his feet and ran around his desk, his fists clenched and teeth bared. Steffens feared he was going to strike or throttle Riis.

"Don't you dare ask me that," TR roared as Riis shrank back. "Don't you put such ideas into my head. No friend of mine would ever say a thing like that, you—you—"

As Riis cowered and Steffens gaped in amazement, Roosevelt put his arm over Riis's shoulder and beckoned Steffens close.

"Never, never, you must never either of you ever remind a man at work on a political job that he may be President," he said quietly. "It almost always kills him politically. He loses his nerve; he can't do his work; he gives up the very traits that are making him a possibility. I, for instance, am going to do great things here, hard things that require all the courage, ability, work that I am capable of, and I can do them if I think of them alone. But if I get to thinking of what it might lead to—"

He stopped, holding his friends off, and looked into their faces with his face screwed up into a knot, as Steffens described it. He continued with lowered voice, "I must be wanting to be President. Every young man does. But I won't let myself think of it; I must not, because if I do, I will begin to work for it, I'll be careful, calculating, cautious in word and act, and so I'll beat myself. See?"

He looked at the two stunned and crestfallen reporters, Steffens noted in his autobiography, "as if we were enemies," then returned to his desk. "Go on away, now," he said brusquely, "and don't you ever mention the—don't you ever mention that to me again."

According to Steffens, neither man did so as long as TR was in Mulberry Street. However, reluctance to tempt the Roosevelt temper on the issue of the White House did not dissuade Steffens from collaborating with Riis and other reporters in testing the mettle of the police under their new boss, and having a bit of fun at the same time.

The plot hatched during the summer in the basement of police headquarters, a cool spot where detectives, prisoners, and reporters gossiped and played cards to beat the heat. A relative newcomer, Steffens enjoyed hearing stories of the underworld. "They were true stories, and true detective stories are more fascinating than the fiction even of the masters," he wrote. "Sometimes a prisoner would give his version of his crime and capture after the detective who had caught him told his. Sometimes the stories were dull, technical, so to speak, and therefore interesting enough to the participants, like ex-soldiers comparing notes of a battle after the war."

One day as Steffens appeared to be dozing he heard one of these stories unfolding and decided it was worthy of the *Post*. As it happened, his was the only account of the crime to appear in print. Other reporters, including Riis, were called on the carpet for having been scooped. The next day Riis turned the tables and beat Steffens with a story on a burglary. Immediately, Steffens found himself called upon to explain himself to city editor Harry Wright.

"I thought you didn't want crimes in the *Post*," Steffens replied.

"No," said Wright, "but a big burglary like that—"

Steffens informed his assistant, a youth named Robert, that they had to "get some crimes." Buttonholing detective after detective, they came up empty. Then Robert learned of the robbery of a

Fifth Avenue club. It was a beat. But that day Riis came up with two scoops.

Other reporters observed what was happening and joined them in digging for stories, while their editors freely borrowed items from competing papers. The effect was to create in the public's mind an impression that the city was in the throes of rampant crime and that the police appeared incapable of checking it.

"It was indeed one of the worst crime waves I ever witnessed," observed Steffens, although the fact was that there was no more crime being committed than before the reporters began their frenzied efforts to beat one another into print. This truth notwithstanding, the new police board found itself red-faced. A furious Roosevelt convened a secret meeting of the board to vent his ire.

"Mr. President," said Parker, "you can stop this crime wave whenever you want to."

"I! How?"

Parker showed him that there had not been an upsurge in crime, only an increase in crime stories in newspapers. "Call off your friends Riis and Steffens. They started it, and they're sick of it," he said. "They'll be glad to quit if you'll ask them to."

TR adjourned the meeting immediately and yelled across the street, summoning Riis and Steffens to his office. "What's this I hear?" he demanded. "You two and this crime wave? Getting us into trouble? You? I'd never have believed it. You?"

An abject Riis confessed. In contrition he said, "I'll tell you where my source is, and you can close it up. I have had it for years, seldom used it. But you can stop it forever."

The wellspring of his scoops, he explained, was within the detective bureau. Into a pigeon-hole in the desk in the outer office of the chief inspector each day went a listing of reports of crimes of a high degree against property.

"I told my assistant Max never to pry into that pigeon-hole, except in emergencies," Riis continued. However, when he had been scooped by Steffens he broke the rule. "I got so mad I told Max to go to it, and, well—"

He informed TR of the location of the pigeon-hole, adding advice that Roosevelt gladly followed. He ordered the crime list kept in a desk of an inside office. The "crime wave" ended. And the president of the police board enjoyed the satisfaction of informing Parker that its source had been sloppiness in procedures within Parker's own bailiwick, the detective bureau.

Although Roosevelt took on the role of speaking to the press on behalf of the board, he could recognize that responsibilities of running the police department had been divided between the four members. If a matter came before the board that was within the domain of a particular commissioner, he yielded the running of the meeting to him. So it was on December 4, 1895, when the board took up the adoption of new procedures for promotions. The meeting was conducted by the commissioner who had been put in charge of administrative affairs, Avery Andrews.

The new rules adopted by the board permitted promotion on the grounds of seniority, meritorious service on the force, and "superior capacity," as judged by the board. They also required promotion to a higher rank only from the next immediately lower grade; there would be no leap-frogging ranks. All promotions had to be made from an "eligibility list," such lists to be drawn up from time to time at the request of the board. To get onto a list a candidate for promotion had to attain a numerical grade, based on an evaluation of his seniority and meritorious service (maximum 65 points each) and superior capacity (35 points). Minimum acceptable total score was 75.

Merit was to be measured in terms of integrity, efficiency, success in current rank, personal character, gallantry, bravery, and zeal in carrying out duties. Should two candidates score evenly, the deciding factor would be seniority. No such criteria had ever been imposed in the history of the police force. But it was in the sixth rule covering eligibility for promotion that the Board both made history and resolved the dilemma of what to do about promoting Acting Chief of Police Peter Conlin to the position permanently. The rule established that a rating for "superior capacity" be determined by a competitive examination. The test would be open to everyone in the proper rank; however, the board appointed to itself the sole authority to "cite" the candidate as being eligible to take the exam.

In issuing the rules and regulations the board announced that the only individual cited for the qualifying examination for the post of Chief of Police was Conlin. They ordered him to present himself before the board for examination at noon on Friday, December 6, 1895. Accordingly, Conlin came, passed, and received the hearty congratulations of the commissioners as the permanent successor to the legendary but unlamented Tom Byrnes.

With confidence in the new chief and pleasure with the historic rules and regulations that eliminated political influence and bribery from the department's promotion procedures, TR accepted the role of guest of honor at a dinner of the Aldine Club in its home at 75 Fifth Avenue. Held on December 11, the banquet offered a motif fitting to the author who was just completing the last volume of *The Winning of the West*. The walls were festooned with Indian blankets, hunting implements, authentic bows and arrows, wampum belts, saddles, lassos, and cowboys' "chappies."

The guests included artists, writers, and publishers, as well as Seth Low, president of Columbia College; John P. Proctor, president of the National Civil Service Commission; Colonel George Waring, who inherited the job of Street Cleaning Commissioner after TR had turned it down; Commissioners Parker and Andrews; and a beaming Jacob Riis.

They heard TR sound many of the themes he had addressed in the recent election. Mindful of adoption of the police department's strict new rules and regulations covering promotions, he boasted of stopping the purchase and sale of police appointments and promotions. "Since we have been in office we have appointed between 200 and 300 patrolmen," he said, "and not a single appointment has been made because of the man's politics or backing, but simply because of his fitness."

Stressing, again, that the principle of the board was that all the laws must be honestly enforced, and pledging to do so, he went on to say, "If all the laws were honestly enforced throughout the State, the legislators would soon repeal those that are oppressive and keep on the statute books only those which are fair and just."

The words amounted to an invitation to the legislature to change the Sunday closing law. In doing so he indirectly associated himself with a move in Albany to seek changes in the law through a referendum on the question of whether businesses might be permitted to open their doors for the sale of beer, ale, and wine on Sundays between the hours of 1:00 P.M. and 10:00 P.M. The legislation had been formally introduced on December 4 on behalf of the Excise Reform Association. It called for voting on the proposition on March 5, 1896.

Three days after the Aldine Club dinner the board received

their new chief of police for a report on the implementation of the new promotion rules. He stated that application forms had been distributed to all precincts, along with the conditions laid out by the board. The commissioners then authorized a certificate of merit and a medal to Patrolman Thomas Craven of the West Thirtieth Street Station for bravery in stopping a runaway horse. TR was so impressed by the act that he announced his intention of "looking up" Craven's complete record with an eye toward possibly promoting the courageous cop to Roundsman.

In hand, too, were two letters praising the officers of the Mercer Street Station for raiding a bawdy house located at 39 Grove Street. The first letter was addressed to the board from Arthur H. Ely, an attorney with offices at 56 Wall Street. It praised Inspector Brooks, Roundsman Kemp, and Patrolmen McConnell, Casey, and Hilton. The second letter had been delivered directly to Inspector Brooks. It came from the Rev. Charles Parkhurst, to whom the raid had special significance. The Grove Street house had been one of those he investigated while gathering evidence of vice and police conspiracies to tolerate it.

As these glowing missives were placed into the record, Commissioners Andrews and Grant noted that the closing of the house had not met universal approval. The board had also received several anonymous letters condemning the police action.

TR offered the next letter received from citizens, though not ones who lived in New York City. Signed by one hundred clergymen in Brooklyn, it had been sent to Mayor Strong and Roosevelt. The ministers lauded the police board and offered "sincere and hearty thanks" on behalf of New York's "sister city" for its work in enforcing the Sunday closing law.

The next item on the agenda seemed as routine as any item the commissioners were called upon to handle. They were asked to approve the appointment of Edward A. Meade to be a stenographer of the Police Civil Service Board at a salary of one thousand five hundred dollars a year. The commissioners assented. They then were asked to sign off on paying a woman who had been employed to fill in for an employee who was ill. Commissioner Andrews reported that the wage that had been recommended by the office supervisor was ten dollars for the week.

Roosevelt asked, "What was the salary of the man for whom she substituted?"

Andrews replied, "Fifteen dollars a week."

With a shake of his head, TR said, "I believe a woman should be paid as much as a man if she did the same work."

The other commissioners agreed. However, for a reason not recorded, the woman actually received twelve dollars a week. Whatever the cause of the difference, it must have satisfied Roosevelt, for it seems unlikely that having enunciated a principle of "equal work for equal pay" the champion of fairness would retreat from that stance without persuasive justification.

With the Christmas season in full bloom the president of the police board told associates, "I should very much like to take a holiday." But the nearest he came to one was spending Christmas with his family at Sagamore Hill, during which time he finished the fourth and last volume of *The Winning of the West*. However, the only business of Christmas day itself was a family tradition of a speech by the head of the family prior to the opening of gifts. This oration was "always mercifully short," he noted in his autobiography, because his children "impressed upon me with frank sincerity the attitude of other children to addresses of this kind on such occasions." The children also performed by reciting "Darius Green and the Flying Machine," "The Mountain and the Squirrel had a Quarrel" and other children's poems.

In event of snow, a sleigh stood ready for rides over hill and dale and to church in Oyster Bay where the Christmas service traditionally began with the hymn "It's Christmas eve on the river, it's Christmas eve on the bay." TR's church was Dutch Reformed but they attended a little frame Episcopal church in the town.

Having witnessed the Roosevelt family of Sagamore Hill at such times, Hermann Hagedorn wrote, "Winter was the time for open fires—and did they need them at Sagamore!—with Theodore telling stories of his hunting adventures or acting them out with the children, with himself as the big bear and the children as the cubs, or Edith reading 'Sir Patrick Spens' or some other stirring ballad, with their father, perhaps, adding 'Sheridan's Ride,' or 'The Sinking of the Cumberland.'"

For Theodore Roosevelt, whom many people predicted in that Christmas season of 1895 was destined to spend future Yuletides as President of the United States, the greatest of all prizes were those connected with the home. "There are many forms of success, many forms of triumph," he wrote after the predictions of a White House future had come true. "But there is no other success that in any shape or way approaches that which is open to most of the many, many men and women who have the right ideals. These are the men and the women who see that it is the intimate and homely things that count most."

Three days after Christmas he traveled to Philadelphia to deliver the principal address at a mass meeting of Republicans in the interest of a movement to reform the city councils of the city of Brotherly Love. An invitation to speak on behalf of a cause so "greatly at heart as that of honest municipal government" was not one that he could refuse, he told them. The speech went on to cite successes in reforming the police.

On the day he went to Philadelphia a movement to change the hated Sunday closing law was gathering momentum in New York City. The German-American Citizens' Union circulated what the New York *Times* called "its monster petition" to the legislature in Albany to pass the proposed law "referring to the voters . . . the question of whether the sale of beverages, milk and food shall be permitted on Sundays under proper restrictions to be fixed by statute." As of December 28, their petitions contained twenty-five thousand signatures. Fanning out from the movement's headquarters in Room 101 at 25 Third Avenue, canvassers carried huge bundles of blanks with room for twenty names each.

"This is a popular movement," said Moses Oppenheimer, the secretary of the Citizens' Union. "The signatures are given readily, and often enthusiastically."

At the same time, enforcement of the closing law went ahead with vigor on the part of the police, although in one instance the enforcement appeared to have gotten out of hand. On December 27, saloon owner J. A. Butler showed up at the district attorney's office to complain that Acting Captain John R. Groo and special duty man, Detective Sloane, smashed the door of his establishment at 25 Prince Street on Christmas Eve with the intention of carrying out a burglary.

Groo heatedly denied the charge. The door had been knocked in, he said, because he found the shades of the saloon drawn, as if the place were closed. Yet he heard the sounds of clinking glasses and rowdy voices, indicating the bar was open and likely to remain so into Christmas morning, when the liquor business was to be closed under the Excise Law. Groo stated that when he tried to investigate by knocking on the door, he had been denied entry. Consequently, he had shoved the door open with his shoulder.

Butler insisted the saloon had not been open for business and that he and a few friends were gathered for a postmidnight Christmas dinner of chicken that was being cooked on a small gas stove on the premises.

Because there had been no evidence produced of liquor being sold and as a result of Groo grudgingly admitting that he might have been overly strenuous in his investigative technique, the case headed for settlement without charges being filed by either man and Butler being reimbursed for repairs to the broken door.

No such misunderstandings had marked the police case against saloon keeper Theodore Allen, better known as "The Allen," when he had been arraigned in Jefferson Market Court on November 28. He and twenty-seven others had been arrested in a raid on an illegal gambling den above The Allen's West Broadway saloon.

The only entrance to the poolroom in which bets were taken on horse races was through the saloon and up an inner stairway. A private door was guarded by a man with orders to admit only those whom Allen had approved. A central office detective had managed to get inside the room and place a bet on Marguerite, a horse running at Pimlico Race Track in Maryland. The following day the detective returned and placed a wager on Tamsen, also running at Pimlico. On the basis of the report of the undercover detective, Inspector Brooks, who was to be lauded for shutting down the bawdy house on Grove Street, and fourteen coppers from the Mercer Street Station swooped down on the premises. But it had not been the first raid. They had done so in June, making an arrest for which The Allen stood indicted and awaiting trial.

What was significant about the raids was that they happened. The Allen had operated his saloon and its upstairs gambling den for years without annoyance by paying off the police to leave him alone and providing money to political bosses to ensure that the police carried out the bargain. With a second charge against him and a conviction at trial likely, Allen looked forward in that holiday season of 1895 to possibly his last Christmas as a free man for some time.

Although contemplation of a prison term dimmed the festivities of the week between Christmas and New Year's Eve for The Allen as 1895 drew to a close, Mrs. Evelyn Byrd Burden and her husband,

Isaac Townsend Burden, the multimillionaire and partner in the Burden Iron Company of Troy, New York, planned a glittery week of gala events. They had invited numerous guests to their mansion at 5 East Twenty-sixth Street.

On the north side of Madison Square and in the shadow of the graceful tower of architect Stanford White's Madison Square Garden, the house stood in full view of Delmonico's, the Hoffman House, St. James, Albemarle, Fifth Avenue, and Bartholdi Hotels, as well as the Metropolitan Life Insurance Company Building, the University Club, and the select residences occupied by families just as conspicuous in society and in fortune as themselves—the Abercrombies, Osgoods, and Iselins.

At 8:45 on Friday evening, December 27, the Burdens left the house with their daughter, Evelyn, for the short carriage ride to the Metropolitan Opera at Broadway and Fortieth Street for a performance of "Romeo and Juliet," while one of their two sons, I. Townsend Burden, Jr., put on his evening wear for an evening of livelier entertainment elsewhere. The other, eighteen-year-old William, elected to stay at home and catch up on reading in a comfortable chair in a ground floor parlor. Seeing after Willie's needs or whims would be seven servants, five women and two men.

When Mr. and Mrs. Burden returned from the opera they found Willie still comfortably ensconced. Bidding him good night, the couple went upstairs to their separate bedrooms. A few moments later, Mrs. Burden's anguished cry brought her husband, son, and servants hurrying to her room. One look at its disarray and a glance at the opened door of a small safe left no doubt in any of their minds that the room had been burglarized.

Highly knowledgeable and discerning, the thieves had made off with only the most exquisite of Mrs. Burden's formidable collection. Its centerpiece was a diamond necklace whose value Tiffany set at thirty thousand dollars. A diamond tiara had been appraised at seven thousand dollars. In all, the thieves got away with loot valued at $58,930.

First on the scene on behalf of the police was Captain Pickett of the Nineteenth Precinct. In the colorful phrasing of the reporter from the *Times,* the infamous Tenderloin station house once commanded by Clubber Williams stood "within gunshot" of the Burden mansion, and in the most important police command of the city.

Immediately upon arriving at the scene, Pickett determined

that the thief or thieves had entered the house through a second-floor window—literally a "second story job." Some detectives saw the possibility that the burglars had reached the Burden house through the rear of the adjacent Brunswick Hotel. This the manager heatedly denied, asserting that his alert staff would have seen anyone who did not belong in that part of the hotel.

In seeking to determine how the robbery of a safe could have been achieved without drills or explosives and consequent noises, Pickett learned to his dismay that Mrs. Burden customarily left the key to the safe on top of it. This information immediately provoked suspicions that the theft had been an inside job, the necessary information having been provided to professionals by at least two of the Burdens' servants.

One of the detectives told reporters, "Our idea that two of the Burden servants were in collusion with the thieves is founded on what we regard as the suspicious actions of the servants. On the evening of the robbery, William Burden sat in one of the rooms reading a book. Two servants were constantly in the hall during the evening, going up and down the stairs, bringing one thing after another to William, and giving him no chance to leave the room for anything. They seemed to be anxious that he should not be disturbed by any want, and should have no occasion to leave the comfortable chair in which he was sitting. It was while he was thus pleasantly engaged, and was being waited on in this unusual manner that the robbery occurred."

Presently, Chief of Police Conlin expressed agreement with that analysis.

Blared from the front pages of all the newspapers, the tale of a robbery of fabulous jewels from a magnificent mansion while a scion of an extraordinarily wealthy family was being pampered by seven servants provoked little, if any, sympathy for Mr. and Mrs. Burden. The hearts of the people of Jacob Riis's "other half" went out to the servants. Rather than feel sorry for the Burdens' loss the public appeared to relish it. And the general population took angry note of the extraordinary measures being taken by police to solve the crime, whereas offenses against less notable and powerful people seemed to languish on the books.

Among the open cases cited by critics of the police was the murder of a "colored" butler, Ferdinand Harris, in the residence of C. D. Borden of 25 West Fifty-sixth Street on May 27. Critics also pointed to the unsolved robbery of Walter's saloon at Brown Place and Southern Boulevard on November 7 in which Richard Pope had been killed. The list went on to the robbery of one thousand seven hundred dollars from the Brentano's bookstore in Union Square on November 23. Nor had the detective bureau caught the person who blew open the safe in the office of Dr. G. H. Modemann, 504 Third Avenue, within a block of the East Thirty-fifth Street Station House.

Stung by these criticisms, and a suggestion floated around town that the police were too busy shutting down saloons to catch crooks, Commissioner Andrew Parker, who was the board member in charge of the detectives, lashed out at the newspapers. "It is not impossible that some criminals may have gathered the impression that this city at present furnishes a good field for their activity. They may have got the impression from the tone of some of the newspapers which have very strongly asserted that to be a fact." He also blamed lenient judges for imposing "inadequate legal sentences" upon professional criminals.

The Burden robbery was "a professional job of the cleverest character," said the head of the detective bureau, Acting Captain O'Brien, to the throngs of eager newspapermen swarming to Madison Square in the early hours of Saturday. "So far we are baffled."

The crime-solving picture was not totally bleak, however. The Morrisania Police Station reported to Mulberry Street police headquarters on New Year's Eve that they had caught John Dempsey, "a rough-looking fellow," between Lincoln and Alexander Avenues in the act of attempted burglary as he climbed through a second-story window of an apartment house at 494 Bergen Avenue. He had been spotted by a janitor, who called the police. When they came upon the scene Dempsey leapt from a fire escape into the yard, breaking his leg in the process. Under arrest, he had been taken to Harlem Hospital.

Although Theodore Roosevelt knew the Burden family and might have used his position as president of the police board to speak about the robbery and rise to the defense of a beleaguered and frustrated detective bureau, he chose to leave the field to the man responsible for it, Commissioner Andrew Parker. Details of particular criminal cases offered little appeal to TR, unless they were the offenses of police, elected officials, or those who chose to thumb their noses at his efforts to make a point about the principle of enforcing laws fairly, as in his pursuit of full compliance with the

Sunday closing law. That so many otherwise decent people opposed him on that principle had left him increasingly disappointed.

Very late in 1895 he wrote to friend Henry Cabot Lodge, "It really seems that there must be some fearful shortcoming on my side to account for the fact that I have not one New York City newspaper, nor one New York City politician of note on my side." But, he went on in a typical mixture of determination and gloom about his future, "Don't think that I even for a moment dream of abandoning my fight; I shall continue absolutely unmoved from my present course and shall accept philosophically whatever violent end may be put to my political career."

Chapter 10

Other Half, Other Hat

Because of the manner in which the New York City government was organized, the president of the board of police commissioners also sat as a member of the health board. This was the body that held the power to address all the societal wrongs Jacob Riis had exposed in *How the Other Half Lives* in 1890, and a second volume, *The Children of the Poor,* in 1892. Each preached a simple gospel, that with elimination of the slum the immigrant population of the city would take its place in society. The cure for urban ills was decent housing, parks, good schools, playgrounds, and sunlight. In Theodore Roosevelt's donning of his other hat as a health board member Riis believed he found exactly the helper TR had promised to be when he left his calling card at Riis's office in 1890.

Very few, if any, alliances between politician and journalist match the one formed by the pair whom Lincoln Steffens affectionately called "Teddy and Jake." It was a bonding that would last all their lives. Roosevelt thought so much of Riis that he mentioned him on the first page of the chapter in his autobiography dealing with events of TR's experiences in Mulberry Street. He wrote, "The man who was closest to me throughout my two years in the Police Department was Jacob Riis." But even earlier, in an essay written in 1901 for *McClure's Magazine,* he said, "The countless evils which lurk in the dark corners of our civic institutions, which stalk abroad in the slums, and have their permanent abode in the crowded tenement houses, have met in Mr. Riis the most formidable opponent ever encountered by them in New York City. Many earnest men and earnest women have been stirred to the depths by the want and misery and foul crime which are bred in the crowded blocks of tenement rookeries. These men and women have planned and worked, intelligently and resolutely, to overcome the evils. But to Mr. Riis was given, in addition to earnestness and zeal, the great gift of expression, the great gift of making others see what he saw and what he felt."

Riis was equally laudatory regarding TR in his own memoirs, *The Making of an American,* and in *Theodore Roosevelt, the Citizen,* a 464-page plea on behalf of the election of TR to be President of the United States, published in 1904. Before Roosevelt, Riis wrote, "we had all the ammunition for the fight, the law and all, but there was none who dared begin it till he came."

The law Riis mentioned gave power to the health board to seize and destroy tenement-house property that was a threat to the city's health. But Riis viewed the law as "a dead letter." When Roosevelt came on board he promptly handed him a list of the sixteen worst tenements in the city outside of the notorious Mulberry Bend. The most egregious of these was an area known as the Mott Street Barracks. In 1888 the infant death rate among its Italian population had been 325 per thousand, that is, one-third of all the babies died that year. In a four-year period the death rate in ninety-four tenements stood at 62.9 when the death rate city-wide was 24.63.

Little wonder, then, that when Riis became TR's guide for the midnight rambles whose purpose was to catch slacking cops he saw to it that Roosevelt's attention was drawn to the conditions of the people who slept, lived, and frequently worked in the dismal tenement neighborhoods that TR's rambles encompassed.

"The midnight trips that Riis and I took enabled me to see what the Police Department was doing," Roosevelt wrote in his autobiography, "and also give me personal insight into some of the problems of city life. It is one thing to listen in perfunctory fashion to tales of overcrowded tenements, and it is quite another actually to see what the overcrowding means, some hot summer night, by even a single inspection during the hours of darkness."

Roosevelt soon learned that his guide brought to their tours personal experiences of life amongst the other half. As an immigrant himself, Riis had gone through the hard struggle of going out with no money to seek a future in a strange and alien land. He had known what it was like to sleep in doorways and go for days without food. In Jake Riis, Roosevelt discovered "certain qualities the reformer must have if he is to be a real reformer and not merely a faddist; for of course every reformer is in continual danger of slipping into the mass of well-meaning people who in their advocacy of the impracticable do more harm than good." He found in Riis "high courage, disinterested desire to do good, and sane, wholesome common sense," as well as a sense of humor.

Riis embodied Roosevelt's own brand of practical idealism. He wrote of Riis in "Reform Through Social Work" for *McClure's Magazine,* "He sets himself to kill the living evil, and small is his kinship with the dreamers who seek the impossible—the men who *talk* of reconstituting the entire social order, but who do not *work* to lighten the burden of mankind by so much as a feather's weight."

Long before Roosevelt arrived at the uptown end of Mulberry Street a prime Riis target had been the downtown, curving stretch of the street known as Mulberry Bend. In his years of acquaintance with it as a reporter not a week went by, he wrote in *The Making of an American,* "in which it was not heard from in the police reports, generally in connection with a crime of violence, a murder or a stabbing affray."

Although a law passed by the legislature in 1886 had decreed that the Bend's tenements be demolished and the area redeemed, Riis noted that nine years later he could not remember "that a cat stirred to urge it on." He had once asked at city hall why the demolition had not been carried out and was told that no one had ever shown "any interest in the thing."

He had fought to clean up the area for so long he considered himself the recognized crank on the subject. But with the advent of Roosevelt in 1895, "I had at last an ally in the fight with the Bend." Exactly one month after TR took on the role of health commissioner, the *Times* printed a headline concerning the Bend to cheer Riis's reformer's heart.

ALL THE STRUCTURES MUST BE TORN DOWN WITHIN THIRTY DAYS

Demolitions began that day, June 6, 1895. The plans for use of the land also pleased Riis. It was to be cleared for a park. Ironically, shortly after sod had been laid, Riis in a moment of exultation ignored a "keep off the grass" sign and was promptly "whacked by a policeman for doing so."

"But that was all right," he wrote. "We had the park."

As he removed himself from the grass he recalled that he had been "moved on" by a cop of an earlier time when he sat shivering in reeking hallways on that very spot.

Curiously, Riis was not invited to the ceremony marking the park's formal opening. He did not mind. It sufficed that he was "mighty glad" that he had had a hand in making the Bend go.

Next in his sights were the "lodging houses" that the law authorized to be established within police stations. These consisted of bunk rooms for a growing number of homeless. The system had been in existence for decades. As early as 1867 the police department's board of surgeons expressed an opinion "that it would be recreant to its duty did it not strenuously urge upon the Board of Police the propriety, the economy, nay, the absolute necessity of discontinuing the practice of using the station houses as lodging houses for vagrants." In 1876 an investigation made by the State Charities Aid Association found appalling conditions and called for an end to the system. In the fall of 1891 a grand jury recommended in "the best interests of the city" that the lodging houses be abolished.

Roosevelt wanted a firsthand look at the conditions and Riis readily agreed to become his guide. The police station he chose to show was one in which he had lodged in 1870, the Church Street Station. Down the cellar steps they went. Riis found it unchanged, "just as it was the day I slept there."

Typically, Riis saw behind grimy faces and tattered clothes to the human beings. He bore bitter memories of having been one of them. He told Roosevelt that in his vagabond years before he became the sage of the police department press shack he had come to the point of killing himself. Teetering on the edge of a river and about to throw himself into it, he heard a little whine from a small black and tan stray dog he had befriended. Scooping the dog into his arms, he set aside thoughts of suicide, swallowed his pride, and went to the very police station lodging room in which he and Roosevelt now stood. When he awoke in the morning, Riis continued, he found that a gold locket that was his only connection to his past had been stolen. He reported the loss to the sergeant at the station house desk. The policeman scoffed. How should a tramp such as Riis come honestly by a gold locket?

The sergeant summoned the doorman of the police station and ordered him to throw the "liar" onto the street. As the doorman attempted to do so, the little dog growled and bared his teeth.

"A policeman seized the dog and clubbed it to death," Riis concluded.

Roosevelt gasped in disgust. His face turned alternately red and white with anger. Looking round at the dismal place that had not changed in the twenty-five years since Riis had slept there, he clenched his fists and declared of it and the city's other twenty police department lodging houses, "I will smash them tomorrow."

When he requested a report on the lodging houses from Chief of Police Conlin, he found a voice in agreement. "The practice is fraught with numerous evils; the huddling like cattle of a large number of drunken, dirty, and oftentimes diseased wretches, contaminates the air breathed by patrolmen in the same building. It engenders typhoid and other idiosomatic diseases and is a prolific and traceable source of sickness among the officers and men," Conlin said.

The chief of police reported to the board on January 28, 1896, that in the past year lodgers in the twenty precincts had totalled 65,556. Yet only two-percent of them, he said, had been truly in need and worthy of police assistance. The remainder were described in the terms that would be applied to the homeless of New York City a century later. Conlin viewed the lodging houses as havens for "lazy, dissipated, filthy, vermin-covered, disease-breeding and disease-scattering scum of the city's population."

The chief of police then proposed moving the occupants of the lodging rooms to a facility operated by a private charity, the Wayfarers Lodge and Woodyard of the Charity Organization Society at 516 West Twenty-sixth Street. Those who agreed to go to the new location would be issued vouchers entitling them to dinner, lodging, a bath, disinfection and clean clothing, in return for "a required amount of work."

Conlin concluded with as much forcefulness as he could summon that "the police station lodging houses must go, and go at once."

TR agreed that they were "a fruitful encouragement to vagrancy." When the board considered Conlin's report on January 29, 1896, it voted to adopt the voucher system and abolish the police lodging rooms as of February 15.

To be certain that only worthy persons received assistance the board authorized Conlin to create a squad of "three or four officers to go through the city to locate and identify "confirmed and habitual beggars."

The record indicates no one suggesting that a system of spying on citizens, even "tramps," might not be in keeping with the spirit and the letter of the U.S. Constitution. Neither did there exist organizations to defend the rights of homeless people such as those formed during the homeless crisis a hundred years later.

The "tramp and beggar squads" carried out their assignment throughout the balance of Roosevelt's term and beyond.

Concurrently with the police board's actions regarding the lodging houses, an investigative panel of the State Legislature, known as the Reinhardt Committee, reported on the condition of women and children employed in "mercantile establishments." This was a nice way of referring to the sweatshops that Jacob Riis had documented in his books. The committee was charged with determining not if they ought to be outlawed, but if they should be brought under supervision of the State Factory Inspector.

The findings of the committee's report of January 15, 1896, were as dismal as those described and pictured in *How the Other Half Lives* five years earlier. They also indicated no difference in conditions from those discovered by Assemblyman Roosevelt's Cities Committee in 1884. The 1896 report stated that the evils of the sweatshop system and of tenement work could not be exaggerated. While doubting the authority of the legislature to impose a wage structure, it did contend that laws could require improvements in working conditions regarding cleanliness, ventilation, light, and working hours. It especially recommended strict attention and prompt action regarding the use of children in factories.

The report stated, "No child under sixteen years shall be permitted to work in any manufacturing establishment unless the compulsory education law is complied with and there is first obtained a certificate from the local Board of Health stating that such board is satisfied that the child is of the age of fourteen years or upward and physically able to perform the work."

Regardless of age, thousands of children were working in these factories, most of which were actually the children's homes. In the rooms of slum tenements they labored side by side with their parents to make a bewildering array of products listed in the committee's report as "coats, vests, trousers, kneepants, overalls, cloaks, hats, caps, suspenders, jerseys, blouses, waists, waistbands, underwear, neckwear, furs, fur trimmings, fur garments, shirts, purses, feathers, artificial flowers, cigarettes and cigars."

The last item on the list, cigars, had attracted Roosevelt's attention as an assemblyman. Because they were being manufactured in
tenement sweatshops the Cigar-Makers' Union lobbied in Albany to
prohibit the practice, though the union's motivation appeared to
stem from its concern for its members' jobs, not out of a deep outrage
at the exploitation of the poor and their children. In connection with
the bill TR was appointed to a committee of three to investigate
conditions in the tenement cigar factories. One of the members took
no interest in the measure. The second was a Tammany man. Because Tammany Hall benefitted from tenement owners who ran the
cigar factories, he opposed the bill and wanted no part in an investigation. This left TR, in effect, a one-man committee. However, those
who had appointed him did so because they expected him to come
out against any interference with the exercise of a *laissez faire*
economy. They were wrong.

Roosevelt's first visits to the tenement-house districts made him
feel that, "whatever the theories might be, as a matter of practical
common sense" he could not conscientiously vote for the continu-
ance of the conditions he found. He recalled in his autobiography,
"These conditions rendered it impossible for the families of the
tenement-house workers to live so that the children might grow up
fitted for the exacting duties of American citizenship."

Appalled by the conditions, he voted for the bill. When Governor
Grover Cleveland seemed reticent to sign it, he made a direct appeal
on its behalf. Cleveland signed. But opponents of the law carried
their opposition to the Court of Appeals, which ruled the measure
unconstitutional. The decision awoke TR to "a dim and partial understanding of the fact that the courts were not necessarily the best
judges of what should be done to better social and industrial conditions."

A dozen years after the cigar-making law was invalidated, Police and Health Commissioner Roosevelt toured with Riis and found
conditions of cigar-making tenement dwellers unchanged from Roosevelt's first investigation and Riis's description of them in his book.
"Probably more than half of all the [immigrants] in this city are
cigarmakers," Riis had written, "and it is the herding of these in
great numbers in the so-called tenement factories, where the cheap-
est grade of work is done at the lowest wages, that constitutes at
once their greatest hardship and the chief grudge of other workmen
against them. The manufacturer who owns say, from three to four to

a dozen or more tenements contiguous to his shop, fills them up with these people, charging them outrageous rents . . . deals them out tobacco . . . and devotes the rest of his energies to paring down of wages to within a peg or two of the point where the tenant rebels in desperation. . . . Men, women and children work together seven days a week in these cheerless tenements to make a living for the family, from the break of day till far into the night."

The Reinhardt Committee of 1896 heard testimony from a woman who had inspected one of the cigar sweatshops. Joy Ross told the members about a factory run by the Liberty Cigar Manufacturing Company. She said she had seen children at work stripping tobacco and that the tenement rooms were unclean and that children with bare feet and legs worked with tobacco laid across their knees. She noted two boys who looked pale and unhealthy. The eyes of one of them appeared badly inflamed. When she inquired of a physician about the health risks in such work the doctor informed her that young children working upon tobacco in close rooms would be subject to digestive troubles and a functional disorder of the heart commonly known as "smoker's heart."

In going after the owners of tenements who permitted their use as sweatshops, TR discovered that "not a few of the worst tenement-houses were owned by wealthy individuals, who hired the best and most expensive lawyers to persuade the courts that it was 'unconstitutional' to insist on the betterment of conditions." Jacob Riis noted in his autobiography that when the Reinhardt Committee reported to the legislature it said that "the net result of the Factory Law was a mass of perjury and child-labor."

Another situation regarding children also drew Roosevelt's attention in both his capacity as health commissioner and police board president. It was a long-standing policy under which children, often infants, who were found abandoned were taken to the nearest police station, then to headquarters where matrons would care for them until they could be collected by the Department of Charities and then removed to Bellevue Hospital.

TR told fellow commissioners, "The exposure of the infant for a greater or less period of time before discovery, the added exposure on the journey to the police station, thence to the Central Office, and the long journey and unnecessary delay in getting the child to some place where it could receive proper nourishment and skilled medical attention, almost invariably causes the death of the foundling."

Departmental procedures were amended, requiring the police to transport an abandoned child by the most direct route to the nearest hospital, with immediate notification to be made to the Department of Charities.

Nothing infuriated Roosevelt more than the use of children in obtaining liquor in saloons and carrying it out to adults. On an occasion when Jake Riis reported observing a steady stream of "little ones with mugs and bottles going through the door" of an East Side saloon Roosevelt issued orders to arrest the saloon keeper. But to accomplish this it was necessary to employ a boy to obtain the evidence. The one chosen, according to Riis, was "a regular customer who had gone there a hundred times for a bad purpose, and now he was sent in once for a good one." When word went round that TR had employed a child in such a way a howl went up. A magistrate freed the saloon keeper and rebuked the police officer who had arrested him.

In addition to encouraging and supporting TR's attention to children going into saloons to fetch booze for adults and working in sweatshops Riis expressed concerns about the conditions in the city's schools, especially regarding lack of playgrounds. He also believed that a special school was needed for truants. When his demand was greeted with scorn and ridicule by those who denied that truancy was a problem he produced figures showing that out of the city's third-of-a-million school-age children 251,235 were actually in school, 28,452 were employed, and 50,069 were on the street or at home.

Truancy might have appeared to be an area far afield of the jurisdiction of either the police or health commissioner, but TR believed that the answer to criminality lay in shaping the lives of children in a way that would ensure their growing up to be good citizens. In that enterprise he ranked education beside a good home and sound religious underpinning. Together they created patriotism, and in Roosevelt's book patriotism formed the bedrock of good citizenship.

The state of education in the city came as an eye-opening shock to TR when he discovered that some of the men applying to the police force, when asked to name the thirteen original states of the Union had replied, "England, Ireland, Wales, Belfast and Cork." One who aspired to become a policeman stated that Abraham Lincoln had been "murdered by Ballington Booth." Still another asserted with certainty that on occasions when Mayor Strong was away, the Fire Department was in charge of the city.

While there was nothing Roosevelt could do directly to influence what was taught in schools, he did have the right as a city official with two hats to express himself and to take action regarding playgrounds (a health issue) and truancy (a matter of enforcing the law). Furthermore, playgrounds and a school for truants were ideal institutions for keeping a boy from growing into a youth and an adult likely to find himself in jail. To prevent a life of crime was, after all, a laudable enterprise that ought to be a high priority of the police force.

Riis reported that in the whole of Manhattan there existed but one outdoor playground attached to a school, and it was an old burial ground in First Street that had been "wrested from the dead with immense toil." As for a truant school, he wrote, "the lack of one was the worst outrage of all, for it compelled the sending of boys, who had done no worse harm than to play hooky on a sunny spring day, to a jail with bars in the windows."

Riis believed deeply that when a boy found himself in jail the failure belonged to society as a whole. "That such conditions as were all about us should result in making 'toughs' was not strange," he had written in 1890. "Rather, it would have been strange had anything else come of it. With the home corrupted by the tenement; the school doors closed against them where the swarms were densest, and the children thrown upon the street, there to take their chance; with honest play interdicted, every natural right of the child turned into a means of oppression, a game of ball became a crime for which children were thrust into jail, indeed, shot down like dangerous criminals when running away from the policeman; with the lawlessness of the street added to the want of rule at home . . . it seemed as if we had set out to deliberately make trouble under which we groaned."

Quick to point out to Roosevelt and others that he did not believe that there were no boys who ought to be in jail, he was just as prompt in insisting that to put truants behind bars would be "the poorest use you can put them to . . . to learn all the tricks the jail has to teach, with them in the frame of mind in which it receives them, for boys are not fools, whatever those who are set over them may be, and they know when they are ill used; I know of nothing so wickedly wasteful."

As Riis had set his course on ridding the city of the ills of Mulberry Bend, he determined to have the sun shine on children at play. His words might have been spoken by Roosevelt: "That is a child's right, and it is not to be cheated of it. And when it is cheated of it, it is not the child but the community that is robbed of that beside which all its wealth is but tinsel and trash. For men, not money, make a country great, and joyless children do not make good men."

When a Tenement House Commission of the legislature made it law that no public school should ever again be built without an outdoor playground, Riis seized the opportunity. Putting a playground next to a future school was fine. But what about existing schools? Turning to TR's police department, he obtained a list of locations where the police experienced trouble with boys. Finding the same sad story in each place, he pointed out that the troublesome boys had no place to play but in the streets. They broke windows. The police came.

"By hitching the school and the boys' play together we should speedily get rid of the truant," he argued. He did not care where they were, on the ground or on the roof, so long as areas were opened to children. He went on to propose that schools be opened at night as recreation areas for children.

This scolding voice in society's ear, and a kindred one in TR's, found a new platform in the spring of 1896. The Council of Confederated Good Government Clubs appointed Riis to the post of general agent, draping him in a mantle that afforded him further opportunities to lobby Roosevelt on the issues of playgrounds, truants, schools, parks, sweatshops, and slums.

He even campaigned against conditions in the city's prison, the dreaded Tombs. This was another project close to the heart of Theodore Roosevelt. He had been secretary of the Prison Reform Association after graduation from Harvard. The lockup had been built in 1838 and officially named the Halls of Justice. But its architect, John L. Stevens, designed it after an ancient Egyptian mausoleum, lending the prison the name "the Tombs." Soon after it opened in 1838 it received its first female prisoner, Catherine Hagerman, sentenced on June 15, 1838, to six months for prostitution. Besides its roster of notorious inmates, the gloomy jail also claimed a unique position in the history of crime and punishment in 1890 as the site of the first execution of the death penalty by electricity. In 1896

Jacob Riis wanted "the horrid old pile" torn down and replaced by a modern, humane jail.

Roosevelt inspected the Tombs himself, then threw his backing to its demolition. The old Tombs came down. "And a good riddance to it," Riis wrote. Although the original building fell before the wrecking crews, its name persisted. The primary jail for men waiting to go to trial in New York City would be known in perpetuity as the Tombs.

The investigative team of Roosevelt and Riis also turned its attention to a program for dispensing soup to the needy, a project launched with great fanfare by William Randolph Hearst's *Journal.* Inviting Riis to witness their charity, editors offered to send a carriage to convey him to the site. Riis replied that he would arrive "on foot" and that he would be in the company of Theodore Roosevelt. When they questioned the ragged men queued for the meager soup, they learned that many had come from out of town, in Riis's words, "to take it easy in a city where a man did not have to work to live." Following children toting away pails, they discovered that the soup ended as "free lunch" in saloons where it was exchanged for beer that the children carried home to their parents or other adults. Roosevelt denounced the "charity" as "a nuisance." Soon after, the newspaper abandoned its soup lines and moved on to other ways to enhance its image and thus sell papers.

Bringing together Roosevelt's responsibilities as police commissioner and health board member, a letter from the secretary of the board of regents in Albany, James Russell Parsons, drew TR's attention to the existence of illegal and fraudulent practitioners of medicine. The letter asked if Roosevelt could help in locating them so that they could be put out of business.

TR's response was sealed orders sent to the commanding officer of each city police precinct. They were to be opened and read at morning roll call. They required each patrolman to note the full name and address of every doctor's shingle encountered on their beat. The lists forwarded to Mulberry Street provided data on every individual in the city who advertised himself as a doctor. The names and addresses were then sent to Albany for a comparison with the lists of accredited physicians. "Scores of pretended physicians were brought to book or driven from the city," TR recorded with satisfaction in his memoirs.

But the most troubling social problem confronting Roosevelt in his twin capacities as guardian of law and order and public health was "the social evil," prostitution. It had been this blight more than any of New York's myriad vices that had propelled the Rev. Charles Parkhurst into his pulpit in 1892. He had said, "Social vice has been so protected and encouraged by the filthy officials who control the (police) department that the number of abandoned women and disorderly houses now existing in the city is no measure of what it would be if we had a police force, from top down, who conceived of sexual crime as an evil to be suppressed, not as capital to draw dividend from."

Roosevelt viewed dealing with prostitution as "one of the saddest features of police work." His approach was a tough one and it extended to the men engaged in the sordid business as well as to the women. He felt they should be treated "on an exact equality for the same act." He favored a proposal by Rev. Charles Stelzle of the Labor Temple that called for publication of the names of the owners of property used for immoral purposes, after the individual had been warned to desist and given time to do so. He backed vigorous prosecution of the keepers and the backers of brothels, men and women, punishing them "as severely as pickpockets and common thieves." Fines would not suffice. They must go to jail.

"As for the girls, the very young ones and first offenders should be put in charge of probation officers or sent to reformatories," he wrote. "We would thus remove from this hideous commerce the articles of commerce."

He found a cause for girls and young women going into prostitution in "wages inadequate to keep them from starvation, or to permit them to live decently," so that a certain proportion of them were forced by their economic misery into lives of vice.

"The employers and all others responsible for these conditions stand on a moral level not far above the white slavers themselves," he wrote.

Toleration of the vice as Clubber Williams had suggested, because houses of prostitution were "fashionable," TR viewed as unacceptable. "There should be no toleration of any 'tenderloin' or 'red light' district," he insisted, "and, above all, there should be the most relentless war on commercialized vice. The men who profit and make their living by the depravity and awful misery of other human beings stand far below any ordinary criminals, and no measures taken against them can be too severe."

In going after the flesh trade he greatly expanded the scope of the central office detective bureau, authorizing the use of plainclothesmen in finding and arresting prostitution operations. The detectives were permitted to pose as clients and to offer marked money in order to obtain evidence.

When the use of "spies" drew protests from some quarters he replied, "The present methods are not only entirely proper, but they are the only methods by which it is possible to enforce obedience to the law, and the only methods which honest officials can employ if they honestly desire to see the law executed. A failure on the part of the police to resort to them would inevitably result in plunging the city into a state of open depravity and vice."

In carrying out this strict policy one of the undercover men arrested a woman who gave her name as Mrs. Ardenne Foster, a resident of England. The officer charged her with soliciting. The woman and her husband heatedly denied the accusation. Furthermore, they charged, in making the unfounded arrest the detective had "roughed up" the woman. These objections notwithstanding, the couple was put in jail overnight. When news of this event reached the editorial offices of London's *Daily Mail* the newspaper protested the "outrageous behavior" of the New York police toward a visiting British couple.

Deciding to investigate, TR soon learned that Mrs. Foster was well-known to the police as a prostitute and her husband as her pimp. The arresting officer informed his commissioner that, in fact, Mrs. Foster had propositioned him. Forwarding these results of his investigation to London, TR suggested that fairness required an apology by the *Daily Mail* to the police of New York. The request proved unavailing.

In waging war on the social evil, however, Roosevelt left no room for sentimentality "which grows maudlin on behalf of the willful prostitute." He rebuked those who confounded the woman who went into prostitution willingly with those whom circumstances forced into the trade. He told them, "There are evil women just as there are evil men, naturally depraved girls just as there are naturally depraved young men, and the generous thing to innocent girls and decent men, is to wage stern war against the evil creatures of both sexes."

Ranked below prostitution on the Roosevelt list of targets, though not far down, was gambling, whether it took the form of games in illegal dens, horse-betting parlors, or the most widespread of all, the numbers-based lottery known as policy. Because this was readily available to the entire population and because it victimized those least able to afford losing money, the racket was especially targeted.

Raids on gambling houses and rooms and private clubs saw a quantum leap in numbers. Typical was the manner in which the men of Captain Adam Cross's Leonard Street squad on October 19, 1895, hit the Tuxedo Cafe at 392 Canal Street. Owned and operated by Moritz Tzschentke, the establishment served as poolroom, saloon, and gambling "resort" for Cuban cigar makers. Its purpose was hardly a secret. Tzschentzke distributed coupon tickets for a lottery. Each bore a number that might prove to be a winner of one of two weekly prizes. A customer put part of the coupon in a box and retained a stub, each bearing a number. When one reached Captain Cross he read:

3,001
Compliments of the Tuxedo Cafe
Drop the coupon in the box

3,001

This ticket is given away gratis, Holders of these tickets will please deposit the coupon in the box.

Please keep your tickets until the lucky numbers are drawn on Saturday of each week.

PRESENTED BY THE TUXEDO CAFE
392 Canal Street

On the reverse of the ticket was an advertisement for the Danbury Hat Company, 22 Debrosses Street, evidence that Moritz had found a way to deflect some of the costs of his lottery.

Swooping down on the Tuxedo Cafe, the men of the Leonard Street Station arrested him, his bartender, and thirteen of the Cuban patrons. They confiscated hundreds of intact coupons, a bag containing two thousand portions that had been dropped into the tin box from which winning entries were drawn, and the prizes that would be presented to two lucky holders of that week's winning draws, a cheap ersatz-gold watch and a meershchaum pipe.

Tzschentke was charged with keeping a gambling house. The others were booked as disorderly persons.

The effect of this vigorous antigambling campaign was reflected in police department annual tabulations of arrests. The total doubled between 1894 (776) and 1895 (1,443). Arrests for keeping gambling houses rose from 483 in 1894 to 1,059 in 1895. In the year before Roosevelt the cops had confiscated not one poker chip. In 1895 they collected 5,654.

Zero policy slips confiscated in 1894 rose to fifty-three the next year, not counting the list of hymn numbers grabbed from the hand of the hapless Sunday-school superintendent whose case had both amused and embarrassed the police board as the outraged churchman brought charges against the arresting officer.

Observing Roosevelt as he alternated between his two hats, Jacob Riis grew more and more admiring of him and increasingly consulted him concerning matters of which TR unabashedly admitted a lack of sufficient information or background. Such was the case in a crisis between police and working men who reverted to the tactic of calling strikes against employers. The recent record was replete with violent clashes between men on picket lines and the police force.

One of these sensitive situations came to a head when Roosevelt decided to meet with a group of strikers. He asked Riis to go with him to the union gathering. Trudging through a blinding snowstorm they arrived at Clarendon Hall. The savvy newspaperman immediately sized-up the situation as one in which the strikers expected to find in Roosevelt a typical politician "playing for points." They hinted there would be trouble if Roosevelt failed to meet their demands.

Riis described Roosevelt's reaction.

"'Gentlemen!' he said, with the snap of jaws that always made people listen, 'I asked to meet you, hoping that we might come to understand one another. Remember, please, before we go farther, that the worst injury any one of you can do for the cause of labor is to counsel violence. It will also be worse for himself. Understand distinctly that order will be kept. The police will keep it. Now we can proceed.'"

The union men burst into applause. TR reddened with pleasure, for, as Riis wrote, "he saw that the best in them had come out on top, as he expected it would."

Roosevelt's views on labor had undergone a transformation; he had parted company with most of his fellow Republicans by becoming a strong believer in the rights of labor. He wrote in his autobiography, "For that very reason I was all the more bound to see that lawlessness and disorder were put down, and that no rioter was permitted to masquerade under the guise of being a friend of labor or a sympathizer with labor. I was scrupulous to see that the labor men had fair play; that, for instance, they were allowed to picket just so far as under the law picketing could be permitted, so that the strikers had ample opportunity peacefully to persuade other labor men not to take their places. But I made it clearly and definitely understood that under no circumstances would I permit violence or fail to insist upon the keeping of order."

One of the labor leaders, Henry Weismann, secretary of the Journeyman Bakers' and Confectioners' International Union, would say to him as he left the police department in 1897, "I am particularly grateful for your liberal attitude toward organized labor, your cordial championship of those speaking on behalf of the toilers, and your evident desire to do the right thing as you saw it whatever the cost."

Perhaps Weismann knew of Roosevelt's experience with workers in the manufacture of baked goods who did not have the protection of a labor union. Employed at sweatshop wages in kitchens set up in some of the tenements TR had inspected with Riis, they made crullers. The process involved boiling the dough in huge vats of fat standing over open flames in the early-morning hours when the warren-like tenement rooms were crowded with people sleeping. Each year many of them perished, trapped by the conflagrations started by sparks from the stoves. Countless others had suffered burns from spilled or spattering cooking fat.

Nor were labor unions available to champion rights of those trapped in all the other kinds of tenement factories. For them the only hope lay in the possibility that one day the conditions in which they had to live and work would be eradicated, as Jacob Riis's hated Mulberry Bend was being demolished. Yet Riis could point to a scrapbook from the year 1883 to 1896 that was one running comment on the Bend and on the official indolence that delayed demolition nearly a decade after it had been decreed.

In venturing into the slums with Riis to see for himself how the other half lived Roosevelt was presented with the forceful reality of tenement living, especially in summertime. One of the heat waves impressed upon him in both his roles as president of the police board and member of the health board that at times there could be nothing that he could do in either capacity to solve a problem.

"We did everything possible to alleviate the suffering," he recalled in his autobiography. Especially heartbreaking was the "gasping misery of the little children and worn-out mothers."

Every recourse of the health department, the police, and the fire department, which flooded the scorching streets, was taxed in the effort to render service, TR remembered.

The heat was especially disastrous for horses. Scores of complaints came into Mulberry Street from citizens about the dead horses in front of their homes, some of them festering for two or three days. One complainer sent furious demands for action to remove a carcass from in front of his shop. Presently, a large wagon was sent, albeit already loaded with the corpses of eleven other horses. When it lumbered to a stop to collect the one about which the shop owner had been so vociferous, the overloaded dray collapsed under the weight. Suddenly, the shop owner had a dozen dead horses at his doorstep. In desperation he sent TR "a final pathetic letter" requesting Roosevelt's police force "to remove either the horses or his shop, he didn't care which."

Chapter 11

Very Rough Work

On February 25, 1896, Chief of Police Peter Conlin presented an historic recommendation. He proposed abolition of the Broadway Squad. Organized in the spring of 1857, it was almost as old as the police force itself. Located on East Twenty-ninth Street and carried on the police roster as the Seventeenth Precinct, it ran from Bowling Green at the southern tip of Manhattan to Thirty-fourth Street. Members of the squad had been especially selected to cope with fearsome and dangerous traffic on the city's main thoroughfare.

In the words of an article published in *Harper's Magazine* in March 1887, the forty-four officers and men, all over six feet in height, were "far more commanding in presence" and just "as famous in the police-world as the gigantic grenadiers of Frederick the Great in the military." Their sole function was regulating "the endless procession of vehicles passing up and down that magnificent thoroughfare." They had gained a deserved reputation for courtesy, gallantry, and daring in shepherding New Yorkers safely from one side of the perilous, traffic-clogged Broadway to another.

Nine years after the *Harper's* article the attractions and the traffic of Broadway had spread farther uptown, persuading Chief Peter Conlin to propose extending the street-corner postings to Forty-second Street. But in outlining the proposal he stressed that he was not doing away with the work of the squad but simplifying the administrative structure in which the Broadway cops functioned. Rather than having the officers assigned to one long, ever-extending precinct, he wanted the Broadway beat men transferred to precincts in which their respective posts were situated. He told the police board, "The expense of maintaining one station house would be saved; jurisdiction would in each and every case be well defined, which it is not now; in any case of emergency, accident, riot and so forth, assistance could be more promptly had and police work more effectively performed."

Fresh in the memory of the commissioners in February of 1896 was exactly the kind of emergency to which Conlin alluded. It had happened on an evening three months earlier. Monday, November 25, had witnessed the opening of a theatrical extravaganza that in itself exemplied the northward expansion of the city's colorful and exciting nightlife, previously defined by the terms "Bowery," "the Rialto," and "Tenderloin," but increasingly being replaced in the lexicon of New Yorkers by "Broadway."

The south-to-north, downtown-to-uptown street had gotten its name quite naturally. It had been laid out as a broad way, though over the years its width had narrowed considerably, becoming the wagon, cart, and carriage-clogged artery that required a special squad of tall, brave men to police it and escort frightened pedestrians across it. As the city spread northward the thoroughfare segmented itself into districts designated by the type of commerce pursued there.

Below city hall grew the financial center, commonly known as Wall Street, bounded on the north by Tom Byrnes's *cordon sanitaire*, until, as we have seen, an outraged magistrate ruled the "dead line" unconstitutional. North of the seat of city government and the Tweed Courthouse on Chambers Street had settled the garment district, dominated in the early 1890s by the mammoth firm of drapers, A. T. Stewart & Co. Farther up stood warehouses of numerous furriers and clothiers, then blocks of booksellers.

Bending from a directly northern line at Tenth Street, site of Grace Church, the street ran four blocks to Union Square, long dominated by the Academy of Music and Steinway Hall and noted as the addresses of Luchow's and Tammany Hall. At Twenty-third and Broadway stood Madison Square Park, surrounded by Delmonico's, the Hoffman House, and Brunswick Hotels (suspected as having been used by the second-story men who burgled the Burden family), the Tiffany jewelry emporium, and the staid Madison Avenue Church of the crusading Rev. Dr. Charles Parkhurst.

Between Madison Avenue and Thirty-fourth Street flowed the Rialto/Tenderloin with its restaurants, gambling parlors, bawdy houses, and theaters. Illuminated by Thomas A. Edison's electric lights it was soon called the Great White Way. Here stood the world-famous Casino, the Bijou, Koster and Vial's vaudeville house, the Standard, and the Garrick. In these entertainment palaces New Yorkers took in shows written by Victor Herbert, produced by Florenz Ziegfeld, and starring Eddie Foy, Weber and Fields, Anna Held, Lillian Russell, the Floradora girls, Ethel Barrymore, Otis Skinner, Fanny Davenport, and Fay Templeton.

"All the world came to Broadway to flirt, to dine, to gamble, to find amusement, to meet acquaintances," wrote the editor of *Valentine's Magazine,* Henry Collins Brown. He added that if one stood in the Broadway portico of the Fifth Avenue Hotel any person "would one day meet any long-sought acquaintance whensoever he might come."

In 1893 the reach of Broadway-based theater had made a small leap of both geography and faith. The American Theater opened for business just off a patch of former farmland known as Long Acre, at the crossings of Broadway, Seventh Avenue, and Forty-second Street. Opened on May 22, 1893, at 260 West Forty-second Street, the American Theater offered "The Prodigal Daughter," an occasion that has been enshrined in American stage history as the birth of "the Broadway theater." Long Acre had become known by then as Longacre. It would be renamed Times Square in 1904, after the firm that had built its offices in the triangle of land formed by Broadway, Forty-second Street, and Seventh Avenue, the *New York Times.* Later generations would also claim that if someone stood long enough in Times Square, that person would encounter everyone he or she ever knew. (*Author's note:* When I was about eight years old and enchanted by the lights and crowds at that very corner during a 1942 visit to an uncle who lived in Brooklyn, my father repeated this claim to me, and, lo and behold, a few minutes later another family on a visit to New York from my hometown in Pennsylvania sauntered past us, proving my father and the maxim true.)

But it was under the auspices of the noted impressario Oscar Hammerstein that Broadway witnessed a far more grandiose debut than that of the American Theater. An orthodox German Jew born in 1848, Hammerstein made his money from a cigar-making machine he invented, permitting the rolling and cutting of twelve cigars at once—far beyond the capacity of a slum child in a tenement cigar factory. In love with show business of all kinds, he once won a bet of one hundred dollars that he could write a complete opera in twenty-four hours. But when he produced it at great expense it was a flop. In 1888 he had built the Harlem Opera House. Purchasing a plot of real estate that had been the location of the Seventy-first Regiment Armory until fire destroyed it, Hammerstein set out to build on the west side of Broadway between Forty-fourth and Forty-fifth Streets an entertainment center such as had never been seen. Under one roof would be a great music hall, a concert hall of noble design and ample proportions, a theater called the Lyric and built on unique lines that he intended to house comic opera and burlesque and other light diversions and a rooftop that would offer a garden, an Oriental cafe, smoking rooms, billiard room, cloak rooms, and lounges. The music hall alone would boast 128 boxes and seat more than 2,800 people. Best of all, admission to these theaters was a single ticket priced at fifty cents. It was what motion picture exhibitors claimed to have invented in the next century, a "multiplex theater."

Hammerstein called his establishment "Olympia." And with a blizzard of publicity, including newspaper advertisements, he announced the opening date: November 25, 1895. Fay Templeton was to star in the Olympia's Lyric Theater production of a burlesque called "Excelsior, Jr." by R. A. Barnett, with music by Messrs. Tracy, Sloane, and Rice, fresh from a triumph in New Haven. In the American theater of the 1890s, no star shone as brilliantly as Miss Templeton. Her name alone would have drawn a large turnout and provided a decent evening's profit. However, the overzealous and probably nervous impresario, who had sunk a fortune into its building, oversold the house.

The total capacity of all the theaters and halls was six thousand. Hammerstein's box office and publicity mill distributed ten thousand tickets including complimentaries to the cream of society that numbered Roosevelt's friend and mentor Elihu Root, Senator-elect Jacob A. Cantor, District Attorney Nicoll, and the brewer Colonel Jacob Ruppert, Jr. Dressed in evening clothes and accompanied by wives with puffy sleeves (the latest in ladies' high fashion), they arrived by handsom cabs and private carriages to find a mob. Gathered in rain, mud, and slush and in the garb of ordinary people, they had come by cable cars or on foot until, by eight o'clock, their numbers filled Broadway and the side streets in a portent of the next century's Times Square New Year's Eve throngs.

Dismayed and impatient, they forced open the doors in what a reporter from the *Times* recorded as "mediaeval warfare," then "a modern gridiron, with nobody to retire the injured from the field and nobody to count the yards of gain or loss."

Puffed sleeves wilted and crimped hair became hoydenish in the crush and rain. Elegant dresses ripped. Toes were stepped on and crushed. Patent leather shoes and trousers were splashed with muck. For those lucky enough to get inside there were other hazards. Not all the paint had dried. Presently, Elihu Root was seen with green and yellow stripes lacing the back of his coat. Others sported slashes of red and white. District Attorney Nicoll picked up a rainbow of hues garnered from brushing against walls and railings, or finding himself shoved into them.

"Gracious, Harry, I'm glad I didn't wear anything good," gasped one woman as she found herself shot "like a cannon ball" through one of the doors and into the jam-packed lobby.

"Move on," cried a harried ticket-taker. "Move somewhere, ladies and gentlemen." But there was nowhere to move to. The inside was already jammed, in the colorful phrasing of the *Times* observer of the melee, in a "denser mass than was ever the crowd at an international wedding."

Mr. Hammerstein blurted, "Close the doors. Call the police."

Not since the Astor Place riot had the police force been summoned to quell such a disturbance at a theater. A score dashed afoot from the nearby station house. "Oh, Lord," grumbled one of them, a strapping six-footer, "I've played football and you can get a fair show for a rush in that game. You can't get it here."

Struggling against the crowd, the police managed to close the doors, only to have them battered open again. At ten o'clock the crush was as great as ever. But the mob's spirits soon sagged and they drifted away. No one had been killed. But that had been pure luck. Yet even good fortune petered out. The day after the riotous opening night a hot water pipe broke in the basement, its gusher sending two workers to their deaths under a drivewheel and scalding others. Turning out to be too big to fill and too costly to run, the Olympia adventure pushed Hammerstein into bankruptcy in 1898. However, motivated by the maxim that the show must go on, he bounced back a year later with the more modest Victoria at Broadway and Forty-second. Managed by his son Willie, it became the vaudeville center of the city and the world, furthering the reputation of Broadway as the place to go for a night out.

Faced with this reality of a new and burgeoning stretch of

Broadway and the impracticality of trying to police the traffic of its larger and larger crowds with a special squad that could only grow more cumbersome and unmanageable, Chief Conlin came to the police board in February 1896 with his radical proposal to disband the Broadway Squad. He told them, "The immense and constantly growing traffic in this street makes its proper policing one of the most important duties of the entire department, and any change in the conditions of service that tends to its greater efficiency, merits the prompt consideration of your board."

Conlin chose the right word. Nothing appealed to Roosevelt more than efficiency. He gave Conlin wholehearted backing and New Yorkers learned on March 8 that the Broadway Squad would pass into history at eight o'clock next Thursday morning, March 12.

The board also voted to eliminate another venerable part of the department, the steamboat squad. It had been established in 1876, primarily to battle organized criminal gangs known as river pirates. Again the reasoning was that efficiency dictated that it made no sense to maintain a separate facility when the tasks and the men could be reassigned, thus saving the costs of operating one station house.

A second motivation in shifting the men from specialized squads and merging them with the general police population was a shortage of manpower. In addition to numbers of corrupt cops who had been retired, fired, or prosecuted and sent to jail the force had had to be stretched to cover the new precinct of Westchester. By Chief Conlin's count the force was under strength by eight hundred. On May 1, 1876, the roster had totalled 2,261 in a city with a population of 1,075,532, or one patrolman to every 475 residents. On February 1, 1896, there was one patrolmen for every 540, for a total force of 3,584. In London the ratio was 1/330, in Paris it was 1/306, and in Berlin 1/447.

Conlin's manpower report on March 14, 1896, also provided a thumbnail sketch of how the city had expanded, especially in Manhattan. He stated that the area north of Fifty-ninth Street, west of Central Park, and extending to 110th Street "has grown wonderfully in the past ten years, and the police force is not adequate in this district to cover the territory as it should be covered."

Harlem was even more of a problem, the area around 125th Street having become "one of the most busy and important streets of the city." This was especially true at night. Conlin said, "This street is thronged by as large crowds as are any of the streets downtown." Harlem alone could use three hundred more men, he told the commissioners.

North of the Harlem River in the villages of the Bronx, he continued, another crisis existed in force undermanning. Yet this section was one of the fastest growing in the city.

Overall, the city's population was increasing by fifty thousand per year. Added to the residents were thousands more who visited the city on business or looking for the thrills on the sidewalks of New York, especially Broadway. In Conlin's view, as well as Roosevelt's, these out-of-towners were particularly susceptible to criminals of the kind depicted in the 1891 hit song "The Bowery" by Percy Gaunt (music) and Charles Hoyt (lyrics) in their show *A Trip to Chinatown*. It recounted the tribulations of a country hick who found himself swindled, mugged, and cheated at every turn. Lamenting, "I had one of the Devil's own nights," he vowed. "I'll never go there anymore."

Seeking to bolster the ranks of the police department to protect residents and keep out-of-towners from being fleeced, TR traveled to Albany on March 19 in company with Commissioner Avery Andrews to lobby both houses of the state legislature. Appearing before the panel he had chaired in 1884, he asked the Committee on Cities to endorse a police manpower bill introduced the day before. Drawing on Conlin's ratios of cops and citizens, he asked for the eight hundred new officers cited in Conlin's report. But this was no ordinary supplicant coming hat-in-hand to the State Capitol, as evidenced by a standing-room-only audience of legislators in the Assembly chamber. Most were rural politicians who had never seen Theodore Roosevelt in person and were not about to pass up an opportunity to do so.

Appearing before the Senate's Cities Committee he was asked his position on a police measure, known as the Pavey Reorganization Bill. Although it was opposed by Commissioner Andrew Parker and contained some objectional provisions, he answered that he was for it because extraordinary conditions cited by the Lexow Committee still existed in the police department, some of which the bill addressed. However, he added, the situation in the police department had been "greatly improved." He added that he would back a new bill, to be presented "in a few days," designed to change aspects of the methods of making promotions in some grades of the force. It was a rather casual mention of a bill that would lead to a great deal of trouble in Mulberry Street.

In seeking additional men for the department Roosevelt was not attempting to build a bigger empire for himself to rule. He saw in the rapid expansion of the city a genuine challenge to the police in maintaining law and order and in protecting the lawful. And he saw in an insufficiently strong force a real danger to the men who carried a police badge. He recognized the difficulties of their job. "It is," he said, "very rough work."

He also appreciated the need for two approaches to fighting crime. In his essay on administering the New York Police written for the *Atlantic Monthly* in 1897 he explained, "The man with the nightstick, the man in the blue coat with the helmet, can keep order and repress open violence on the streets; but most kinds of crime and vice are ordinarily carried on furtively and stealthily—perhaps at night, perhaps behind closed doors. It is possible to reach them only by the employment of the man in plain clothes, the detective. Now the function of the detective is primarily that of the spy, and it is always easy to arouse feeling against a spy. It is absolutely necessary to employ him."

Accordingly, he enthusiastically backed the introduction of a new detective system that went into effect on January 2, 1896. Assigning four detectives in each precinct, it placed the men under the local commander but made them responsible, as well, to the chief of detectives at police headquarters. These men were not only permitted to carry out their duties and investigations in ordinary clothes, they were expected to do so.

When bills were immediately introduced in Albany to prohibit the use of "spies," Roosevelt shot off a letter to New York City corporation counsel, John Proctor Clark, assailing the measures. He argued, "The passage of bills of this character would greatly lessen the labor of the police, for it would relieve them of all responsibility for the numerous kinds of crime conducted in secret behind closed doors, and which can never be successfully interfered with by policemen in uniform."

He cited the case of the "Molly Maguires," a Pennsylvania group that had terrorized through murder, arson, and violence of every kind. They had been broken up as the result of being penetrated by a police undercover informer.

"Moreover, there are certain kinds of crime which can be

reached only by the use of detective methods—gamblers, keepers of disorderly houses and law-breaking liquor dealers can hardly ever be touched otherwise. It would be almost useless to try to enforce the law against any of them if we continued to employ uniformed police," he continued.

He suggested it would be far better to repeal laws against gambling, prostitution, and illicit liquor sales than to nominally keep them on the statute books "and yet to pass other laws forbidding us to take the only possible methods of obtaining evidence against the law breakers."

As to allegations that the police had a policy of using children as spies, he heatedly denied the charge. "So far as the outcry can be said to have any basis at all, it presumably refers to a single case of the use of the evidence of a minor to whom liquor had been sold in trying to procure the punishment of the man who had illegally sold liquor to very many other children," he said, a case in which two policemen had employed a child to collect evidence without approval of the police board. However, he did not mention the instance Jacob Riis had brought to his attention in which TR had sent a child into a saloon to obtain liquor so as to prosecute the seller. He went on to vow that the board would not "allow any liquor dealer who practices this particularly revolting form of debauching children to feel that in the last resort (the Board) would refrain from using against him the evidence of one of his victims in order to save that victim and the hundreds of other children upon whose lives he preys."

Although he was not directly in charge of the day to day operations of the force—that job was shared by Commissioners Andrews and Parker—TR did bear responsibilities as the formal spokesman for the police department. In that capacity he took considerable interest in the functions of both the uniformed and plainclothes officers. This included backing Andrews when he proposed introducing a means of identifying criminals, developed in France, the Bertillion System. It consisted of a complicated procedure of measuring physical traits of criminals—hands, ears, noses, height, weight, eye and hair color, etc.—and keeping them on file, along with their photographs. The system was developed by the French police, the Sureté, and had recently been adopted by Scotland Yard. Andrews proposed its use by the New York Police Department in January 1896. (Fingerprinting would not come into use for another decade.)

Among the cases of the detective bureau that Roosevelt could not have failed to pay attention to was the Burden jewel robbery. Since the daring theft in late December, newspapers had continued to give it a high profile, affording great display to the offer by Isaac Burden of a reward of ten thousand dollars. This was announced in the papers on February 28, two months-to-the-day after the theft. In the meantime, the newspapers pointed out, none of the purloined gems had turned up and the police appeared no nearer an arrest than on December 28.

Soon after the notice of the reward was announced, a letter arrived advising Burden to look for a newspaper item that would list a telephone number at which Burden would get information on the robbery. The ad appeared, giving a telephone number at the Holland House Hotel. He was instructed to expect a call at three o'clock sharp on the afternoon of Saturday, January 4, 1896.

The phone rang at the exact moment but Mr. Burden was too frightened to speak to the caller. He dropped the receiver. Fortunately, Detective Sergeant William Evanhoe had the call traced and the caller arrested. The episode was a hoax concocted by an enterprisingly greedy clerk, Henry Figer, employed in the office of Lewisohn Brothers of Fulton Street.

A more promising development caught the attention of TR and the entire city in the form of a confession blurted out in the Tombs by Joseph Sylvester, a known crook being held on a charge of burglarizing a boarding house. Sylvester said he knew the three men who pulled the Burden heist. However, the head of the detective bureau, Acting Captain Stephen O'Brien, was dubious. He told reporters that if a man of Sylvester's ilk knew anything he would have made a play for the reward money and not wasted his time breaking into a cheap rooming house.

The break in the Burden case came not in New York City but London, thanks to the detective work of one of the most dogged sleuths at Scotland Yard, Inspector Frank Froest. In mid-April he spied a pair of men in Bond Street, one of London's most exclusive commercial avenues. Froest thought the dress and manner of the pair looked very suspicious. Enlisting the aid of another detective, he stopped them for questioning.

A search of their pockets produced a trove of diamonds. The men gave the names Dunlop and Turner and said they were from New York. Froest heard an English accent in Dunlop, deepening his suspicions. The pair also claimed they had come by the jewels legit-imately. However, when Froest searched their rooms he turned up even more gems—the bulk of the Burden loot.

Froest's breaking of the case was not his last triumph for the Yard. In 1907 he became the first head of Scotland Yard's "Murder Squad" and went on to play a crucial role in the 1910 case of Dr. Hawley Harvey Crippen, who butchered his wife and ran off with a young woman, then found himself the object of a trans-Atlantic chase that ended with his arrest aboard a boat bound for Canada in one of the most written-about homicide cases in the literature of crime.

Further investigation in the Burden case showed that the two men picked up by Froest were William Roberts Dunlop, a native of England and formerly a butler in the Burden mansion, and William Turner, who had been a Burden family footman. The names had been well known in police headquarters and in the press shack across the street. At the time of the robbery both had been suspected by O'Brien's detectives, but nothing could be proved. At the same time the two had enjoyed themselves by granting interviews to the reporters who had covered the robbery. Lacking evidence, O'Brien had been unable to stop them from leaving the country in March.

Next came a revelation that left O'Brien and his men red-faced. A third member of the inside gang of thieves was arrested, Edna Steimquist, a maid. She had been amourously involved with Dunlop. Abandoned and brokenhearted when he sailed for England without her, she had turned to drink and was so often drunk on the job that she was fired. Then she turned talkative, informing another Burden employee that it had been Dunlop who had arranged the theft.

As to her role in the scheme, Edna confessed to the police that she had hidden the loot in a ham in a pantry. That was the embar-rassing part for the detective bureau. On the night of the robbery a detective had confiscated the ham along with other possible pieces of evidence. Greeted with laughter and ridiculed by the servants, who suggested the cops were being silly, he returned the ham to the pantry. Later, Edna removed the cache of gems and passed them to Dunlop.

The position of Stephen O'Brien illustrated the peculiar position in which Roosevelt and his fellow Commissioners found themselves when they wished to promote able men. Their own new rules re-quired that promotions be made from the immediately inferior rank, and based on an acceptable score on an examination. A member of the force since 1875, O'Brien had risen to detective sergeant in 1885. But for technical reasons the validity of that rank was questionable. Therefore, to remove any doubt as to his qualifications to become Captain O'Brien, the board took the unusual step of reducing him to patrolman, then promoted him up the ranks to sergeant again and then to captain. He had no trouble with the qualifying examination, scoring 83.5 out of a possible 100 points.

O'Brien was exactly the kind of policeman Roosevelt wanted on his force: good record, faithfulness, industry, vigilance, and unimpeachable character. He welcomed endorsements of these traits from supporters of candidates for promotion, so long as they did not smack of attempts to use "pull."

Novelist Owen Wister saw for himself how far someone got if TR sniffed the slightest whiff of impropriety. The author would become famous for *The Virginian* (published in 1902), but in 1896 he was known for two short stories in *Harper's Magazine* and as a friend of TR's, as well as an ardent advocate of the outdoors and of living a strenuous life. While visiting TR's office he observed as a surgeon named Marvin Palmer presented a letter recommending him as a departmental physician. The letter had been written by the surveyor of the port. A Republican, he held that a Republican ought to get the job in question, pointing out that Palmer was a Republican.

Roosevelt allowed that a Republican appointment might be timely, adding, "And I am quite sure, Dr. Palmer, that you are qualified for the position." The surgeon smiled in anticipation of appointment. "And here's the way you can get the position," TR continued. "Stand first on the Civil Service list!"

Palmer wheeled about and strode to the door, then stopped and looked back long enough to blare, "You can go to hell."

Another eyewitness to Theodore Roosevelt's application of standards in placing people on the force was twenty-four-year-old Cornelius W. Willemse. An immigrant from Holland, he had been employed as a bouncer in rough establishments on the Bowery and, most recently, a counterman at the Eagle Hotel. These jobs in places that served liquor had been cited as the reasons for his having been rejected as a police recruit. He decided to appeal to Roosevelt.

"I was taken into his office and faced a stockily-built man, vigorous and decisive in his appearance and quick in his movements," Willemse recalled. "I wasn't kept in doubt long."

Roosevelt told him, "I'm sorry, but you're not wanted in the police department."

"But Commissioner, I'm only a lunchman at the Eagle Hotel and never drink, myself," Willemse pleaded.

"That makes no difference. As long as you work in a place like that, you never will be allowed to become a policeman. Good day!" Willemse departed quickly.

"I knew there was no use in arguing with a man who had a jaw like his," he remembered in his book, *Behind the Green Lights*. A memoir of Willemse's distinguished career as policeman and the commander of the first detective division, the book carries the reader forward a few years from that disappointing meeting with TR in 1896 to a day when Theodore Roosevelt visited New York City as President of the United States. By then Willemse had become a member of the force and was detailed to a squad protecting Roosevelt while he stayed at the Waldorf Astoria Hotel.

TR shook Willemse's hand and asked, "Did I appoint you to the police?"

"I'm sorry, Mr. President, but I tried to get on when you were Commissioner, and you wouldn't have me," Willemse replied.

"Is that so? There must have been a reason. Why?"

"Because I worked at the Eagle Hotel on the Bowery."

"Reason enough," said TR. "I didn't want any man who was connected even in the faintest way with the liquor traffic to be on my police force. Still, I see you've made good. You are a detective now, eh? Well, I'm glad of it. I congratulate you."

Willemse had finally donned the uniform in 1899 and went on to become so effective and famous as a detective that he had no trouble in selling his autobiography to publisher Alfred A. Knopf in 1931.

Once on the force, a man who wanted rapid promotion could count on it if Roosevelt learned the individual had demonstrated bravery. More than five pages of Roosevelt's autobiography are devoted to stories of heroism by policemen. The acts fell into four categories: saving somebody from drowning, rescuing someone from a burning building, stopping a runaway horse or team of horses, and arresting a violent lawbreaker under exceptional circumstances.

One of the deeds recorded in TR's memoirs was also recounted by Jacob Riis in *Theodore Roosevelt, the Citizen*. It involved a gray-haired veteran of the Civil War. In his twenty-two years on the police force he had rescued twenty-eight people from drowning or being burned to death. In carrying out the latest of these rescues he ruined his uniform. But when he applied to the police board that preceded Roosevelt's, the commissioners had refused to allot him money to buy a new one. Told the story by Riis, TR saw to it that the hero received reimbursement, then pushed through a new policy under which the clothes of a policeman ruined at the risk of life on duty were a badge of honor, of which the board was proud to pay the cost. A few months after getting his money the fifty-five-year-old officer added a twenty-ninth rescue to his record by plunging into the East River in the middle of the night to pull out a man who had fallen from a dock.

On May 23, 1896, Roosevelt brimmed with pride over the men of the Oak Street Station who repeatedly entered a blazing building in New Chambers Street, saving one hundred fifty people. Four days later it was Policeman Thomas Donnelly who impressed TR by braving the ire of a mob of angry, stone-throwing onlookers to arrest a group of tough characters. Known as the "Kettle Gang," for months they had been looting a portion of East Seventy-fifth Street called Cooley's Hill.

Although an ardent advocate of good physical conditioning as a requirement for a member of the police force, the president of the police board marshalled all his energies in May of 1896 to oppose a proposal that the minimum height required of all new police officers be increased half an inch. At a meeting of the board on May 16 he argued that stocky men were more suitable physically than men of great height and reach and therefore must not be penalized for being short. That Theodore Roosevelt had a personal interest in the issue was not lost on the reporter for the *Times*. He wrote, "Mr. Roosevelt is himself not tall," then went on to say that Roosevelt was "perfectly proportioned, and would make the ideal police model as to height and weight. His gait is springy."

TR's objections failed to prevent the raising of the minimum height. The board voted in favor of the taller men. "I bowed to their combined judgment," he said to reporters. "That's all there is to it."

As of that date the minimum height was set at five feet eight inches and minimum weight 140 pounds. The previous standard was five feet seven-and-one-half inches and 133 pounds. The board also set a maximum age of thirty for applicants to the force. The maximum had been thirty-five. Periodic physical examinations were also to be required of all members of the force for the first time in departmental history.

Hand in hand with these stringent new physical requirements, and the previously unknown expectation that a police officer must be of sterling character, came an examination by the commissioners of the administrative structure of the department and the system of rules, regulations, and guidelines under which these fit and honest public servants were to carry out their duties. Learning that the department's policy manual had not been looked at and revised for several years, TR appointed a committee of ranking officers to review it and recommend improvements. His orders to the panel directed them "to consult with the various officers of the department, who are invited to suggest, in writing, changes and new rules and regulations as the welfare of the department may seem to require." Nothing like it had ever been done and decades would go by before the notion of management consultation with the rank and file would find a permanent place in American law enforcement.

In all of the reforming going on nothing struck Roosevelt as more vital than remaking the detective bureau and placing it more under the control of the central office, that is, police headquarters. Much of the mischief that had provoked the Rev. Parkhurst and brought the Lexow Committee into being had stemmed from a lack of centralization of the detectives. Accountable to their precinct commanders, who were corrupt, the detectives had been tainted, and discredited in public opinion.

Convinced that the success of reform depended on reshaping the detective bureau, while at the same time sustaining pride and spirit among the men in plain clothes, the president of the police board staunchly defended them at every opportunity. He denounced those who scorned the detectives as "spies." He hoped that the detectives would come to appreciate that they would be beneficiaries of the reforms.

To preach that gospel and to reassure the members of the detective bureau that he had their interests at heart, he had an order posted on Saturday, May 30, requiring all of them to be present at a roll call at police headquarters on Wednesday, June 3, at nine in the morning. In the meantime he would conduct a Sunday whirlwind personal inspection of precinct station houses to "see how things were going on generally."

Like so many recent events at 300 Mulberry Street the roll call of all detectives had no precedent, or, if it did, no one could remember the last time the president of the board of police commissioners had addressed the detective bureau en masse, and if one had, it surely would not have been at such an early hour.

The lesson preached was pure Rooseveltism. The future of each man was in his own hands. The men who did well were surer than ever before of receiving proper recognition. The only thing that would be considered by the board was service rendered to the department and the public. The incompetents and shirks would be rooted out. Pull was out. Merit was in.

"If you do your duty well," he concluded, "you have nothing to fear. The Commissioners will pay sole heed to what you do."

Recognizing that work performance depended on the tools that were at hand, he embraced advances in technology that held out the promise of a more efficient police force. Soon after the introduction of the Bertillion System of criminal identification, there could be found no more enthusiastic supporter of it than Theodore Roosevelt. He praised it for being simple and inexpensive and for providing "a full public and complete record of the criminal classes."

Just as vigorously, he reached out to improve an antiquated communication system that linked 300 Mulberry Street with the precincts. A telegraph system in place when he came into office dated to the 1850s. He ordered its modernization. The telephone had been introduced in 1890, but in only three of the thirty-five precincts. He found this appalling. He was also distraught over a lack of effective, rapid communication between a patrolman on his beat, his station house, and the central office. The board voted to upgrade the communication system to "provide for a modern and complete telephone and electrical signal communication between the station house and each part of the precinct." The board required it to be "simple in construction, capable of being readily understood and operated, yet strong and durable, and involving all modern improvements in the line of police signal systems."

To ensure prompt response to a call for help from a man on a beat and to convey arrested parties to jail, sixteen new horse-drawn patrol wagons were bought.

Anyone examining matters having to do with transportation in the middle of the decade of the 1890s had to come to terms with the phenomenon of the bicycle—or, more accurately, the bicycle craze. In 1896 there were between two million and four million of them in use in America. Hundreds of factories were turning them out as fast as possible, yet they had a hard time keeping up with demand. When a bicycle show was held at Madison Square in January of 1896 the *Times* headlined:

BICYCLE BOOM CONTINUES
Not Room Enough for the Big Madison Square Garden Show

EVERY INCH OF SPACE TAKEN
The Biggest Exhibition of Wheels
and Their Attachments Ever
Given—Some of the
Novelties

James C. Young of Madison Square Garden said, "If the Garden had been three times as large we could have rented every available space. Fully as many applicants for space have been rejected as have been accepted."

Anyone interested in buying a bicycle or simply looking at what was available—and who wasn't?—would find a bewildering array of models and prices. A Columbia cost nineteen dollars. A Liberty was priced at twenty-three dollars. A Mohawk was listed at twenty-nine dollars. At the bottom end of the scale a bicycle could be had for nine dollars. In addition to those with bikes and biking equipment to sell, scores of purveyors were on hand to hawk souvenirs of the event, ranging from catalogues of models and makes to spoons, knives, pipes, pocketbooks, scarf pins, necktie stickpins, watch charms, buttons, and badges.

The "wheel" had also reached Broadway. On November 19, 1895, at the Grand Opera House the audience was afforded a performance by Nellie McHenry in Louis Harrison's timely play "The Bicycle Girl," all about "the new woman," "the new man," hypnotism, and, of course, the bicycle. Noted the critic of the *Times,* "A bicycle woman with fin de siecle taste in bicycle costume would enjoy the various bloomer styles that are shown by the young women who say things to give Nellie a chance to sing and talk."

Wheeling clubs blossomed simply for the fun of bicycling and to organize races. Brooklyn had its Kings County Wheeldmen and the Brooklyn Bicycle Club. The latter promised that at one of its gatherings in January 1896 there would be a stirring rendition by the orchestra of "The Brooklyn Bicycle March."

While it seemed unlikely anyone would be able to whistle the song a century later, one number written in 1892 by transplanted Englishman songster Harry Dacre found immortality in songbooks with its jaunty tune and the words

> Daisy, Daisy, give me your answer do;
> I'm half crazy, all for the love of you;
> It won't be a stylish marriage;
> I can't afford a carriage;
> But you'll look sweet upon the seat,
> Of a bicycle built for two.

To assure that "wheelmen" and lady wheelers had smooth rides a national organization was formed to demand improved roads. The Good Roads Association declared, "We say to all riders of the wheel who are not members, join! To those who are members, get others to join."

The challenge for the police as the craze appeared to show no signs of waning was reckless wheeling. The problem had become so acute in New York City in the spring of 1896 that Acting Chief of Police Moses Cortright (Chief Conlin was visiting Europe) felt compelled to issue a warning to the wheelers.

"There are many thoroughfares in the city where the traffic on vehicles of all kinds, and especially bicycles, is so great that it is necessary for the protection of life and limb that such traffic should be properly regulated," he said.

A possible answer to this new challenge took the form of a letter to the Board from E. J. Tinsdell, chairman of the Cyclists' Federation. It stated that at a meeting of the group in November a resolution had been adopted asking the police commissioners to make special posts of Eighth Avenue from Fourteenth to Fifty-ninth Streets and on the Boulevard (the name applied to Broadway north of Fifty-ninth) to 108th Street, and to have these posts patrolled by policemen on bicycles.

Avery Andrews, himself a bicycle enthusiast, liked the idea. TR was also a wheelman, using a bicycle to get to and from the railway station in Oyster Bay; yet, inexplicably, the president of the board expressed skepticism. However, the uncertainty soon evaporated and he became as fervent an advocate of putting cops on wheels as Andrews. The board voted to experiment.

"For the present we shall try two men, to see how the plan will work, and what sort of duty they can perform," Andrews said on December 10, 1895. "If the policemen on bicycles are a success we shall organize a bicycle squad. The man on a bicycle certainly can go faster than a man on a horse."

Beside him as he disclosed the plan stood two policemen who had been selected because of their proven expertise as wheelmen. They were Dennis Gleason and Henry Negglesmith. At the end of the announcement they and Andrews left 300 Mulberry Street for the nearest bicycle dealer to pick out the bikes to be used in the test. As to their uniform, the board approved a plan proposed by Andrews. It consisted of a double-breasted box coat of regulation blue cloth that would come down a quarter of the way between the hip and the knee. It was to have two rows of seven buttons each, a rolling collar, and side pockets. (In summer the coat would be replaced by a standard blue police shirt.) Trousers would be the same as the standard patrolman's but worn tucked into army-style brown leggings. Instead of the patrolman's helmet, the wheelers would sport a blue cloth cap. The date set for the beginning of their historic assignment was December 12.

In the interim the board decided to authorize a squad of four men for the experiment, beginning with Gleason and Negglesmith at 6:00 P.M. When the big day arrived rumor spread like wildfire through the environs of the West Sixty-eighth Street Station that the entire precinct was to be on wheels, causing a large crowd of men and boys to gather to watch the wheel brigade set out on its way. Disappointment rippled through their ranks when only two wheelmen rolled into view, but it was momentary. Cheers rose as Gleason and Negglesmith peddled off toward the Boulevard. There they separated, Gleason heading uptown and Negglesmith turning south toward Fifty-ninth Street.

A reporter tagging along on with Gleason, presumably on a bicycle of his own, noted that the unique policeman attracted hardly any attention, "as his identity was not always discovered, and wheelmen were plentiful along that way." Negglesmith had the opposite experience as he left the Boulevard at Fifty-Ninth to swing down Eighth Avenue. Wheelmen were also plentiful on the busy thoroughfare, noted a newspaper reporter, but a bluecoat riding a bicycle was a curiosity. Both men were back at their station house at ten o'clock.

The next morning a different pair of police officers set out to patrol. Thus, Policemen John Gillis and John Lake found themselves going into history as the third and fourth men to police on bicycles, a status somewhat akin to the plight of the American astronauts seven decades later who followed Neil Armstrong in setting foot on the moon.

After nearly three months of trial Chief of Police Conlin told the commissioners "the service has been of great benefit to the public, that it has much increased the efficiency of police service on the thoroughfares patrolled by the bicycle squad, and has been instrumental in the accomplishment of police work that could not possibly be accomplished under the conditions of the police service existing along bicycle posts prior to the organization of the bicycle squad."

In their initial weeks of duty the wheel-mounted cops had good results in the regulation of travel on bicycles and vehicles of all descriptions. Runaway horses had been stopped. Racing on bicycles, with its attendant dangers to people on foot, had been largely prevented. A considerable number of arrests had been made for various traffic violations.

Conlin proposed making the bike squad permanent and extending it to three more precincts immediately, concentrating them in the uptown neighborhoods where streets were paved. To fund them Roosevelt authorized transfer of monies from other departments. They proved to be funds well-spent. In its first year of service, with its ranks expanded to twenty-nine, the Bicycle Squad accounted for 1,366 arrests. Eventually the squad expanded to a corps of one hundred wheelers with their own station house. And, proving once again that what is old is new again, a century after biking policemen were introduced to the streets of upper Manhattan, the New York Police Department announced with great fanfare that bicycle squads would be returning to service, chiefly in parks and residential areas, though mounted on bikes with the benefit of a century of improvement, and wearing rugged plastic helmets.

As usual, TR was impressed not only by the efficiency of the innovation but by the prowess and bravery of the men. He wrote of the Bicycle Squad in his autobiography: "They frequently stopped runaways, wheeling alongside of them, and grasping the horses while going at full speed; and, what was even more remarkable, they managed not only to overtake but to jump into the vehicle and capture, on two or three occasions, men who were guilty of reckless driving, and who fought violently in resisting arrest. They were picked men, being young and active, and any feat of daring which could be accomplished on the wheel they were certain to accomplish."

No such glowing tribute had passed Theodore Roosevelt's lips in December 1895 regarding the abilities of three members of the force in the handling of firearms. Rather, TR gritted his formidable teeth as he read a report that in attempting to kill a mad dog one of the trio of cops fired wildly, sending a bullet across the street and hitting a young girl in the leg. For a marksman such as TR this was too much to countenance. He ordered a study of the state of the force's pistol readiness.

Although carrying a Smith & Wesson pistol had been mandated in the New York Police Department since 1888, Roosevelt's survey found that comparatively few cops possessed one, a still smaller number were in good and serviceable condition, and numerous officers who did have guns carried cheap ones that were likely to be out of order and dangerous to the cop carrying them, as well as being a threat to others. But just as alarming was the fact that at no time in the history of cops carrying guns had anyone been required to undergo firearms training.

He told the police board, "The importance of having officers of this department, who must at all times when on duty have about their persons a loaded revolver, thoroughly instructed in the use and care of their arm, cannot be questioned. Numerous accidents on record in this department from careless handling of revolvers, and the not infrequent injury to innocent persons in the public streets, emphasizes the importance of this instruction, while, upon the other hand, when it becomes necessary for an officer to protect his own life, or to apprehend a dangerous criminal, he must be able not only to shoot promptly but to shoot well."

Responding to TR's appeal, the board passed a resolution "with a view of increasing the efficiency of the Police force, and of establishing systematic instruction" in the use of guns. The action set up the School of Pistol Practice, another first in the history of the N.Y.P.D.

A culling of the lists of officers for someone capable of conducting the training produced the name of Sergeant William Petty, who happened to be assigned to the central office and an expert pistoleer and target-shooter with several medals attesting to his skills. With someone outstanding selected to take charge of the training the next question was where to conduct the classes. Chosen for the historic event was the basement of the Eighth Regimental Armory at Ninety-fourth Street and Park Avenue. The order requiring attendance also expected each man to bring a .32 caliber, double-action Colt revolver with a four inch barrel. The department would supply the ammunition.

This ruling caused Tammany Hall to stir in outrage, charging that the police were being forced to pay ten dollars for a gun that sold on the public market for four. Roosevelt and Andrews shot back that, in fact, a Colt .32's regular price was fifteen dollars.

Telling reporters that he did not expect many, if any, of the men to be able to "hit a barn door," Petty said, "Why, don't you know that half the men on the force never used their pistols? Chances are that you could tackle ten policemen before you would find one with his gun loaded. But I'll wager that in a couple of weeks I can turn out a company of twenty that will shoot the cotton out of anything in New York."

"How about a target?" a reporter asked.

"Well, now, you want to go easy on that," Petty said. "You see, we will have to encourage the men in some way, so I'll start off with a target two-and-a-half feet square, shooting at a distance of ten yards. There will be an iron plate behind, placed at an angle of about thirty degrees, slanting, so that the bullets will fly upward. There they strike another plate and drop to the floor harmlessly."

The first group to undergo Petty's instruction was from the Old Slip Station. Thirty-nine nervous men under the command of Sergeant Jacob Braun, they reported to the armory on December 30. Petty allotted each fifteen rounds. Four military targets stood ten yards away from the firing line. But before anyone was permitted to shoot Petty first had to make sure the men knew how to handle a pistol. Most did not. Said one anxious gunman, "This is the first time I ever fired a revolver."

When the men finally opened up, the highest number of hits

was scored by Patrolman James J. Dennin, 62 out of a possible 75. Minimum for qualifying was 45. Two of the gunners scored zero.

Afternoon brought twenty-eight men from the Church Street Station of the Second Precinct. They did better, the highest score being 49 and the lowest 2. However, one man got off one shot that missed the target and took off the handle of a gas jet.

The pattern of groups taking to the firing range on weekday afternoons between one and five o'clock would continue until the entire force had been trained. In keeping with the Rooseveltian policy of encouraging performance through rewards, a grading system was established and medals given for the categories of Sharpshooter (minimum of 70 points) and Marksman (65). In its first year of operation Petty's School of Pistol Practice was attended by 5,841 officers, who fired 130,000 rounds. Presently, the average of scores improved by ten percent. The only pistol-training program for a police department in the United States at the time, the school was to become the foundation of the Police Academy, formed in 1909.

The pistol training paid off on May 8, 1896, for Patrolmen Patrick Ried and Daniel Ryan, operating in plainclothes out of the Morrisania precinct. They surprised William O'Connor and an accomplice hanging around a house at 156th Street and Prospect Avenue at 1:30 A.M., apparently casing it prior to breaking and entering. Attempting to question the men, Ried and Ryan found themselves in a footrace to catch them and were shot at. One bullet ripped through Ryan's hat. Another tore the shoulder of Ried's coat. As the suspects fled, both officers opened fire. Ryan missed. Ried's shot hit O'Connor in the neck, a mortal wound. Roosevelt thought highly enough of the actions of Ried and Ryan that he remembered the event in his autobiography.

Although Roosevelt admired heroism, there could be instances when it was not enough, as in the case of an officer who was shot while attempting to break up a fight between a pair of toughs in a restaurant. Despite the cop's exhibition of bravery, Roosevelt recorded that "this same officer was a man who, though capable of great gallantry, was also given to shirking his work, and we were finally obliged to dismiss him from the force."

On the broad, philosophical issues of crime and punishment he took a hard line. He favored the death penalty and noted that the trouble with "emotional men and women" who opposed it was that they saw only the individual whose fate was in the balance but "neither his victim nor the many millions of unknown individuals who would in the long run be harmed by what they ask." Yet he believed in the possibility of the rehabilitation of criminals. Punishment was an absolute necessity from the standpoint of society, but if a criminal who had been punished showed "a sincere desire to lead a decent and upright life, he should be given the chance, he should be helped and not hindered; and if he makes good, he should receive that respect from others which so often aids in creating self-respect—the most invaluable of all possessions."

That he believed in the value of women in the workplace he had demonstrated at the beginning of his commissionership by hiring Minnie Gertrude Kelly as his secretary, and again when he argued for a woman temporary clerk getting equal pay with a man for equal work. This appreciation of a role for women in the police department found expression in 1896 with the creation of thirty-two new positions of matron in police stations. At the same time the hours when a matron was to be on duty were extended around the clock, thus assuring that whenever a female were arrested she would be processed at the police station by a woman. However, another quarter-century would go by before the New York Police Department admitted women to its ranks of fully-sworn officers.

Roosevelt's police department was also to be open to others who previously had been discouraged from joining the "finest's" predominately white Protestant ranks, especially Jews. TR had not hesitated to encourage and assist Otto Rapheal in getting on the force. But perhaps the episode that was most illuminating of his attitude toward Jews involved a virulently anti-Semitic preacher from Berlin, Rector Ahlwardt. When he declared his intention of visiting New York City to speak, the city's Jewish population expressed outrage. They demanded TR ban Ahlwardt from any podium in the city.

This was impossible, TR told them. Besides, he added, if he were to keep him from talking it might turn him into a martyr. Instead, he combed the departmental roster until he found a Jewish sergeant and as many other Jewish cops as possible. He then detailed them to form a squad of bodyguards for the city's unpleasant visitor and thoroughly enjoyed the knowledge that the offensive fellow "made his harrangue against the Jews under the protection of some forty policemen, every one of them a Jew."

Four decades later in answer to a demand from Nazi Germany

for police protection for its New York consulate against Jews, Mayor Fiorello LaGuardia took a leaf from TR's book and saw to it that every member of the squad was a Jew. It seems inescapable that if TR could have been present he would have told the Little Flower he was "dee-lighted" at being copied.

Chapter 12

"Pistols or anything else."

Two years after Theodore Roosevelt graduated from Harvard, a brash seventeen-year-old son of a millionaire California miner and rancher arrived in Cambridge to begin his college education. Kicked out in 1885 as unscholarly, ungentlemanly and, therefore, unworthy of a Harvard sheepskin, William Randolph Hearst shunned taking over his father's ranching interests. Instead, he bought the *Examiner,* a foundering San Francisco newspaper. Having turned it around so that it produced a profit in 1890, he realized he had a real knack for newspapering and, bolstered by five million dollars from his mother, took over the New York *Journal.* Repeating his *Examiner* success, he became in the process exactly the sort of newspaper boss who was anathema to TR.

Hearst's evening paper returned the sentiment by borrowing from the city's favorite song. "'East Side, West Side, all around the town,' yesterday went King Roosevelt I, ruler of New York and patron saint of dry Sundays," sniped the self-appointed champion of beer-drinking working men, the *Evening Journal,* in the autumn of 1895. That more than a smattering of New Yorkers agreed with Hearst's sheet, rather than with Roosevelt's policy of enforcing Sunday closings, had been thumpingly demonstrated in the Tammany Hall victory in November.

This message was not lost on the boss of the Empire State's Republican Party, Thomas Collier Platt. The savvy, cunning, and realistic politician had designs on being a king-maker when the day arrived for the party of Lincoln and Grant to choose its candidate for the White House in 1896. Consequently, Platt viewed the drubbing dealt to his machine as a setback in that scheme. How could Platt be a king-maker at the nominating convention if he went into it perceived as the head of a split state party that could not deliver New York City? In his mind blame for the defeat deserved to be pinned on the hard-headed, high-minded individual who had brushed aside exhortations that for the sake of the Republican Party he ease up on the saloon crusade. According to Platt's approach to politics, such a blatant demonstration of party "disloyalty," not to mention a lack of personal fealty toward the Republican boss, deserved swift and sure comeuppance.

Born in 1833, Platt bore the scars of an adulthood devoted to political warfare. He had been elected to Congress in 1872 and the U.S. Senate in 1881, making him unquestioned top dog of the Grand Old Party in the Empire State. Tall, bearded, and elegantly clothed, he held court in a quiet recess of New York City's Fifth Avenue Hotel that became known as "the Amen Corner," because no one who met with him there ever told him "no." However, no matter how rough his wheeling and dealing became he never presented himself as less than courtly and a gentleman in every way, the opposite of his rough-edged nemesis, Boss Dick Croker of Tammany Hall. Platt shouldered the mantle and nickname of "Easy Boss."

Without his canny guidance, reformers hoisting the banner of William Strong could not have been swept into city hall in 1894. That Roosevelt refused to wink at the Sunday closing law and had cost the Republicans dearly in November 1895 smarted as surely as if TR had slapped the Easy Boss in the face. Therefore, as the new year came, Platt determined to take revenge on Roosevelt and all who chose to back him in reforming New York City, which had thereby thwarted Platt's own plans for the city.

They were breathtaking in scope. In the short term he set out to change the Sunday liquor law in expectation of winning back droves of imbibing drinkers whom Roosevelt's police force had sent flocking into voting booths to cast ballots for Tammany, as well as to cash in on graft associated with their operations. Long term, he planned to capitalize on the growing movement for amalgamating Manhattan, the Bronx, Brooklyn, Queens, and Staten Island into the single governmental entity of Greater New York. In the proposal, first presented in 1868, and given impetus in the explosive growth of the New York region in the 1890s, Platt saw an opportunity for a Republican windfall. In *The Rise of Theodore Roosevelt,* published in 1979, Edmund Morris succinctly described him as "gearing up his organization for the most massive gerry-mandering in American history."

The grand scheme for Greater New York City would spell the end to the existing police department and require the formation of a new and larger one that promised to provide Republicans a banquet of patronage and opportunity for graft that would make Tammany Hall's previous pickings seem like one of the paltry free lunches served at Cornelius Willemse's Eagle Hotel on the Bowery.

On the issue of Sunday drinking Platt threw his considerable backing to a measure introduced by Senator John Raines, a small-time politician from the town of Phelps. The bill was neatly devised to blunt traditional upstate prohibitionist sentiments by assuring that excise taxes collected from state-licensed saloons and other drinking establishments in besotted New York City would be shared with poor rural counties, towns, and villages, whether they were dry or wet. The system was to be administered by three or more state officials, thereby removing any opportunity for local corruption, transferring graft to Albany where Platt held sway. Existing Excise Commissioners would be legislated into oblivion as of April 30, 1896. Most important, the bill had a provision which would permit any establishment claiming to be a hotel to serve liquor on Sundays. This would prove an invitation to mischief eagerly accepted by wily liquor purveyors. The term employed to describe such operations by opponents of the Raines bill was "side door saloons."

When Senate and Assembly committees took up the measure on January 21, 1896, there was no doubt it would sail through to enactment in the Platt-controlled legislature. "The committeemen of the majority who revealed anything of their sentiments were evidently not impressed (by opponents of the bill)," noted the *Times*. "They had the air of men who had determined on a course of action and listened that they might give the appearance of having 'a decent respect for the opinions of mankind,' rather than any disposition to be convinced."

With the "side door saloon" portion of his double-barrelled master scheme on target, Platt prepared to fire the second round, aimed directly at Roosevelt. Unwilling to wait for passage of the law creating Greater New York that would of necessity abolish the police department, which TR commanded, and create a new, bigger force, Platt moved to legislate him out of office immediately. The vehicle was to be a supplement to the Greater New York bill that would shift the power to remove police commissioners from the Mayor of New York to the Governor.

Not without allies in Albany and within the ranks of supplicants of the Amen Corner, TR got wind of what was going on in the
capitol. With no way of confirming what amounted to rumors of the
plot against him, he did what he had done in Dakota when he had
been told that Jake Maunder was out to shoot him. He went looking
for the purported enemy. He asked his oldest political ally in the
Republican Party, Joe Murray, to find out if Platt might prove amenable to a meeting. Presently, Platt sent word that he would be available at the Fifth Avenue Hotel on January 19.

Thomas Collier Platt was not to be treated like the Dakota brag-
gart. Platt was twenty years older than TR, frail, and pained by
acute arthritis. A United States Senator, he was an esteemed figure.
He was also a gentleman. So was Roosevelt. Courtesy and amenities
were exchanged, followed by a bit of banter concerning national
affairs before TR felt comfortable in getting down to the point of the
conference. Here, he became as blunt and direct as he had been in
confronting Maunder. He asked Platt if it were true that a Platt
plan was afoot in the state capitol that would end in TR being
"kicked out."

Platt replied, "Yes." Roosevelt could expect to be removed from
Mulberry Street "in about sixty days."

The next day TR filled a long-standing speaking commitment
and found himself among friends. He addressed a morning meeting
of the Methodist Ministers Association at 150 Fifth Avenue, not far
from Amen Corner. He told the Methodists that he had heard of a
boast by "the most famous gambler in New York, long known as one
of the most prominent criminals in this city" (TR did not name him
but he referred to "The Allen") who had told reporters covering him
in the Tombs as he awaited trial for his arrest on gambling charges
that by February everything would again be running in the open.

"In other words," TR told the Methodists, "that the gambler, the
disorderly-house keeper, and the lawbreaking liquor-seller would be
plying their trades once more."

The Methodists stirred anxiously. When he told them that The
Allen (name not mentioned) expected that "the present Board of
Police would be legislated out of office under cover of some bill
supplementary to or included in the Greater New York bill" the
Methodists gasped.

"Undoubtedly there are many politicians who are bent on seeing
this," TR continued. Still naming no one, he predicted the politi-

cians would "bend every energy to destroy us, because they recognize in us their deadly foes."

With his jaw jutting defiantly, he went on, "These politicians are men who hate honesty in public office with a bitter hatred, who look upon politics as a game to be pursued only for the basest personal advantage, and who naturally war against men who will do neither the foul work of political bosses on the one hand, nor, on the other, permit any kind of criminal to go unpunished. The politician who wishes to use the Police Department for his own base purposes, and the criminal and the trafficker in vice, who wish to ply their trades with immunity, are quite right in using every effort to drive us out of office."

He told the audience, "It is for you decent people to say whether or not they shall succeed."

The plot against Roosevelt and TR's combative reaction to it came as no surprise to Jacob Riis. He had long-since taken the measure of the politicians and the man who had told him, "We are not playing 'puss in the corner' with the criminals. We intend to stamp out these vermin, and we do not intend to consult the vermin as to the methods we shall employ." What surprised and amused Riis and Lincoln Steffens was that it had taken the politicians so long to recognize that Roosevelt was their nemesis, as well as the criminals'.

Three days after the speech to the Methodists, they and similarly minded citizens picked up the *Times* to find a most unusual set of double-column headlines. The sensational, alarming banners blared:

THE REPUBLICAN PLOT TO OUST ROOSEVELT
Political Cowards and Assassins Would Strike Him
Down for His Honesty and Courage.

Below this attention-grabber the newspaper reported, "The Platt politicians of this State have determined to remove Theodore Roosevelt, President of the Police Board in this city, from office. They intend—if they can—to legislate him out of office as a punishment, mainly, for his persistent, untiring and courageous efforts to enforce laws framed by Republicans.

"They have found they cannot frighten or cajole him into ignoring the provisions of the excise law. So they propose to get rid of him.

"This will be done, unless the law-abiding element of this State comes to Mr. Roosevelt's rescue and makes it known to the Legislature that any attempt to degrade an official for doing his duty will bring political ruin on those engaged in such a despicable movement."

In a three-day series of detailed front-page lead-stories in the manner and style of the next century's exposés by the *Times* of the "Pentagon Papers" and the Watergate Scandal, investigative reporters presented chapter and verse of the Platt scheme. Along with the facts came such stinging editorializing phrases as "the foes of Mr. Roosevelt are hypocrites and cowards." Unlike TR, the paper excoriated Platt as "the leader of the politicians who are casting about for a chance to use the Police Department of New York and render it subservient to their own ends." It went on to assert, "All the patronage will go to the Platt crowd if the plan is carried out, and they will control the liquor saloons. Through it, Mr. Platt, his choice henchmen and lieutenants in this city, in Brooklyn and in all the rest of Greater New York, will have the naming of policemen, firemen and health officials."

On January 25 the third of the articles warned, "A greater political machine than Tweed ever dreamed of—a machine that will dominate cities and State, and prove a mighty power in National conventions—is to be constructed by the Legislature of the State of New York, unless the people rise in protest."

The paper then took a swipe at Mayor Strong, stating, "It is quite plain to all (except our innocent and confiding Mayor) who have been watching the movements of the Platt machine men that these conscienceless political bandits intend, if possible, to rule the people of this city and Brooklyn, through legislative commissions."

Once again, Strong proved to be less a man than his name suggested. He offered no repeat of pledges of unmitigated support for police reforms he expressed on appointing Roosevelt. Rather, he had come to regret having voiced them. He also grew to resent being denied under the Bi-Partisan Police Law powers to effect any influence over what was transpiring up on Mulberry Street. He had also come to envy the attention garnered by Roosevelt from the press. Moreover, he felt he had been unjustly held to account for Roosevelt's vigorous enforcement of the Sunday closing law when he as Mayor had gone on record as favoring allowing saloons to be open at specified hours on the Sabbath. He had pleaded with TR to go easy, especially in the weeks leading up to the November election, and suffered the results of Roosevelt's refusal to fall into step.

Reporters who covered city hall had also made note that the official they called "Col. Strong" had felt personally insulted when Roosevelt and the other police commissioners did not bother to attend the New Year's Day reception he gave at city hall in honor of aldermen. The journalists also sensed resentment on the part of the Mayor that while the police force went all out to locate illegal saloons, gambling dens, and bawdy houses it had taken a Scotland Yard detective to nab the Burden jewel thieves.

Therefore, it was with considerable fascination that police reporters and their city hall brethren heard a rumor on January 30, 1896, that Strong had summoned the police board to his office for a lecture on how dismally he perceived their performances in office. With dismay and disappointment the reporters heard Strong deny any such meeting was in the offing. Mindful of his hopes for a future in public life and keenly aware of a large outpouring of support for Roosevelt as a result of the revelation of the Platt plot, he appeared to have taken to heart a remark by Tammany Boss Dick Croker. "Roosevelt is all there is to the Strong Administration," he had said in May 1895, "and Roosevelt will make or break it."

Although Strong nurtured hopes that Roosevelt might decide to leave Mulberry Street voluntarily, resignation was unlikely in the face of the plot to depose him. Everyone who knew Roosevelt appreciated he was not a man who would walk away under attack.

Presently, public exposure of Platt's maneuverings to oust Roosevelt proved so embarrassing to Platt that he ordered faithful minions in Albany to scrap the idea. No supplement to the Greater New York bill surfaced. TR said he was delighted. And he advised friend Henry Cabot Lodge that he harbored no hard feelings and that, being a good and loyal Republican, "I shall not break with the party." There could be no blame affixed to Roosevelt's name for splitting New York Republicans with an election coming up. "The Presidential contest is too important," he said to Lodge.

February passed in wintry cold and with the flurry of innovations described earlier, including adoption of the Bertillion System, acceptance of the design of the uniform for the Bicycle Squad, the reorganization of detective districts, and abolition of the Broadway Squad. On the penultimate day of that Leap Year February the board convened for what was expected to be a routine meeting.

However, February 28 provided something unexpected and disconcerting. When TR brought up the names of Acting Inspectors Nicholas Brooks and John McCullagh for what he expected to be a routine approval of changing the pair's rank to permanent status, he listened with disbelief as Andrew Parker voted "Nay."

While the Democrat had always been an enigma TR hesitated to accept the warning of his friend Joseph Bucklin Bishop, editor of the *Evening Post,* that Parker was not to be trusted. Bishop said he was "a snake in the grass." Nor did he listen to others who held that at a propitious moment Parker would stab Roosevelt in the back.

Reluctance to regard Parker as a wolf in sheep's clothing did not mean that Roosevelt failed to appreciate that Parker was a secretive and mysterious fellow. His discernment of Parker's nature had been evidenced when he sent Lincoln Steffens to see Parker regarding the rehabilitation of Max Schmittberger, telling Steffens that "espionage" was more in line with Andrew Parker's character than Theodore Roosevelt's. But if Parker were a Judas, how to explain a speech Parker had given to the Patria Club at a meeting at Sherry's on January 11? He had noted the bragadoccio on the part of the city's most infamous and talkative gambler. "It may be as 'The Allen' has said, that the Board of Police will be wiped out of existence by February 5, and then everything will be run wide open again," he had said, "but if this is to come to pass, then the Commissioners will be cannonized instead of being cannonaded, and the people of this city will be soon sighing for the good old days of Theodore Roosevelt."

Had these words been a sham by a man motivated by mendacity, treachery, and duplicity? Were they a cunning cover for a snake in the grass? Was Parker's unexpected blocking of the appointments of Brooks and McCullagh a signal that Parker had chosen to drop all pretenses? The next few days provided further evidence that something was amiss. Parker boycotted subsequent meetings of the police board.

Unanimity was required to promote the two men, but there was a provision in the rules governing the board that permitted the three commissioners to take action without Parker if they obtained written assent by the chief of police. Accordingly, they called Peter Conlin to a meeting of the board on March 12. But when Roosevelt asked Conlin if he would recommend Brooks and McCullagh for the permanent rank of Inspector, Conlin refused. He then went on to put the trio of stunned commissioners on notice that he had no intention of rubber-stamping any promotions unless they were submitted to him in advance, pointing out to the board that under the Bi-Partisan Police Law it was his right to do so.

The board, minus a vote by the absent Parker, passed a resolution ordering Conlin to put his position in writing. This was their legal right to do, but they could not compel Conlin to endorse Brooks and McCullagh. Despite their majority, they found themselves deadlocked. All they could do was ask, "Why?"

As usual, TR hoped to find an answer to a puzzle as he had in the threat of murder on the part of Jake Maunder and plotting by Thomas Platt, by going straight to the horse's mouth. Such an opportunity seemed to present itself in the form of a previous invitation to Parker to dine on March 13 at the Roosevelt Madison Avenue town house. However, the guest list also included the Rev. Parkhurst and Joseph Bishop. TR's prudence and good table manners prevailed. He chose not to confront.

While Parker's puzzling demeanor did not come up at dinner, a clue to his mindset burst from his lips after the gathering. Walking with Bishop, he gave the astonished newspaperman a quick look at his attitude toward Roosevelt that had been simmering but now was on the verge of boiling over. "I wish he would stop talking so much in the newspapers," Parker grumbled. "He talks, talks, talks all the time. Scarcely a day passes that there is not something from him in the papers. The public is getting tired of it. It injures our work."

Bishop replied, "Stop Roosevelt talking! Why, you would kill him. He has to talk. The peculiarity about him is that he has what is essentially a boy's mind. What he thinks he says at once, says aloud. It is his distinguishing characteristic, and I don't know as he will ever outgrow it. But with it he has great qualities which make him an invaluable public servant—inflexible honesty, absolute fearlessness, and devotion to good government which amounts to religion. We must let him work his way, for nobody can induce him to change it."

The next morning, Parker walked into Roosevelt's office. "You think Bishop is a friend of yours, don't you?" he said with a smug smile.

"Yes," replied a puzzled TR.

"Well, you know what he said about you last night?" Parker asked. "He said you had a boy's mind and it might never be developed."

Roosevelt's recorded response was not to Parker but to Joe Bishop. He telephoned and invited him to lunch. As soon as they were seated at a narrow table, TR leaned forward. With his pince-nez within three inches of Bishop's face he related the morning's report by Parker and waited for an explanation.

Unflinchingly, Bishop replied, "Roosevelt, I did say that. Did he tell you what else I said?"

"No, that is all I want to hear."

Bishop persisted in relating the rest of his analysis of the Roosevelt character.

When he finished TR banged a fist on the table. "By George, I knew it."

"There, Roosevelt," Bishop said glumly, "is your snake in the grass, of which I warned you—the meanest of mean liars, who tells half the truth."

Determined to break the deadlock over Brooks and McCullagh, TR took the issue to the city's lawyer. The Corporation Counsel informed the president of the police board that both Parker and Conlin were within their rights. When this assertion reached the newspapers the heavy weather that many sages of the press corps had long been forecasting for Mulberry Street burst forth as a tornado of hard news, wild rumor, analysis, and speculation, the latter colored by the papers' attitudes toward TR—pro and con.

Lincoln Steffens provided *Evening Post* readers with his view that a parting between Roosevelt and Parker had been inevitable because they had always "run on radically divergent tracks." He painted Parker as "secretive" and Roosevelt as a man who "seeks the open." When two such "able and obstinate men . . . disagree," he wrote of the situation, "it is idle to say that there is even a semblance of peace in Mulberry Street. There is war and nothing but war in prospect."

When TR expressed himself on the subject of a rebellion in Cuba by recommending that the United States use force of arms to drive out the Spaniards who ruled the island and urged the nation to be ready to uphold its honor by an appeal to the sword, Steffens' boss, E. L. Godkin, offered an editorial that esteemed Roosevelt as police commissioner but thought "his value to the community would be greatly increased if somehow he could somewhere find his fill of fighting."

Some speculation regarding the internecine skirmishing of the police board found roots of Parker's obstinacy in Tammany Hall; for Parker was, after all, a Democrat, and the election had shown the anti-Tammany reformers to be vulnerable. If it were true, as Boss Croker had told Steffens, that the people would tire of reform and bring back Tammany, why should a Democrat help a Republican, especially when no less an authority on public mood than The Allen had predicted doom for the do-gooders? Others who assessed Parker's sudden revelation of his true political stripes found it more likely that Parker was taking orders from New York County Democratic leader Jimmy O'Brien than directly from Dick Croker.

Even more cynical interpreters said the one behind Parker was not a Democrat at all, but the Republicans' Easy Boss. Tom Platt was seeking revenge for the foiling of his plot to get rid of Roosevelt by legislation. Some credence to this theory stemmed from the failure of Commissioner Fred Grant to enlist Platt's aid in bolstering Roosevelt. The old man of Amen Corner told the son of Ulysses S. Grant, "I would like to please you, Colonel Grant, but I don't care nearly as much to please you as I do to worry Roosevelt."

Soon the reporting of the hostility between TR and Parker took the shape of journalistic jesting. Jacob Riis's *Sun* said, "Look Out for Epithets." The *Evening News* depicted the battling commissioners as the Montagues and Capulets of Shakespeare's "Romeo and Juliet" and wondered when they would stop "biting their thumbs at each other and engage in armed combat."

How was Roosevelt bearing up? On March 30 the *Times* quoted him. "Though I have the constitution of a bullmoose," he said, "it is beginning to wear on me a little."

Seeking a way out of the stalemate, he enlisted Grant and Avery Andrews in an effort to win the war by shifting the field of combat to Albany. They petitioned the legislature to kill the Bi-Partisan Police Law and substitute a statute that would drop the all-or-nothing voting system and strip the chief of police of his veto power over appointments. For once the Easy Boss proved to be slow out of the starting gate, failing to muster his ranks of faithful in time to prevent the Assembly from giving TR what he wanted. Boss Croker was quicker. Goaded by a panicky Parker, he marshalled enough Tammany stalwarts in the Senate so that not even a personal appearance by Roosevelt in Albany could keep the measure from going down to defeat.

When TR got back to his office on Monday he found Chief of

Detectives O'Brien waiting for him. He reported that at 10:30 the previous morning a package had been mailed at the General Post Office addressed to "Theodore Roosevelt, Police Headquarters." It had "Medicine" written upon. To determine if the parcel contained glass and required special handling, a post office clerk opened a corner of the package. He found a bundle of matchsticks and what appeared to be a fuse. Further inspection by the police, who took the precaution of first dunking the package in a bucket of water, revealed a bomb made of black powder. If it detonated it would have at least blinded whoever opened it. The chances of that being TR were slim. Usually the job of opening mail belonged to Minnie Kelly or a policeman who was assigned to the police board, John Rathberger.

TR said, "Whew! If infernal machines were all I had to contend with in the Police Department, I would sleep mighty easy," and proceeded to his desk.

Although the legislature had turned thumbs down on TR's bid to rewrite the police law, it was forging ahead at full steam in changing the statute that lay at the heart of the struggle going on at police headquarters, the Sunday closing law. Pending before the lawmakers was the Raines Liquor Tax Bill. The crux of it was a provision allowing "hotels" to sell liquor *with meals* in their dining rooms *or to patrons in their rooms* on Sundays and other Christian holidays. Precisely what would constitute "rooms" was left obscure.

With passage a foregone conclusion, interpretation of its clauses became an urgent Roosevelt priority. To deal with this he convened a meeting of the police board on Friday, March 28, 1896. Parker attended. When TR raised questions about the true meaning of the language of the Raines Law, Parker responded by informing the board that Chief of Police Conlin had sent a letter to the city Corporation Counsel, Francis M. Scott, seeking elucidation.

Roosevelt was astounded. He pointed out the proper procedure in cases in which an interpretation of law was required was for the board's own legal counsel to contact the city's attorney. But the deed had been done. There was nothing Roosevelt could do but await a response to Conlin's request and quietly seethe over the improper manner in which Chief Conlin had acted, evidently with Parker's knowledge and blessing, if not connivance.

The law known as "the liquor tax law," constituting Chapter 112 of the Laws of 1896, was to go into effect as of May 23, 1896. Unfortunately, the police who had to enforce it still had not received definitive interpretation of its scope from Scott. When he did reply, he read the law as requiring that henceforth it would be illegal for any place selling alcoholic beverages to offer the traditional free lunch.

News of this provision hit the down-and-out denizens of the Bowery especially hard. When a *Times* reporter surveyed men he called "Weary Willies" he found a state of "consternation" but no lack of enterprise. Gathered into groups along the curb and indignantly discussing the new state of affairs, they "resolved to eat up at once all the free lunch left on the counters. No sooner was this resolve formed than it was put into execution, and the frowsy gentry alighted in a body on the pickled-herring, the potato salad and liver pudding, and devoured it in a jiffy. It was as though a horde of locusts had swarmed through the Bowery in search of wild honey."

The commander of the Nineteenth Precinct, the Tenderloin, with most of the city's hotels and a large number of saloons, reported to headquarters that operators of those establishments had wasted no time in bending the law their way. "Saloon keepers have canvassed the situation thoroughly and have many plans," he noted. In drinking establishments that once handed out free food, sandwiches were suddenly being sold, albeit for one cent, thus legalizing an enterprise that would have been subject to closing if it gave away food.

Said Captain Pickett of the Nineteenth, "There is even a plan to give away drinks and sell the lunch. Besides, supposing they raised the price of the lunch to ten cents or a quarter for a portion? What law is there to compel a seller of drinks to collect what is due? He can evade the law by putting a price on the lunch and not seeing to it that consumers pay. It's going to be a great muddle for the police."

TR decided to survey compliance himself. During a whirlwind tour of the city he found ample evidence to bolster Pickett's report. He learned that for a nickle he got a sandwich and a beer, plus unlimited refills of the brew.

The law also codified Clubber Williams' suggestion that saloons and other hard-drink dispensers be required to raise their shades during hours when they were supposed to be closed so as to allow a passing patrolman to see inside. When some establishments pointed out that their windows had wooden shutters or were made of frosted glass, TR promised them that while the fancy panels and opaque panes would have to go, replaced by transparent glass, no arrests would be made until sufficient time had gone by to permit the renovations.

The definition of "hotel" and "rooms" also presented the cops with a problem. When Raines specified a minimum of eight bedrooms as qualification new hostelries appeared on the Bowery overnight. Many of them had draped wires with blankets to convert stables into "rooms." One posted a sign warning, "Sleeping in this hotel positively prohibited." Whorehouses transformed themselves into hotels, affording customers the added amenity of a meal, at an extra cost, of course, so as to keep within the law.

TR's survey revealed establishments where "dining rooms" were no larger than ten by six feet. "Hotels" did not require guests to register.

The Raines Law became even more complex when the Corporation Counsel decreed that "clubs" were exempted from the law. This came as a profound relief to such established bulwarks of society as the Union League and others. For New Yorkers with a penchant for stretching Raines to their advantage the ruling presented a golden opportunity. As fake hotels had sprung up like mushrooms, new "clubs" sprouted all around the town. Admission was to members only. Sentinels guarded the doors. Passwords were required. And the drinking population began employing a funny new word to describe such a place. Reported the *New York Times* on May 11, 1896, "A struggle between policemen of the East Twenty-third Street Station and the patrons of a 'speak-easy' at 391 Avenue A occurred last night."

Whether it was a "speak-easy," "hotel," "club," "side-door saloon" or an old-fashioned, pre-Raines Law barroom, in enforcing the new liquor-sales statute the police force had on their hands an even more complex challenge than under the despised old law. Changing certain aspects of the law to allow limited Sabbath Day liquor sales did not spell eradication of illegal operations in the off-hours. Going after these illicit establishments required as many detectives as before. And plainclothes squads retained their mandate to go after the gambling and prostitution. In all these enterprises the detectives would accumulate out-of-pocket expenses, such as the money wagered in a gambling resort, paid for an illicit drink, or given to a charmer in a bawdyhouse. The money was confiscated and impounded as evidence. To reimburse these men the police board, like its predecessors, had authorized the commissioner charged with department business affairs to draw from a contingency fund. The transfers had to be approved by the City Comptroller.

Early in 1896 Andrews requested seven thousand five hundred dollars from money that had been appropriated in 1892 for a new police station in the Ninth Precinct but not spent. To his shock, Comptroller Ashbel Fitch refused to allow it. A Tammany man who had somehow missed being swept away by the reform broom of 1894, Fitch announced that the use of contingency funds for paying back "spies" was illegal.

When Andrews protested that such practices had been common in the department Fitch said, sarcastically, "No matter what the old boards did, this board is expected to do better than the old ones, isn't it?"

Mayor Strong retorted, "It's pure cussedness, nothing else, and to get political capital, that's all."

Roosevelt snapped his belief that Fitch was exerting efforts "in behalf of the criminal classes."

The Comptroller lashed back, asserting that Roosevelt "is constantly saying that everybody in journalism, in office, or in politics who disagrees with him on any subject is 'aiding the criminal classes.' He probably honestly believes that it is criminal to oppose him in anything."

Fitch then drew Mayor Strong into the affair, wondering if TR ought to consider the man who had appointed Roosevelt a member of the criminal classes because Strong, at a dinner of the North Side Board of Trade on March 7, 1896, had said, "I have my beer on Sunday and I do not ask Theodore about it either."

Amidst the heat and smoke of the battle between Roosevelt and Fitch there occurred an event in the Roosevelt-Parker contest that amazed onlookers. At a meeting of the police board on the first of May the routine agenda was disrupted by a motion from Andrew Parker that Roosevelt be reelected president.

Astonishment silenced the room. TR responded that his term had a week more to run. Parker brushed aside the formality. The motion carried and the commissioners proceeded to the next item on the regular agenda. They approved a design for a new uniform for the mounted policemen (those on horses, not bicycles). It was to be colorful raiment of shades of blue, silk braid, chevrons, and rows of brass buttons. Roosevelt voted for it despite expressing the opinion that the outfit made the cavaliers look like bandmasters.

Five days later the contenders in the growing flap concerning reimbursements for detectives found themselves face to face in Mayor Strong's office. The occasion on May 6 was a routine meeting of the Board of Estimate and Apportionment, the panel that had the final say on expenditures, but always guided by recommendations by Fitch.

When the issue of the reimbursements came up TR opened with, "The Comptroller is now in the position of forcing this Board (of Estimate) to hold up the money due to these poor people."

An aggravated Fitch interrupted. "Why didn't you take some action? I sent you a report on the matter a month ago, and politely suggested that you begin legal proceedings at once, and have the points of law settled by the courts. You read my report. You said it was a move in the interests of the criminal classes, and you have done nothing else since."

Roosevelt railed, "It was a move in the interests of the criminal classes. I said so and it was the truth."

The Comptroller then referred to TR's public argument with Commissioner Parker, alleging that it was that dispute that had diverted Roosevelt's attention. Leaning back in his chair with what an observer called "one of his exasperating smiles on his face," Fitch asserted, "If anyone is the blame, it is you."

"That is not so," Roosevelt cried, almost leaping from his chair. "If you want to go into these outside matters, Mr. Fitch, I can go into them, too. I can give enough of it, if you want to fight on these outside issues."

"I know you are a fighter," Fitch answered, condescendingly. "You have a great reputation in that line."

"Well you are not a fighter," TR shot back. "You would run away from a fight. If you want to fight in this matter, I can give you all that you are looking for."

Fitch waved a dismissing hand. "Oh, come on. I don't want to fight with you."

Roosevelt leaned across the table separating them. "I know you won't fight, you would run away," he said, teeth snapping.

"I would never run away from you," Fitch said, smilingly.

TR reared back. "You would not fight."

Fitch smirked. "What shall it be, pistols or—"

"Pistols or anything else," Roosevelt growled as he rose.

At this point, according to an observer from the *World,* two reporters who knew that Fitch had come out the winner in some thirty sword fights when a student at the University of Heidelberg realized they stood in the line of either fists or fire. They dropped their notes and ducked under a table.

From their secure hiding places they heard the agitated voice of Mayor Strong, "Gentlemen, gentlemen, I warn you right now that if this thing goes on, I shall call in the police and have you both arrested."

"Oh, this man Roosevelt is always getting into a row," said Fitch. "He had a row with Parker, now he wants a row with me."

The Mayor declared that he would refer the contentious issue of reimbursing detectives to the Corporation Counsel for ajudication. As he spoke, a red-faced Roosevelt stormed out.

Later, Fitch told reporters that if there were to be a duel he would ask "Fighting Bob" Evans of the United States Navy to be his second, adding, "If he has other engagements there are some fellows who fought their way through Heidelberg with me, and I guess I will have to call on one of them."

Back in Mulberry Street, TR had cooled down, but he had not given an inch on the issue. He informed the mob of bloodthirsty reporters who congregated around his desk, "I have no personal quarrel with Mr. Fitch, but I have too deep a sense of my responsibility as President of the Police Board under Mayor Strong's administration to submit to any effort to cripple this department without protesting as strenuously as I am able. As a self-respecting official I could all the less submit to this when an effort was seemingly made to prevent me by what amounted to bullying from standing up for the needs of the department and therefore the needs of the city."

The next day Mayor Strong called in reporters to show off a wood-and-tin pistol that had been given to him by a friend, along with a note. It stated, "Thinking you might not be at all times armed in the board meetings, permit me, with other friends, to present this." Chuckling, Strong said, "I will not have to call in the police now."

Coincidentally, Fitch and Parker met that day. They agreed that the entire matter of reimbursements required settlement in court. But Fitch could not miss the opportunity for another dig at Roosevelt. He said, "It was a matter easily arranged with a sane person."

When the issue of the money reached the courts the verdict was not to Roosevelt's liking. The judge declared that many of the bills that had been submitted were "monstrous and illegal." Roosevelt and Andrews fired off a response, warning that if the police board were to have no authority to incur such expenses "then the department is absolutely without the power to regulate or control in any manner disorderly houses in this city, which is their duty under the law." While Grant concurred, Andrew Parker declined to make a public statement, much to TR's chagrin.

More trouble came when the office of the Corporation Counsel declared that Chief of Police Conlin was acting within his rights in insisting that the Bi-Partisan Police Law vested powers of promotion in him, not the police board. As a result, on March 24 TR listened with quiet restraint as Conlin read into the record a letter in which he exercised those powers by making appointments and shifting personnel, none of which had been discussed with TR and the other members of the police board. Conspicuous on Chief Conlin's list were retentions of Brooks and McCullagh in the position of "Acting" Inspector.

Furious over a turn of events that he believed had gutted the authority of commissioners, Roosevelt consulted with Avery Andrews. They worked out a resolution that would put the board on record in favor of revising the police law in a way that would strip the chief of police of his veto over appointments. When it was presented to the board, Parker surprised Roosevelt by casting a favorable vote. Asked by reporters why he had done so, Parker replied with the same inscrutability that had made him such an enigma: "I thought it adviseable."

It may have been that Parker anticipated a day when Roosevelt would be gone and Andrew Parker or some other Tammany Democrat might ascend to president of the board, at which time he would not care to be stymied by a recalcitrant underling such as Peter Conlin. Some credence to this tactic could be found in Parker's opposition to naming Moses Cortright, a Roosevelt man, to the post of deputy chief of police. Because Conlin was close to retirement age, Cortright would then be in line to succeed, thereby denying Parker a valuable ally in Mulberry Street against Roosevelt.

As to Peter Conlin, views around town varied. Some felt that he was in cahoots with Parker out of political sympathies. Others held that Conlin just did not like Roosevelt. And there was the suggestion that Conlin simply found Parker useful in protecting the perquisites of the office of chief of police for whomever assumed it after Conlin. At age fifty-five, he had been a policeman most of his life. Over the past several months he had been required to preside over a series of historic changes, as well as to run a department that had been called on to intervene in several strikes, supervise police response to crime, deal with the embarrassment of the Burden case, and cope with the intricacies of enforcing the Raines Law. Added to these woes was the fact that he was tired and not in the best of health. Consequently, he notified the warring commissioners that he wanted to take a vacation by traveling to England, promising to return in time to lead the annual police parade scheduled for June first. Unsaid was the likelihood that following the parade he intended to retire.

The board voted unanimously on April 21 to grant him leave for fifty days. In his stead at the pinnacle of the force would be Inspector Cortright. Accordingly, Conlin sailed away, leaving the Mulberry Street civil war in his wake.

Although no one had been able to produce evidence of the existence of a Parker-Conlin cabal whose aim was to thwart and frustrate Roosevelt to the point that TR would resign, this was widely believed amongst observers in the press shack and between the canny politicians of city hall and the state house. What a Conlin retirement and likely accession to chief of police by Cortright might mean were question marks.

In mid-April a link between Parker and Republican Boss Tom Platt came to light. In meetings Parker had with a lieutenant of Platt in Albany, Parker alleged that Roosevelt had been playing politics by stacking the upper echelons of the police force with Republicans, but only those exhibiting a pro-Roosevelt stance. He went on to say that it had been himself, Parker, a Democrat, who had to fight to get Republicans appointed, regardless of how they felt about Roosevelt. In fact, he said, Roosevelt had appointed more Democrats than Republicans. The intended effect of this unusual situation in which a Tammany man claimed the credit for putting Republicans on the force was to doom any likelihood that Platt would support the police reorganization bill being pushed by Roosevelt aimed at limiting the powers of the chief of police in matters of appointments.

When Roosevelt traveled to Albany to lobby for the measure he was handed a copy of Parker's allegations. He exploded with wrath, branding the assertions "unqualifiedly false." A letter to that effect addressed to Albany Republicans was signed by Grant and the police board's other Democrat, Andrews, TR's everfaithful cross-party ally.

Speculation bubbled up in the city that Roosevelt would appeal to Mayor Strong to apply pressure on Parker to hand in his resignation. With what one reporter called "the soft and gentle smile of some of his Quaker ancestors" Parker told reporters, "I have no intention of resigning my office as police commissioner. I shall simply continue to perform my duty with care and fidelity to the public interest."

Asked about his charges that Roosevelt played politics with the police department and TR's allegations that Parker was the source of all the turmoil in Mulberry Street, Parker answered, "I am not going to blow the embers of discord so that the flames of passion may rise any higher than they have done. I have always given considerable attention to detail and my conclusions (that Roosevelt blocked some Republicans from appointment to the force) have been formed from abundant premises. At no stage of these differences between the members of the Police Board have I been the aggressor."

Lincoln Steffens analyzed the contest between Roosevelt and Parker and became convinced that the trouble had nothing to do with party politics but was due solely to different characters. TR liked to lead cavalry charges while Parker preferred to direct his troops mysteriously from the rear, unseen.

Jacob Riis also looked to the role of personal character in the struggle and, as usual, found Roosevelt's to be exemplary. His memoirs relate an incident in TR's office in June, observed by Riis. A police official of superior rank, whom Riis did not identify, whispered something to Roosevelt that caused TR to recoil. "No, sir!" TR said loudly. "I don't fight that way." After the crestfallen police officer left, TR told Riis that the man had informed him that Parker could be found that night in a "known evil house" uptown. The police officer, who was under a cloud himself in the department, had offered to raid the house in order to "get square" with Roosevelt.

For reformers who had placed their hopes on Roosevelt as he barged into police headquarters just one year earlier the events of May 1896 were disheartening. The remaking of the police force appeared to have been stopped dead in its tracks, victim of the unbecoming public squabble between Roosevelt and Parker. Yet even as vituperation and vitriol appeared to be the *soupe de jour* at headquarters, the people who hungered for changes were informed they had gotten a large measure of the menu they had ordered.

After an exhaustive examination of police appointments and promotions during the past year, a blue-ribbon panel of the Civil Service Reform Association issued a glowing report card. And it credited Roosevelt, not only for assuring that the investigators were not impeded in their work, but for having gotten across to the rank and file of the force that advancement in rank depended solely on merit.

The report concluded, "The testimony of those familiar with the conditions at police headquarters under the old regime and since the change of administration is that the influence of the new plan is felt throughout the entire department. The men are said to appreciate generally that their advancement in the future is to depend on the character of their service, and the increased efficiency shown in the general work of the department is due principally to this cause."

While this endorsement of the progress that had been made cheered Roosevelt, he faced disconcerting news from the courts regarding two of the men who had been exposed by the Lexow investigation as leading figures in the old system of corruption. A jury of the Criminal Branch of the State Supreme Court found Captain William S. Devery not guilty of bribery. This finding was compounded by a decision by District Attorney Fellows to dismiss three indictments of Devery on grounds of insufficient evidence. While this was happening, William McLaughlin remained free on bail pending appeal of his conviction on bribery charges. The only glimmer of satisfaction in this disposal of the remnants of the Lexow exposé was dismissal of all charges that had been lodged against the reformed "big broom," Max Schmittberger.

Meanwhile, analysts of the favorable report on police reform by the Civil Service investigators concluded that if their report had been critical of results, a fair reading would lead to the conclusion that the battle between Roosevelt and Parker might have originated in a dispute over who should bear the blame for failure. But the report had pointed to successes, allowing all commissioners to bask in shared credit. Therefore, whatever lay at the root of the titanic tug of war between TR and Parker, it did not involve apportioning responsibility for making a mess of reform. Nor did these observers go along with Lincoln Steffens' assessment, that the trouble was simply a clash of personalities. The inescapable conclusion was that the cause of the chaos and the stalemate was the old bugaboo of Mulberry Street: Politics.

The only doubt left in the situation was how it would come out once the dust settled.

What these outsiders and Parker could not know as they anticipated the next clash was that TR held in his pocket an affidavit, signed on April 20 by a Patrolman named McMorrow, that might prove more explosive than the mail bomb that had been directed at TR. If Roosevelt chose to publish it the contents would be far more damaging to Parker's reputation than a visit to an uptown whorehouse.

Chapter 13

Nothing of the Purple

On May 20, 1896, Mayor William L. Strong read a letter from Theodore Roosevelt. A year and fifteen days had passed since the mayor had sworn him in and sent Jacob Riis flying down the stoop of the press bastion opposite police headquarters shouting to Lincoln Steffens that Roosevelt was en route to Mulberry Street, a modern Hercules bent on cleaning out the Aegean stables. With the letter from Roosevelt was the McMorrow affidavit. In it the patrolman swore he had won appointment to the police force by paying four hundred dollars, with the understanding that the bribe would clear the way for an endorsement of the application by Andrew Parker. Weighted with memories of the bad old days when such bribery had been common and redolent of the struggle between him and Parker, TR's letter asked the mayor to intervene.

Strong wasted no time in addressing a missive of his own.

City of New York
Office of the Mayor, May 20, 1896
Andrew D. Parker, Esq., Police Commissioner:

MY DEAR SIR: When I appointed the Board of Police Commissioners about a year ago, I fully expected that each member would discharge his full duty, having at heart the best interests of the city, and work out a complete reformation of the department. And I really felt that in securing you for one of them, that your work would add greatly to the accomplishment of that result, but your course during the last four months has convinced me that you have lost your influence with the public and the board. Consequently, I feel that your resignation would be for the best interest of the Police Department.

I regret the necessity of this decision. However, I feel that in coming to this conclusion, it is in the interest of good government, and while I

have no one in mind to fill your place, I would like your resignation on
receipt of this, to take effect when your successor shall be appointed.

Respectfully yours,
W. L. STRONG, MAYOR.

In Strong's experience as a businessman that should have ended
the matter. Were a resignation not forthcoming he simply could
have fired the man. But under the Bi-Partisan Police Law the Mayor
of New York City had no such power, short of *proof* of corruption.
Patrolman McMorrow's affidavit was hardly that.

Coincidentally, with this private exchange of notes, Parker
chose a public forum to vent his ire. He granted an interview to the
Recorder in which he charged that Roosevelt "has assumed that he
is the Alpha and Omega of the Department." He claimed that for
eleven months he had "patiently endured this arbitrary assumption
of authority." He said he felt impelled to act in self-defense.

A full week passed before Strong received a reply. "I must decline your request for my resignation," Parker said. He then proceeded to tell the mayor he had "an imperfect understanding of the
facts" and had ignored Parker's attempts to arrange a meeting
"touching on the affairs of the Police Board." Asserting Strong had
gone so far as to set a date, he ended the letter with, "I have never
heard from you since."

Strong shot back on May 28. Expressing "astonishment," he
answered that the meeting Parker had asked for had, indeed, been
arranged and that Parker did not attend it, leaving Strong, Elihu
Root, and the city's Corporation Counsel to cool their heels till
eleven o'clock. Whether Parker or Strong was right is impossible to
say. However, it seems most likely that the men had suffered a
failure in communication. Each of them being a gentleman of their
era, it is difficult to picture either deliberately snubbing the other.

That code of propriety was much on Strong's mind as he went on,
"Now, Mr. Parker, I simply want to say that when I appointed the
four gentlemen whom I appointed as Police Commissioners, I felt
very sure that each one of them was a gentleman and, as such, I felt
that any time I asked either one of them for their resignations I
would get it promptly, and you can judge my surprise when I received your note of last evening. I can only say that I think it would
save you a great deal of trouble and me a great deal of trouble and

the Police Department some severe criticism if you promptly forward your resignation to me."

Whether Parker read between the lines to interpret saving himself "a great deal of trouble and the Police Department some severe criticism" as a hint that Strong possessed a trump card in the form of damning facts about Parker is not known; however, the references to personal trouble and severe repercussions for the police clearly conveyed something dark. That fact notwithstanding, Parker again refused to quit. He retorted in a May 28 letter, "The trouble which may be made for me I shall have to bear; the trouble which may be made for you will be of your own making and any criticism of the Police Department which may ensue will not be properly chargeable to me."

The timing for all this could not have been worse. Parker's May 28 letter arrived at city hall as the State Court of Appeals ruled that the Raines Law contained nothing offensive to the constitution of the Empire State. So it stood as law, vexing as it was to enforce by a police department racked by a controversy at the top. Second, drawing the mayor's office into the feud came on the eve of a grand march by the entire force up Broadway and past a reviewing stand from which Strong, Roosevelt, Parker, and the other commissioners were expected to salute and be saluted.

The parade itself had become a bone of contention. This was the yearly event that Roosevelt had demanded the board cancel in 1895 out of concern that it would have proven offensive to a public made sick by the Lexow Committee's exposé of departmental corruptions. Although there was a sense that much had been done in the intervening year to fix what was wrong with the police, the 1896 parade planners found themselves haunted by two of the most notorious specters of the Lexow investigation, Captains William Devery and Max Schmittberger.

The former had been as much a living symbol of the failings of the police as Tom Byrnes and Clubber Williams. The Parkhurst Society had forced his indictment on a charge of failing to close a particularly noisesome whorehouse that Parkhurst had investigated in Devery's Eleventh Precinct. Saloon-keeper Charles Priem had told Lexow probers that Devery continued a system of blackmail and payoffs when he succeeded Captain Adam Cross as a precinct commander. At trial for not closing the bawdy house he was acquitted. After the police board tried and then dismissed him, a court ordered reinstatement. This was followed by another charge of extortion, causing him to be suspended for more than a year. That charge also fell through at trial. Now he was back in uniform. But the parade organizers banned him from marching, a decision deeply resented by Devery's numerous friends on the force.

What made the Devery blackballing worse was the second cause for concern about how the parade might unfold. Permitted to take part was Max Schmittberger, still widely regarded by the public as a crook and by police rank and file and many superior officers as a squealing turncoat. This was a real worry. In an article on the day before the parade the *New York Times* reported, "It is whispered among police officials that Schmittberger's presence in the parade may have the effect of besmirching the entire force of paraders, as hints have been received that he will be hissed along the route, if something worse does not happen to him."

Monday, June 1, 1896, dawned sunny and warm across the city—anxiously at city hall and 300 Mulberry Street. With the parade scheduled to form at 2:00 P.M. Roosevelt left headquarters for the drive downtown wearing a silk top hat and black frock coat, as he had done for the last big parade he attended, the anti-Roosevelt march through Germantown in November. Mayor Strong awaited him at city hall. Together in a smart caleche complete with a liveried coachman and footman and drawn by a pair of prancing bays they rode back uptown to the reviewing stand at Madison Square.

Proceeding along Broadway they found colorful throngs on the sidewalks. Hundreds more leaned from windows. Flags flapped from nearly every building. Cheers arose from the spectators as the coach passed and they spotted the famous police commissioner's unmistakeable toothy grin and glasses. But not all those along the way felt kindly toward him. A cardboard placard affixed to a fire escape of a brokerage firm featured a crude caricature of TR. Flanked by a sketch of a whiskey bottle and beer stein were the words "Three cheers for Teddy" and "Sunday, Monday, Tuesday and Everyday."

Mayor Strong and the president of the police board took their places on the reviewing stand a few minutes before the first units of marchers were due to go by. Andrews and Grant arrived soon after. Parker appeared last. Taking a spot beside them and among a host of other dignitaries was a genuine hero of police department history. Thomas C. Acton had been president of the police board during the draft riots of 1863 and was credited with having saved the city from being taken over by mobs. Having contended with a myriad of troubles and controversies and facing open hostility between himself and Parker, TR had the consolation of not having had to contend with a civil disorder anywhere near that magnitude. The closest the police had come to a riot on his watch had been the Olympia fiasco, and the cops fared admirably.

Moments after the dignitaries assumed their places on the stand the leading contingent of the marchers appeared, led by a handful of mounted officers whose future promised the new and more colorful uniforms that TR felt were more becoming to men in a band. Into sight behind the horsemen, and to a rolling wave of cheers, wheeled the brand new Bicycle Squad. One observer thought they moved anxiously and a little wobbly but looked smart as they pedalled slowly by in their soft blue caps, blue jackets turned up to permit free wheeling, and leggings.

Eyes turned next to a gallant-looking lone horseman. The commander of five battalions of cops that stretched behind him as far as one could see down Broadway, Chief of Police Peter Conlin sat in his saddle with the practiced ease of an old soldier. Swinging his steed toward the reviewing platform, he snapped a salute to his political bosses and then positioned himself, still mounted, to take the salutes of all who followed the banner borne by the next marcher, Roundsman Wendal. It proclaimed the motto of the department since 1871: "Faithful Unto Death."

Presently, Captain William Devery appeared in line. This was a surprise. The ban against him had been rescinded at the last minute by Chief Conlin. Now Devery gratefully acknowledged what the reporter from the *Times* called a "vociferous" welcome. It was not joined in by the four commissioners of the police board who had tried and failed more than once to remove Devery from the force and who could not have been happy as he passed in triumph.

The greeting for Max Schmittberger was far different. The moment he appeared there arose a noise from the spectators that sounded like escaping steam. Punctuating the hisses were boos and shouts of "squealer." However, all this was promptly drowned out by a claque of Schmittberger admirers who had come equipped with wooden rattles to signal their support. This provoked even louder hisses and yelling from the detractors of Lincoln Steffens' experiment in rehabilitation and Roosevelt's "big stick."

But the mounted officer who stole the show was one of the two men who had become the bone of contention between the president of the police board and Chief Conlin. When Acting Inspector John McCullagh rode into view with the fifth battalion, led by the band of the Seventy-first Regiment, the crowd went wild with admiration for McCullagh and his spritely horse.

The show certainly impressed the *Times'* man along the line of march. He wrote, "He is a very Centaur, and rode a beautiful but very skittish charger. As it passed the Hotel Brunswick it developed a disposition to dance to the march music, then to curvet and caracole, and finally to chasse over the pavement. The rider, who is young and well favored, appeared to regard the pranks of his steed as mere ambling, looked ahead and made the salute in precise form as the charger was pirouetting in a very dizzy fashion."

When all had marched by, Conlin again saluted the mayor and the commissioners and listened to their compliments for the fine display. Reddening face and teary eyes conveyed what those on the stand had expected for weeks, that this would be Conlin's first and last review as chief of the police force he had served all his life. Presumably, TR looked forward to the day he would go.

The man Roosevelt preferred to succeed Conlin had also been in the parade. But whether Moses Cortright would move up to chief of police could not be Roosevelt's decision alone. The Police Law required a unanimous vote of the police board that, because of the war between Roosevelt and Parker, had been unable to take action on anything substantive for months.

As battle lines hardened each had found an ally in another member of the board from the opposite political party. TR had the support of Democrat Avery Andrews. A man in the tradition of the "Long Gray Line" of West Point graduates who pledged themselves to "Duty, Honor and Country," he did not appreciate Parker's conspiracies.

According to Steffens, the Republican Grant sided with Parker out of a combination of cold and cynical calculation on Parker's part and personal pique on Grant's. Discussing the clash with Steffens, Parker said he knew that if the personification of obstinacy and son of "Unconditional Surrender" Grant of the Civil War "voted once, unexpectedly, with me, TR would land on him. Grant has one trait of his father's genius. He will fight it out on this line if it takes all summer." Parker also confided to Steffens that he (Parker) compared Grant to the daily report of the Chicago hog market: "dull but firm."

However, Parker's mainstay was the most important Republican of all, the Easy Boss. Thomas Collier Platt saw Roosevelt as his true enemy in his determined effort to draw back to the GOP ranks the hordes of German-Americans whose votes had been handed to Tammany in 1895 by Roosevelt's saloon-closing obstinacy. Then Roosevelt came out against Platt's favorite for the Republican nomination for President in 1896. Platt was for William McKinley; TR wanted Thomas B. Reed. This added fuel to Platt's desire to do whatever he could to get Roosevelt out of office and out of the way.

Increasingly frustrated by Parker's refusal to hand in the resignation demanded by Strong, TR wrote to Henry Cabot Lodge, "I cannot shoot (Parker) or engage in a rough-and-tumble with him—I couldn't even as a private citizen, still less as chief peace-officer of the city; and I hardly know what course to follow as he is utterly unabashed by exposure and repeats lie after lie with brazen effrontery."

Equally upset by Parker's refusal to be a gentleman and go away quietly, and goaded by Roosevelt and Parker, assisted by the implorings of Rev. Parkhurst, Mayor Strong finally bit the bullet and asked Roosevelt to draft a bill of particulars through which Parker could be brought before Strong for a hearing that amounted to a trial. TR promptly listed neglect of duty, malfeasance, and misfeasance. He omitted bribery (the McMorrow affidavit notwithstanding), prompting Jacob Riis to note in *The Making of an American* that TR "struck no blow below the belt."

When the announcement was made that public hearings would be convened to try the charges in Strong's office beginning on June 11, 1896, the public learned that the prosecutor would be Elihu Root. Appearing in Parker's defense would be General Benjamin F. Tracy, a well-known Platt ally and frequenter of the Amen Corner.

Coming as no surprise to Roosevelt, Peter Conlin assumed the role of a witness friendly to Parker. At one point he said that he had been referred to Parker so frequently by the other board members "that I concluded he was the master spirit of the Board."

Roosevelt was so astonished that he nearly dropped a note pad on which he was scratching down points of interest. His eyes went wide. His jaw dropped. He tapped a pencil noisily against his teeth.

When the moment came for Conlin to leave the witness chair at the end of his testimony he did not do so. Instead, he broke into an unsolicited monologue. "I want to say right here," he declared, "that before this little trouble the Board was all of a unit, working together for the good of the force. They worked hard and well and did all they could to uphold my hands, for which I am grateful. I think the people of New York ought to be grateful to them, too. Col. Grant is an energetic and untiring worker. Mr. Andrews has his heart in the work. As for Mr.—"

Perhaps anticipating phrases somewhat less admiring, Elihu Root shouted, "Oh, stop. How is this relevant?"

Tracy retorted, "Go on; let's hear what he thinks about Roosevelt."

Overheated by the June weather without and warm attitudes within, Mayor Strong's office exploded with laughter.

As Conlin left the chair Root muttered, loud enough for all to hear, "Was all this prearranged?"

"I would have liked to hear about Roosevelt," jabbed Tracy.

A clearly nettled TR snapped, "I don't care to get certificates of good character from my subordinates."

The moment of high drama everyone waited for occurred on July 3. Parker took the witness chair in his defense. Regarding a charge that he had been absent from his office and meetings of the board twenty-two times, he answered, "On every occasion when I was absent Mr. Roosevelt was apprised of my intention, and he knew the reason."

"Did he ever disapprove?" asked Gen. Tracy.

Parker replied, "Quite the contrary."

Tracy inquired of Parker's opinion regarding the cause of the trouble between him and Roosevelt.

"It's one of those difficulties in which you can't put your finger on any one place and say it began there," Parker said. "It practically started Feb. 4, 1896, when I felt I couldn't vote for Brooks and McCullagh as Inspectors."

"Up to that time there had never been a suggestion of your neglecting your duties?"

"Never, Sir; never."

"And that ill feeling between you and Mr. Roosevelt has continued?"

"Yes, Sir, with growing intensity."

Five days later Roosevelt became the witness. At 10:30 A.M. he sketched a scenario in which Parker had exhibited "mendacity, treachery and double dealing" that left Parker unfit to continue as a member of the board. He said, "It began last October, when I discovered that Mr. Parker was not in sympathy with us in the enforcement of the Excise Law. The Mayor told me that Mr. Parker did not approve of our methods. I grew to think that Mr. Parker was double-dealing, for at a meeting we had with the Mayor, he said that he did approve of our methods."

Gen. Tracy interjected, "Did you not say to him, 'You are a bully colleague, old boy? You stand up for your colleagues.' "

"Indeed, I did not," TR replied indignantly. "Mr. Parker stand up for a colleague? I guess not."

With an incredulous tone Tracy persisted on the point. "Do you not remember once saying, 'You are a bully colleague. Great God, if the other two were only like you?' "

Roosevelt answered by repeating his charge that Parker had utterly neglected his duty and that his presence in the board was demoralizing to the force. "If he had only shown an interest in the affairs of the department," he said, "we would have been glad to yield to him. I did yield to him more than I ever did to any other man."

Tracy smiled. "And you do not like to yield?"

Laughter rippled across the crowded room.

"Yes," said Roosevelt, his voice booming. "By George, I do like to yield . . ."

The laughter became a torrent.

". . . to a man who will make concessions also."

Testifying for most of two days and one evening, Roosevelt recited his litany of Parker perfidies relating to the blocking of appointments and promotions, behind-the-back dealings in the state capitol regarding legislation affecting the police department, and conspiracies to thwart the work of the board in general and its president in particular. As a result of all this, he said, "I thought it would be an admirable thing to get him out."

"When did you make up your mind to get Mr. Parker out?"

"By January of this year. I felt that I wanted to get Mr. Parker out because he was neglecting his duty. If the other Commissioners had not acted in harmony the Board could not have done a stroke of work for six months at least."

Tracy pressed for particular instances in which Parker had been a stumbling block. Roosevelt's answers were frequently short of specifics. He often admitted being unable to recall details, a sharp contrast to Parker's unhesitating recitation of the facts, names, and dates. That testimony by Commissioner Grant and Chief Conlin confirmed much of Parker's view of events underscored a sense among observers that the prosecution's case was amazingly weak. The impression grew that Roosevelt might not have been as motivated by high ideals and concern for the good of the police as he was by ambition, spite, or either an unwillingness to be a team player or an innate inability to be one. The result was a broad expectation that Mayor Strong had no alternative but to dismiss the charges against Parker.

However, none of these observers had the benefit of having read the McMorrow document. Because a decision had been made not to accuse Parker of corruption the entire case against him had to stand or fall on how one defined the terms "duty," "malfeasance," and "misfeasance." Like "beauty" their meaning lay in the eyes of the beholders. By not forcing Parker to respond to the charge of bribery the prosecution was left to build its case on the slender reed of Roosevelt's definition of the proper job of commissioner. His being correct legally and morally and Parker's being so wrong that he deserved to be removed from office. As the trial ended, few informed observers of the proceedings could be found who felt the evidence justified that action.

Parker's lawyer rose to demand dismissal of the charges.

Mayor Strong declared he would reserve a decision until he saw Tracy's plea for dismissal in writing. This was no more than a delay in a case whose resolution, should the Mayor rule that Parker must be dismissed, would be swiftly plucked out of his hands. Under state law only Governor Levi P. Morton had the power to fire Parker. What is more, Parker had made it clear going into the trial that if he were to be removed he had every intention of carrying the issue to the courts.

Having asserted his intention to ponder Tracy's motion to dismiss, Strong informed everyone concerned that he would do his ruminating while treating his rheumatism, by resorting to healing mud baths in Richfield Springs. He announced, "I will do nothing in the matter for several weeks."

Disgruntled and discouraged, Roosevelt wrote a letter to his sister. With a gloomy outlook that often exhibited itself in moments loaded with personal and career significance he confessed to Anna that the work of the police board had "nothing of the purple in it." He bitterly described having "to contend with the hostility of Tammany, and the almost equal hostility of the Republican machine."

Going on in the darkest terms, he wrote, "I have to contend with the folly of the reformers and the indifference of decent citizens; above all I have to contend with the singularly foolish law under which we administer the Department."

He cited "a hostile legislature, a bitterly antagonistic press, an unscrupulous scoundrel as Comptroller," and a system in which "I am but one of four Commissioners, each of whom possesses a veto power in promotions."

If he were "a single-headed Commissioner" who had absolute power he could in a couple of years accomplish almost all he desired. He pictured his work as "grimy," "arduous, disheartening and irritating." However, he concluded on the upbeat: "I have faced it as best I could, and I have accomplished something."

Returning to police headquarters, he appeared to resume the unpleasant tasks he described in his letter with the same ardor of his first day on the job. Trials of police misbehavior went on. The docket of July 24 listed ninety-one cases, including Patrolman George W. Hoefling of the Eldridge Street Station. A Roundsman had caught him reading a newspaper on duty. Hoefling explained that the paper contained a story about him and his arrest of a thief known as "Big Hennessy." Shown a clipping of the article, Roosevelt said, "You did pretty well in arresting 'Big Hennessy,' and in consideration of that I will let you off this time, but don't read newspapers on your post again."

Reporters covering the police board on July 30 witnessed another clash over the prickly issue of promotions for Acting Inspectors Brooks and McCullagh, but this time Parker found the table turned. Previously, actions by the board had been blocked by Parker. This time it was TR, Grant, and Andrews. They held the position that until the Brooks-McCullagh matter was settled no one would be promoted. A furious Parker told reporters, "They are willing to hold up the whole force because of these two."

TR's view was simple. He told the journalists on July 31, "We feel that McCullagh and Brooks are very much the two best men for Inspectors."

The next day found him abandoning the swelter and stink of

Mulberry Street in midsummer for his piazza on Sagamore Hill with its cooling zephyrs from Long Island Sound. A guest on that first day of August was Mrs. Bellamy Storer. Although a casual observer might have assumed she was there at the invitation of Edith, she was TR's friend. They met while he served as a member of the Civil Service Committee and she worked the corridors of power and the lobbies of powerbrokers in Washington on behalf of the Roman Catholic Church.

That doors opened readily to her stemmed from the dual root of her being a very wealthy woman with all the political muscle money engendered, and her astute and formidable behind-the-scenes political savvy in directing the use of her and her husband's cash.

Regarding Theodore Roosevelt, Maria Longworth Storer shared the view of Joseph Bishop that TR was like a child, given to a charming and winning spontaneity coupled with a determination to do right. She wrote of him, "One never knew what he would say next. He was certainly very witty in himself, and he valued wit in others." She also found his vituperation "extremely amusing."

During her visit the Roosevelt wit and vituperation were much in evidence as he discussed the woes of Mulberry Street. Then the talk turned to the nation's future, specifically the role that might be played in it by the Republican candidate for President, William McKinley. TR had opposed him, preferring his old friend and Assembly Speaker Thomas B. Reed. He had confided in Henry Cabot Lodge that he would regard a McKinley nomination "a great misfortune." However, when the Republicans at their St. Louis convention in late June nominated McKinley, TR had shown up at the Parker trial sporting a huge ivory-colored campaign button the size of a silver dollar bearing portraits of McKinley and Vice Presidential nominee Garret A. Hobart.

In discussing McKinley with his guest he knew that she had a close connection to the candidate. This link was not only political. She and her husband had loaned McKinley ten thousand dollars in 1893 when he had found himself in potentially ruinous straits. As a result, the Republican standard bearer in 1896 considered himself in the Storers' debt, both morally and politically. If anyone had the ear of the man most likely to become President it was the woman who shared TR's Sagamore Hill breezes that August day.

Presently, he suggested rowboating out on Oyster Bay. There, as he pulled the oars with seemingly effortlessness he returned to his present job. Suddenly gone were his sunny charm and amusing repartee. Instead, she heard words couched in dark tones of a future in which he depicted himself as an unpopular politician destined to become a "melancholy spectacle" in the form of "an idle father, writing books that do not sell."

A secure future, he suggested, lay in a return to Washington. After rowing in silence for a few moments he looked up at Mrs. Storer with the face of a boy bursting to tell a secret. He said, "There is one thing I would like to have."

Now he seemed like a child anticipating Christmas with the vision of a splendid gift that he knew to be too costly to realize under the tree. Forlornly, he said, "But there is no chance of my getting it."

The oars rose and fell. Mrs. Storer waited.

"McKinley will never give it to me," he blurted.

He ceased rowing and fell silent and thoughtful.

"I should like," he said as the rowboat drifted on the bay, "to be Assistant Secretary of the Navy."

In the tone of the mother of that hopeful, expectant child at the approach of Christmas, Mrs. Storer replied as TR began rowing back to shore that she was sure something could be arranged.

The ultimate fate of Theodore Roosevelt in an administration of President William McKinley notwithstanding, the president of the police board found that he bore an immediate responsibility to oversee the police force in carrying out the most daunting challenge in many years. The candidate of the Democratic Party had chosen to launch his campaign for the White House with a speech and rally on August 12 at Madison Square Garden. In deploying the police to ensure the safety and comfort of William Jennings Bryan he had to set aside his personal view, expressed to a friend in a letter, that a victory by Bryan meant "some years of social misery, not markedly different from that of any South American republic."

In meeting its obligation to provide an orderly evening the police failed. Through the doors of Madison Square Garden passed more gate-crashers than those who had held legitimate tickets to Oscar Hammerstein's oversold Olympia. Newspapers jumped on the police and their leader—who had chosen not to be present—and accused them of gross incompetence. Jacob Riis's *Sun* scorned the cops as "Teddy's recruits." The usually unstinting praise for TR from the *Times* was supplanted by judgment that the evening's work by the police had been "bunglingly done." Whispers were heard in the press shack and elsewhere that no such a fiasco would have taken place under the watchful eyes of Tom Byrnes and Clubber Williams.

As the election season blossomed nothing was heard from TR concerning absences from police headquarters by any commissioner. He was away from his desk himself, hitting the hustings on behalf of McKinley. Decreeing that he had no intention of stumping for votes in person, William McKinley chose to campaign from the comfort of his front porch in Canton, Ohio. However, he fully expected an army of Republicans to march on his behalf from coast to coast. This was an enterprise that a man with his heart set on being Assistant Secretary of the Navy could ill afford to sit out. Accordingly, he threw himself into a whirlwind of speechmaking on behalf of the man of whose firmness he once said, "I utterly distrust," and whose nomination he had said he would "much regret."

Under the guidance of McKinley's manager, Mark Hanna, TR and hordes of other surrogates unleashed a forerunner of twentieth century campaign blitzes, fueled by the biggest war chest in history to that date. It was an effort that promoted TR to remark that McKinley was being sold "as if he were a patent medicine."

Between August and October voters saw and listened to TR all over a part of the country he knew well, the West. From there he moved to the East Coast. Next he concentrated on New York City with as bewildering a schedule as the one he had followed the previous year in defense of his policy of enforcing the Sunday closing law and to hell with the consequences for Republicans and Boss Platt at the polls. Back West on October 15, he took Chicago by storm. In one address he spoke to 13,000 frenzied admirers who shouted "Teddy" as if he were the candidate for President.

Heading home to New York by way of Michigan, he shadowed the Bryan campaign so closely that he once found himself in the same town at the same time, standing incognito in the large crowd as the famed orator spoke. On the eve of election day he was back in the city, worn out and a bit nervous about the outcome.

He need not have been. William McKinley won with a plurality of 600,000 votes.

Soon after the victory, Mrs. Storer and her husband traveled to Canton to discuss with the President-elect, among other items on their agenda, what might be done to assure a position in the government for Theodore Roosevelt. Henry Cabot Lodge undertook the same mission and reported back to TR that McKinley spoke of him "with great regard for your character and your services." He reported that McKinley "would like to have you in Washington." But the President-elect wanted assurances that the stormy and headstrong New Yorker had "no preconceived plans which he would wish to drive through the moment he got in."

McKinley expressed the same reservation to the Storers. "I want peace," he said, "and I am told your friend Theodore . . . is always getting into rows with everybody. I am afraid he is too pugnacious."

Mrs. Storer replied, "Give him a chance to prove that he can be peaceful."

Meanwhile, the war in Mulberry Street remained undecided as another season marking the birth of the Prince of Peace turned New York City traditionally festive. But December 1896 was to see a celebration of a different sort, as well. A blithe young man about town and society dandy by the name of Herbert Barnum Seeley, who had inherited $444,440.40 from his late uncle, the circus impresario P. T. Barnum, decided to throw a bachelor party for his brother, Clinton Burton Seeley. Plans called for a group of the "swell set" to frolic in a private upstairs ballroom of Louis Sherry's fashionable Fifth Avenue restaurant on the evening of Saturday, December 19.

Presently as the affair unfolded, three lovely, exotically clad dancing girls appeared to entertain by belly dancing. But all eyes centered on one of them. A dark-eyed, voluptuous, and sensuous wriggler possessed of rarest talents, with diamonds in her garters, had thrilled—and scandalized—Chicago's Columbian Exposition. Her name was as alluring as her looks: Little Egypt.

She had hardly begun undulating when the door burst open and a sea of blue uniforms flooded in. Led by a Captain Chapman of the Thirtieth Precinct, they threatened to arrest the lot. But as they discovered no naked flesh and thereby nothing incriminating, they withdrew with no one in custody. However, once the news of the raid hit the newspaper headlines, an uproar of public outrage forced the convening of a grand jury. Herbert Seeley was indicted for conspiring "to induce the woman known as Little Egypt to commit the crime of indecent exposure." Her testimony consisted of an outright denial, insisting that she had been fully dressed in a Zouave jacket and a pair of lace pantaloons. The case against Seeley evaporated.

But an intriguing question danced around town and in the Mulberry Street press shack. Captain Chapman had never shown such moral diligence before. Why had he pulled this raid? The answer appeared to be, though no proof could be produced to support it, that certain individuals believed that amidst Seeley's titillated guests the cops might find none other than Theodore Roosevelt.

To anyone who knew TR the notion was ludicrous. This was the man who in 1884 while his cities committee was probing sins of the police department had witnessed the fate of one politician who acted indiscreetly. Here was a fellow who appreciated, as he subsequently wrote, that it was always easier to be a harmless dove than a wise serpent. Besides, ogling belly dancers was not at all in keeping with his character.

When Riis told TR that his enemies in the department may have been trying to catch him in an indiscretion that would have forced him out of office, Roosevelt thundered, "What! And I at home with my babies!"

TR removed himself to the sanctuary of Sagamore Hill for the Christmas holiday. But on December 30 he was back at headquarters presiding over the year's final board meeting. All commissioners were present. The session passed without fireworks.

Upon adjournment TR drew his adversary aside. "Parker, I feel to you as Tommy Atkins did toward Fuzzy-Wuzzy in Kipling's poem," he said. "'To fight 'im 'arf an hour will last me 'arf a year.' I'm going out of town tonight, but I suppose we'll have another row next Wednesday."

With a laugh, Parker replied, "I'll be glad to see when you get back, Roosevelt."

On January 8 the man about whom William McKinley expressed grave misgivings concerning pugnaciousness announced, "I shall hereafter refuse to take part in any wranglings or bickerings on this Board. They are not only unseemly, but detrimental to the discipline of the force."

Andrew Parker voiced agreement. Five weeks later he yanked down the flag of truce and returned to his old ways, causing TR to pen a letter to his sister on February 28 about his "almost intolerable difficulty" with his "cunning, unscrupulous and shifty" nemesis. As to Parker's ally through much of the dispute, he wrote early in March to a friend, "Grant is one of the most interesting studies that I know of, from the point of view of ativisim. I am sure his brain must reproduce that of some long-lost arboreal ancestor."

The fact that Andrew Parker remained a member of the Board eight months after his trial ended and his fate had been taken under advisement lay equally on the doorstep of city hall and the threshold of the state legislature. Despite his pledge to rule on the case Mayor Strong had done nothing. When confronted with this startling reality on March 7 by a reporter for the *Sun* he said, "I am very sorry that I ever appointed Andrew D. Parker. I am just as sorry that it is beyond my power to remove him from office."

This was true. The law blocked him. Nevertheless, a reporter pointed out, no law kept Strong from finally issuing a verdict in the trial and finding Parker guilty. Strong reacted to this goading predictably. He did nothing.

While he procrastinated, momentum was building in Albany toward enactment of new statutes to govern the police department at such time as the entity known as Greater New York became reality (January 1898). Amendments submitted by Republicans would abolish the four-man Police Board, vesting its powers in one commissioner of police and making that individual a gubernatorial appointee. As part of the debate an opponent of putting the city police under state control blasted Strong's inaction in the Parker case. Arthur Von Briesen informed the legislature that he had warned Strong in no uncertain terms that his inaction was feeding the drive to strip the city of its sovereignty.

He said, "I told the Mayor unless he acted promptly he admitted by his inactivity that the city is not able to take care of its own affairs. The law clearly authorizes him to remove heads of departments for cause, and yet he did not act. It seemed to me that the interest of the city that it govern itself was at stake . . . ought to satisfy the Mayor that he sadly neglects an important public duty if he fails to try the Commissioners and remove them from office if he finds them guilty."

Sentiment was also mounting in the city for Strong to take steps to dismiss Parker. On March 11 the *Times* reported, "Many people interviewed on the squabble at Police Headquarters suggested that the Major peremptorily remove Commissioner Parker, and let the other Commissioners straighten matters out while he is suing for reinstatement."

Parker insisted that the mayor had no power to remove him, but could only recommend removal, but that "until the Governor approves the recommendation, it has no effect." He stated that if the mayor took action to fire him he would carry on his duties as a commissioner of police as before.

Five days after this defiant assertion Roosevelt spoke to the Social Reform Club on "The Workings of the Police Department." The Parker problem aside, he judged the situation satisfactory, pointing out an improvement in the moral tone of the force and a decrease in crime. The speech might have stood as his personal valedictory as well, but following him to the platform to speak was a familiar antagonist and frequent critic of Roosevelt's methods. He was Moses Oppenheimer, a member of the Committee of Seventy and a leader in social reform circles. "'By their fruits ye shall know them,'" he said. "Let us then, calmly and dispassionately look for some results of the board's labors."

However, his remarks ignored the police board as an entity and concentrated on its president. "We know all about the great anti-saloon crusade, the Haroun al Roosevelt midnight rambles, the sensational handshakes," he continued as the audience and TR shifted anxiously in their chairs. "In those breezy and bustling days Mr. Roosevelt was in the habit of brushing aside criticism with the accusation that the critics were criminals or the allies of criminals. Result: the Raines hotel, the speakeasy, and the people's verdict in the election of 1895."

He went on to assail "the other crusade against what is called the 'social evil'" for emphasizing that police officers would be judged by the number of arrests they made, leading to many arrests that were later judged by courts to have been illegal. He charted that rules of the police department had been calculated to discourage civilian complaints. "The system encourages lying and intimidation on the part of the force," he said angrily. "The circumlocution office could not frame those rules more successfully."

When Oppenheimer finished the blistering attack Roosevelt rushed forward demanding to be heard in rebuttal. Described by a reporter as going after Oppenheimer "hammer and tongs" on all the points he had raised, TR concluded that if Oppenheimer's policy were carried out the result would be "either a return to the corruption or the open flaunting of vice such as would make Babylon seem an Arcadia."

When Roosevelt finished cheers rang through the hall and the applause was deafening, according to news accounts. The president of the Social Reform Club disclaimed on behalf of the membership any responsibility for or sympathy with Oppenheimer's remarks and called for a vote of confidence in Roosevelt. A single dissent was noted.

Leaving the hall, TR was able to go home to sleep assured that all save two people who had listened to him had agreed with his assessment of his almost two years of stewardship in Mulberry Street. Yet the fact that he had been attacked at all was but one more bit of evidence that in being Police Commissioner there was, indeed, nothing of the purple.

The next day he gained a long-sought victory. Finally, after two further weeks of agonizing and delay, Mayor Strong announced that he had determined that Andrew Parker had been proven guilty of neglect of duty and, therefore, was to be dismissed. A report to that effect was being dispatched to Albany for consideration and approval by the new Republican Governor.

Asked how quickly Frank S. Black might act, one Republican who took a dim view of Strong having passed the hot potato to the freshman chief executive of the state replied, "If Mayor Strong saw fit to wait six or eight months before determining to remove the Commissioner, Governor Black certainly has excuse for taking ample time in which to act."

Andrew Parker wasted no time in giving notice that he would resist the firing and carry the fight to the courts, and pointing out that until or unless Governor Black approved Strong's action the dismissal had no legal effect. This was true. Nothing could prevent Parker from doing what he had been doing for the previous twenty-two months and continuing to be the figure the Roosevelt biographer Edmund Morris called, in *The Rise of Theodore Roosevelt*, a handsome, smiling enigma and "the only associate whom Roosevelt never managed to bend to his own will, and, significantly, the only adversary from whom that happy warrior ever ran away."

That TR might be going, if not running, from Mulberry Street leaked to the press on April 3, 1897. A dispatch from Washington reached New York to the effect that President McKinley, who had been inaugurated March 4, had decided to appoint TR Assistant Secretary of the Navy.

Roosevelt told reporters, "I do not know a thing about it. I have received no communication from the President saying that I had been selected, nor have I had any correspondence with him about the appointment."

With the same aw-shucks disingenuousness employed by scores, if not hundreds, of office-seekers since, he said, "All I know is what I have seen in the newspapers."

Would he accept the job if offered?

He answered as he had replied to speculation that he would be named police commissioner. "I cannot tell what I would do in that case," he said. "Until I get the notice of President McKinley's decision I do not wish to say what I will do."

Lobbying for the appointment had been going on at a feverish pace by Henry Cabot Lodge and the Storers. Boss Thomas Platt had conducted himself in such a way as to not encourage the naming of his on-again, off-again opponent, yet not say "nay" to it. As to the President, he still harbored worries that Roosevelt might in some way push the United States into a war with Spain over Cuba, an eventuality McKinley did not desire.

When word flashed, unofficially, from Washington on April 6 that McKinley had sent Roosevelt's name to the U.S. Senate for its advice and consent as to the nomination of Theodore Roosevelt to be Assistant Secretary of the Navy a reporter asked Roosevelt, "Would it would be safe to say that you would not decline?"

TR boomed, "It would!"

On Saturday, April 17, 1897, TR dictated a letter to Miss Kelly. Addressed to Mayor Strong, it tendered his resignation and went on to say, "For the first time the police force has been administered without regard to politics and with an honest and resolute purpose to enforce the laws equitably and show favor to no man. The whole system of blackmail and corruption has been almost entirely broken up; we have greatly improved the standard of discipline; we have warred against crime and vice more effectively than ever before. The fact we have come short in any measure is due simply to the folly of the law which deprives us of the full measure of power over our subordinates which could alone guarantee the best results."

This was all true.

Presiding that day for the last time as the president of the board of police commissioners, he noted the absence of Parker and Parker's ally, Fred Grant.

"I am sorry," TR said to Avery Andrews and the reporters crowded into the room. "There were many matters of importance which I wished to bring up."

Nor did Peter Conlin bother to drop in to say farewell.

Later as TR strode past Conlin's office a guard at the door threw it open for him.

TR shook his head. "No, I am not going in there."

"Well, goodbye, Mr. President," said the guard.

Roosevelt clasped the man's hand and spoke his parting words to Mulberry Street: "I shall be sorry for you when I am gone."

Epilogue

A Larger Kingdom

"I have never had a better time in my life," said Theodore Roosevelt, "than the two years I have been in the police department."

The audience howled with laughter.

Standing before a room packed to the walls with members of the Good Government Club and a stellar array of the movers and shakers of New York City on Thursday evening, April 15, 1897, the soon-to-be Assistant Secretary of the Navy was in a buoyant mood.

He had been introduced by Jacob Riis.

Before that the club president, Charles H. Strong, had said glowing things about the evening's guest of honor. So had James C. Carter, another leading light of the city and the reformers exemplified by TR's hosts. The Albany lawmaker who had warned Mayor William Strong that reluctance to move decisively against Andrew Parker had created a clear and present danger of the city forfeiting its sovereignty to the state, Arthur Von Briesen, had taken the podium to declare, "Theodore Roosevelt will always be remembered in the history of our city as the courageous and manly leader in this important branch of our public service."

Now it was TR's turn and, as laughter at his little self-effacing jest subsided, he continued, "I thoroughly enjoyed the work, because I felt that I could at least do my utmost to administer the office according to my ideas of justice. It is not necessary to have genius to administer that office properly. What is needed is common honesty, common sense, and common courage. We need the minor, the humdrum, the practical virtues—the commonplace virtues that are absolutely essential if we are ever to make this city what it should be. If these virtues are lacking, no amount of cleverness will answer."

Pointing out that one thousand seven hundred men had been

added to the force, he said with a mischievous twinkle in his eyes, "Under a former dispensation that would have meant $200 apiece." The listeners again roared with laughter.

He finished his last address as police commissioner with an affectionate and admiring tribute to the fundamental honesty and integrity of "the common cop, the man with the nightstick."

One of them who spoke to Lincoln Steffens about Roosevelt's leaving Mulberry Street said, "It's tough on the force, for he was dead square, was Roosevelt; we needed him in the business."

The ever-dubious *World* reflected that, while New Yorkers were glad to see Roosevelt go, few could argue that his record was not impressive. The *Herald* proposed that if Roosevelt did nothing except ensure that the police provided honest supervision of the polls during the previous elections "the political revolution of last year would not have been in vain." The *Times* asserted, "The service he has rendered to the city is second to that of none, and considering the conditions surrounding it, it is in our judgment unequaled."

An editorial in Steffens' paper, the *Evening Post,* declared, "The end of the reign of Mr. Roosevelt is not the end of Rooseveltism. His personality will persist as an active influence in the force for a generation at least, till the youngest 'reform cop' is retired, and then he will not go out of business entirely. He will furnish another example for the young policeman and though most of them may choose to follow whatever the ideals of the majority may be at the time, all will remember Roosevelt."

The editor of the *Post,* E. L. Godkin, who had been a frequent critic of TR as commissioner, wrote him a letter that protested his decision to leave the police department in these words: "I have a concern to put on record my earnest belief that in New York you are doing the greatest work of which any American today is capable, and exhibiting to the young men of the country the spectacle of a very important office administered by a man of high character in the most efficient way amid a thousand difficulties. I cannot think of anything more instructive."

Hardly anyone expected that filling the void would be easy. The individual who faced the task, Mayor Strong, said wistfully, "I suppose they can get along at Police Headquarters for a few days with three Commissioners. The three of them cannot make matters any worse than they have been, and I shall take my time [*Author's note:* no surprise there!] to find a man who suits me fairly well."

Of course, suiting William Lafayette Strong was unlikely to be the chief criterion in the selection process. The Easy Boss, Thomas Collier Platt, would want to have his say. The Republican chieftain had found himself at odds with himself over Roosevelt's departure. Platt did not really want him in a high profile job in Washington, but he could not abide the notion of TR staying in New York. In filling the vacancy in the police board room Platt was not about to say an "amen" to anyone exuding even the slightest scent of turning into another Roosevelt.

As it turned out the decision was not Platt's to make. In the next municipal election the Tammany minions who had abandoned their traditional loyalty in 1894 returned. En masse, they proved Boss Croker right in his prediction to Steffens that the people would tire of their revolt. Tammany Hall's candidate for mayor, Robert Van Wyck, marched into city hall proudly carrying the banner "To Hell with Reform."

In the rain at midnight on January 1, 1898, some one hundred thousand of those who had flocked back to Tammany and the old ways stood in front of Tammany's regained city hall to watch and be a part of an historic event. More than three thousand miles away, Mayor James Phelan of another great city on a bay, San Francisco, pressed a button that sent a charge of electricity across the continent. Atop New York's City Hall it triggered a motor that unfurled a new flag above the seat of government. It was the blue and white ensign of "Greater New York." The fanfare marking its debut was arranged by William Randolph Hearst's *Journal*. It was so grand a thing that even Hearst's archrival, Joseph Pulitzer's *World*, called it the "biggest, noisiest and most hilarious New Year's Eve celebration that Manhattan Island has ever known." Of course, from then on Manhattan was no more a city unto itself, but one of the five boroughs of New York.

This required a bigger police force and a new way of running it from Mulberry Street. The new way proved to be the old way. Jacob Riis held his nose and wrote, "Honest government did not suit New York. It deliberately voted the dishonest crew back with vastly increased powers for mischief."

Elevated to chief of police was William Devery. Among his cronies was William McLaughlin, who had not permitted a verdict of guilty, Roosevelt, reformers, and facts about his corruption keep him off the force. Through persistence and a number of legal loopholes he had won a court-ordered reinstatement to duty a few days before TR resigned.

Trials of policemen continued under the new regime, but it was Devery who conducted them and judged the accused. When one of the roundsmen whom TR would have praised for his honesty found himself before the new police chief he heard Devery say, "If you're the kind of man we get from Civil Service, we don't want any more of them." Another cop who stood trial for recklessly firing his gun was fined thirty days' pay by Bill Devery for "not hittin' nobody." Yet another cop who was brought up on a charge of kissing a girl while on patrol was told by Devery, "I would kiss a girl myself but I'd never get caught." The fine imposed was not for misbehaving on duty but for being nabbed at it.

In time New Yorkers staged another of the uprisings that had amused Rudyard Kipling. The police department was purged again in 1912. Reform struck once more in the 1930s in the shape of Mayor LaGuardia and his "honest cop," Lewis J. Valentine. In the 1950s, beset by a fresh scandal, Mayor Robert F. Wagner opined, "When I go to bed at night I say a special prayer for the safety of the city. Then I say another special prayer of thanks that nothing bad happened in the police department." The 1970s brought the revelations of the Knapp Commission and echoes of Schmittberger in the form of Frank Serpico, testifying about a police force on the take and make. By then and afterward the primary source of the rot was not liquor on Sunday, gambling, and prostitution, but illicit narcotics. One can only wonder what TR would have said about that scourge and cops who profited by permitting it.

Following Roosevelt's departure in 1897 the headquarters of the New York Police Department had three locations. It remained at 300 Mulberry Street more than a dozen years after TR's departure. In 1909 it moved a little to the west and into a magnificent stone edifice with an imposing dome at 250 Centre Street. Designed by the distinguished architects Hopin and Koen in the French Baroque manner of the nineteenth century, this police palace afforded the department's commissioner (only one) an office on the second floor (as had been TR's). Those who ran the force from within did so while occupying the desk that had been Roosevelt's in cramped quarters overlooking rooftops of teeming tenements so hated by Jacob Riis.

With the move to Centre Street the denizens of the press quarters at 301 and 303 Mulberry had shifted their note pads and type-writers to space across the street behind 250 Centre Street.

They and the department moved again in the 1970s to a red brick, square high-rise structure called "One Police Plaza." It stood closer to city hall and in the heart of the governmental complex that had obliterated the old Five Points. Within this ultramodern head-quarters of what was arguably (despite its bouts of corruption and exposé) the finest police force in the world, commissioners continued the tradition of occupying a chair behind Roosevelt's desk, if not always filling TR's shoes.

As to the people Roosevelt left behind in 1897:

William Strong died in 1900 of natural causes.

Peter Conlin passed away in 1905.

Thomas "the actor" Byrnes and Thomas "Easy Boss" Platt died of old age on the same day, March 7, 1910.

Boss Dick Croker lived till 1922. A controversial political figure to the end, he was so rich that his heirs fought a bitter battle in contesting his Last Will and Testament and all the loot that went with it.

Alexander S. "Clubber" Williams died in his bed in January 1918.

Max Schmittberger completed a cop's career with honor and died exactly a year after the man whose "tenderloin" feastings he had detailed in all their gluttony before the Lexow Committee.

Fred Grant died in 1912.

TR's stalwart ally, Avery Andrews, commanded the New York State National Guard as Adjutant General on the occasion of TR's inauguration as Governor of New York and throughout Roosevelt's term. For his soldiering in the First World War he received the Distinguished Service Medal. Of his fellow police commissioner and friend he wrote, "It may be truthfully said that Theodore Roosevelt at no time in his career fought more effectively for the basic princi-ples of free government than he fought for them as New York Police Commissioner." He died in 1959 at the age of ninety-five.

The bane of TR's existence in Mulberry Street, Andrew Parker remained a puzzle. His fate became a mystery. This author found no trace of him in the records after 1897. Nor did TR biographer Ed-mund Morris, who wrote, "He vanishes from history as he entered it, a handsome, smiling, enigma."

The Rev. Dr. Charles H. Parkhurst thrived on his fame as a scourger of the wicked and lived to see Prohibition become the law of the land in 1919, but he died in 1921 without witnessing the years of misery, murder, corruption, and lawlessness that flowed from "the Great Experiment," nor to experience its lasting legacy in the form of organized crime.

The earnest young novice newsman who called on Parkhurst in 1893 on assignment from the *Evening Post,* Lincoln Steffens, went on to journalism immortality as one of a puckish band of reform-minded crusaders and writers known as "Muckrakers." Always a liberal and advocate of social engineering, he became a darling of American communists and "fellow travelers" in the 1920s and 1930s. After a visit to the Soviet Union he declared, "I have been over into the future, and it works." Latter-day history records his view as the biggest misjudgment of his astonishing and useful career. In 1931 he published his *Autobiography.* He died in 1936.

Jacob August Riis died on May 26, 1914, having lived to see the most important man in his life occupy the White House. Save for TR himself, no individual worked harder to bring that dream to reality. In an introduction to an edition of Riis's life story TR wrote, "If I were asked to name a fellow-man who came nearest to the ideal American citizen, I should name Jacob Riis."

The man who pledged "I have come to help" to Riis in 1890 went to Washington seven years later to realize the desire he had expressed to Mrs. Storer, serving as Assistant Secretary of the Navy, while exasperating President McKinley by advocating war with Spain in the cause of the liberation of Cuba. When the war came in 1898 he resigned his Navy post and helped organize a band of hardies to fight it. In the rank of Colonel he led these "Rough Riders" up San Juan Hill and wrote another colorful chapter in the biography of Theodore Roosevelt. The fame of that exploit, added to his already impressive credentials, propelled him into the Executive Mansion in Albany as Governor in 1898. Two years later, unable to stand TR any longer, Boss Platt worked to get a Roosevelt nomination as President McKinley's running mate in 1900. An assassin's bullet ended the McKinley presidency in 1901 and opened the White House door to Vice President Roosevelt who became the twenty-sixth President of the United States. He was forty-three, the youngest to assume the office to that date. He served the balance of McKinley's term and won election on his own in 1904.

In those years he gave the American people "the square deal," the first national park, U.S. title to an ocean-uniting canal across the isthmus of Panama, trust-busting, the Pure Food and Drug Law, and the wedding of his daughter Alice in the White House. Brokering of a settlement of the Russo-Japanese war earned him the 1906 Nobel Peace Prize.

Two years later he was to leave his mark on the future of law enforcement for the entire nation as he had done in New York. During efforts to smash trusts, he discovered a vast network of fraud that had led to the corruption of hundreds of federal officials. Learning that no organization existed to root it out, he ordered Attorney General Charles Joseph Bonaparte to create a staff of detectives within the Justice Department. As a result, the Bureau of Investigation was born on July 26, 1908. After the prefix "Federal" was added twenty-seven years later its initials came to be synonymous with the "honest and efficient" policing TR had fought to instill in 300 Mulberry Street.

Out of office, restless and unhappy, he made a bid in 1912 for the Republican nomination for President. Brushed aside by the GOP, he ran as the candidate of the new Bullmoose Party. During a vigorous national campaign tour, as he crossed a sidewalk toward the hall where he was to speak to a large crowd of enthusiastic backers in Milwaukee, a man stepped out of the crowd, muttered something about "third term" and shot him at almost point-blank range in the chest.

Shrugging off assistance, TR demanded that he be permitted to deliver the speech. He began it by saying, "I am going to ask you to be very quiet, and please excuse me from making a long speech. I will do the best I can, but there is a bullet in my body."

As he drew the script from his coat's inside pocket the audience gasped in horror. The bullet had passed through the pages. They dripped with blood.

"It is nothing," he said. "I am not badly hurt. I have a message to deliver, and will deliver it as long as there is life in my body."

While Americans applauded bravery they had strong sentiments against anyone having a third term in the White House. They also sought a change of policies. They chose to elect Democrat Woodrow Wilson. The precedent of presidential retirement after two terms set by George Washington remained intact until 1940, and the third election to the White House of TR's relative, Franklin D. Roosevelt.

As a private citizen for the first time since he had left Mulberry Street, TR did not break a lifetime's habits and settle into idleness. He published his *Autobiography* in 1913, then went exploring and hunting in South America, where the locals promptly named a hitherto unknown stream in his honor, Rio Teodoro.

When America entered "the Great War" in 1917 he asked for a command but was refused. His four sons enlisted. Quentin, who was an aviator, was killed in action in July 1918. At the time TR was suffering from a severe illness that resulted in a loss of hearing in one ear. Allowed to leave a hospital for Christmas at Sagamore Hill, he seemed to rally. He laid in bed writing letters and a few editorials.

Nearing midnight on January 5, 1919, he completed a short memorandum to the chairman of the Republican National Committee. Settling down to sleep, he said to his valet, "Please put out that light, James."

He died without waking four hours later in his sixty-first year.

Standing honor guard at the funeral at Oyster Bay was Otto Raphael. Astride a horse in command of the police department contingent was Edward Bourke, now a captain. The wise political mentor who had taught TR the difference between Sixth and Fifth Avenues, faithful Joe Murray, attended. So did Elihu Root, along with an array of dignitaries that included the former President of the United States, William Howard Taft.

Bourke said, "I was not the only man who shed a tear that day."

Senator Henry Cabot Lodge was there, as he always had been, the recipient of so many of TR's letters who had told his friend that he would one day leave Mulberry Street to claim a larger kingdom. In a memorial address to a joint meeting of the two houses of Congress Lodge had said, "And so Valiant-for-truth passed over, and all the trumpets sounded for him on the other side."

A search for summations of TR's life and contributions to the cause of better government through individual effort, and what he meant to law enforcement, produces a wealth of material.

Of the latter, Jacob Riis said the Roosevelt era in Mulberry Street, "as brief as was its sway, left a mark which nothing can ever efface." Because no one knew the police before, during, and after TR's two years better than Riis, let his judgment suffice.

As to the essential TR before, during, and after Mulberry Street there were no better words than his own.

It is not the critic who counts, not the man who points out how the strong man stumbled or where the doer of deeds could have done better. The credit belongs to the man who is actually in the arena; whose face is marred by dust and sweat and blood; who errs and comes short again and again . . . who knows the great enthusiasms, the great devotions, and spends himself in a worthy cause; who at the least knows in the end the triumph of high achievement; and who, at the worst, if he fails, at least fails while doing greatly, so that his place shall never be with those cold and timid souls who know neither victory nor defeat.

Sources

Prologue

For detailed observations and interpretations of the events and personalities of New York in the Gay 90s a researcher cannot go wrong in starting with *The Autobiography of Lincoln Steffens*. When he appeared on the journalistic scene in 1892 he brought an objectivity and freshness to covering the police department that served him and posterity well. The edition consulted was the one-volume Chautauqua Home Reading Series, Chautauqua Press, 1931. Newspapers and magazines, particularly the *New York Times* and *Harper's New Monthly Magazine*, provided contemporary biographical sketches of Thomas J. Byrnes, whose own book, *Professional Criminals in America*, offered insights into the workings of his mind, Inspector Alexander Williams, and frequently humorous portraits of criminals of the era.

Chapter 1

Because the full life of Theodore Roosevelt may be found in several biographies, including *The Rise of Theodore Roosevelt* by Edmund Morris, I have summarized the years before his debut upon the public stage with an emphasis on those aspects that appeared to have contributed to the intensity of his interest in reform in general, and remaking of the New York Police Department in particular. A wealth of material related to those years of preparation may be found in Morris, other volumes, TR's autobiography, and in the Theodore Roosevelt collection at Harvard, Theodore Roosevelt birthplace museum on East Twenty-second Street in New York City, the New York Public Library, the Library of Congress, and the Museum of the City of New York. Demonstrating a keen interest in TR as a political phenomenon that would continue unabated even after his death, newspapers and other periodicals afforded coverage of his legislative record and the work of the Cities Committee, which he chaired. Details of TR's family life and the frontier experiences described have been drawn primarily from his memoirs.

Chapter 2

Numerous histories of New York and its police department were consulted in tracing the evolution of the force, including A. E. Costello's *Our Police Protectors*, 1885; Herbert Asbury's *The Gangs of New York*, 1927; *Our*

Police, Irving Crump and John Newton, 1935; *The Astor Place Riot,* Richard Moody, 1958; *The Present Condition of the Police Force,* Francis Greene, 1903; *The Epic of New York,* Edward Robb Ellis, 1966; *Manna-Hatin, The Story of New York,* the Manhattan Company, 1929; and *The New York Cops,* Gerald Astor, 1971. A rich source of data is also maintained in the museum of the New York City Police Department. For insights into social conditions in the city's slums the touchstone work remains Jacob A. Riis's *How the Other Half Lives.* For glimpses into the operations of the police before TR's commissionership there is no better resource than Riis's autobiography, *The Making of an American,* 1901.

Chapter 3

Accounts of the Rev. Dr. Charles Parkhurst's war on vice and corruption abound in the journals of the day and in Parkhurst's reminiscences, *My Forty Years in New York,* MacMillan, 1923; and *Our Fight with Tammany,* Charles Scribner's Sons, 1895; Lincoln Steffens' autobiography; and *The Devil and Dr. Parkhurst,* published by Charles Gardner, written by the detective who escorted Parkhurst during his forays into the dens of iniquity he denounced from his pulpit. The furor over the minister's accusations also received wide coverage in the city's newspapers, as did the work of the Lexow Committee, whose official record is contained in the report of the New York City Police Department Investigating Committee (Senate), *Proceedings Before the Lexow Committee,* 1894. The role of Max Schmittberger in police corruption, his courageous decision to testify, and the repercussions are detailed in Steffens' memoirs. He also discussed the victory of the reform movement in the election of 1894 and recorded for posterity Jacob Riis's exultant assertion that in ridding the police of corruption "TR is enough."

Chapter 4

The process by which TR was appointed to the board of police commissioners is recorded in his autobiography, in the newspapers of New York and Washington, cited within the text and in TR archives at Harvard and at the Roosevelt Birthplace Museum. His views on social reforms were expounded in numerous articles and reflected on in his memoirs. Both Riis and Steffens wrote extensively in their autobiographies in describing TR's arrival at 300 Mulberry Street to take up his duties.

Chapter 5

The daily newspapers of the city devoted considerable space to the new police commissioner and to extensive coverage of the events leading to the resignations of Byrnes and Williams. But the best eyewitness account is to be found in Steffens' memoirs. Both newspapers and official city records provided transcripts of trials of police officers accused of failing to do their duty.

Chapter 6

Nothing demonstrated more vividly TR's innate sense of the value of a favorable press than his personal investigations into the manner in which the officers and rank and file of the force carried out their duties. His "midnight rambles" in search of sleeping or absent cops were begun in the company of Jacob Riis and continued in association with other reporters. Details of the patrols filled the pages of the dailies. Both Riis and Steffens devoted many pages in their memoirs to describing the manner and fervor with which Roosevelt sought to find and root out corrupt cops. TR's autobiography also treats the subject, though with a more generalized and philosophical approach.

Chapter 7

Roosevelt's ethical code may be found throughout his life's writings, in letters, diaries, articles, speeches, interviews, and his autobiography. It is also attested to in memoirs of those who knew him and worked with him in his private and public lives. In bringing that philosophy to reorganizing the police department he addressed many civic and religious organizations. Most of these were reported in the city's newspapers. Roosevelt also recorded in his memoirs the value he placed on bringing upright and righteous men such as Otto Raphael and Edward J. Bourke into the police department. Both Steffens and Riis provided other anecdotes. Steffens was the primary source for the rehabilitation of Max Schmittberger, as well as the candid description of political bossing by Tammany Hall's Richard Croker. Details of Roosevelt's confrontations over the issue of Sunday liquor sales were drawn from the coverage afforded by newspapers, Riis, and Steffens.

Chapter 8

The portrait of New Yorkers as people who liked a night on the town has been drawn from a rich variety of sources, including contemporary journals and newspapers, Herbert Asbury's *The Gangs of New York,* and Michael and Ariane Batterberry's history of the city's eating, drinking, and entertainment styles, *On the Town in New York.* TR's views were expounded in articles, speeches, and in his autobiography. Accounts of the Germantown parade to protest TR's enforcement of the Sunday saloon-closing law, the public controversy, and the resultant defeat of the reformers in the next election, despite TR's vigorous campaigning, were found in the press of the day, Riis, and Steffens, TR's memoirs, and the Roosevelt archives.

Chapter 9

My descriptions of Roosevelt's home life at Sagamore Hill have been drawn largely from Hermann Hadgedorn's book. Battles at Mulberry Street police headquarters were fully reported in the press and in retrospect by TR in his autobiography and in the *Atlantic Monthly* article of 1897 cited in the text. The scene in which TR upbraided Riis and Steffens for asking him if he had his sights set on the White House is based primarily on the Steffens account in his autobiography, as is the story of the fake crime wave. The Burden jewel robbery was widely reported in the press.

Chapter 10

In the entire history of the New York Police Department no commissioner enjoyed so intimate and supportive a relationship with the press as Roosevelt. None who covered Mulberry Street proved more devoted to TR than Jacob Riis. Chapters dealing with Mulberry Street in Riis's autobiography brim with praise, but it was in Riis's *Theodore Roosevelt, the Citizen* that Riis was at his most effusive. Published in 1903 to boost TR's candidacy for President of the United States, it filled 450 pages, citing not only Roosevelt's championing of causes to which Riis was devoted, but extolling personal characteristics of honesty, integrity, and courage. The powerful influence of Riis on Roosevelt in the area of the social reforms described in this chapter cannot be overemphasized and was duly acknowledged in TR's memoirs. Incidents in the battle against all forms of vice related in this chapter were reported in newspapers and by Riis, who also recorded TR's meeting with union leaders. The story of the hapless merchant with a dead horse in front of his establishment during a heat wave was related by TR in his autobiography.

Chapter 11

Although Roosevelt, Riis, and Steffens provided some details regarding the reforms that TR brought to the police department, the evidence of the day-to-day challenge of policing New York was found in stories filed by reporters from their offices opposite 300 Mulberry Street, and frequently at the scene of a crime, as in the Burden jewel robbery and the mob-scene associated with the opening of Oscar Hammerstein's Olympia. Much of my account of the event was based on extraordinary coverage filed by the reporter, not bylined, alas, of *The New York Times*. That paper and others also committed vast amounts of newsprint to the biking craze that led to the formation of the police force's bicycle squad. Details of the other innovations were also available in a press showing no signs of flagging interest in TR's police department.

Chapter 12

TR's struggles with Republican Party boss Thomas Platt have been described in numerous memoirs, including TR's. The extent of the Platt plot to force Roosevelt out of office was a major scoop for the *Times* that provided the people of New York a fascinating picture of political machinations. In their memoirs, Riis, Steffens, and Roosevelt provided a general discussion of the subject, but it was the daily press coverage that afforded details of the controversy and the growing impasse between TR and his chief opponent on the police board, Andrew Parker. Riis, Steffens, and Roosevelt archives also provided details. The vituperative battle between TR and City Comptroller Ashbel Fitch in the office of Mayor William Strong was based on newspaper accounts, especially by the *Times*.

Chapter 13

Much of the war of words and struggle for power between TR and Andrew Parker was fought on the record, either in official statements and correspondence, or through the press. Newspapers also provided details surrounding the controversies of whether William Devery and Max Schmittberger would take part in the police parade of 1896. My account of the parade itself was based on coverage by the *Times*. Although there exists a public record of the trial of Andrew Parker, the color and excitement of the event was found in the work of journalists. The events that led to TR's decision to give up his commissionership have been noted in several sources, including TR's archives, reminiscences of Riis, Steffens, Mrs. Bellamy Storer, and Henry Cabot Lodge.

Epilogue

TR's departure from police headquarters, reaction to it, and his post-Mulberry Street activities before leaving for Washington were widely reported in the press. His fate and that of others who played major roles in the drama that was TR's two-year tenure as police commissioner were drawn together from a variety of sources, including biographies by some of the participants, press accounts, and, finally, obituaries.

Bibliography

Abbot, Lawrence F. *Impressions of Theodore Roosevelt*. Garden City, N.Y.: Doubleday, Page and Company, 1922.

Andrews, Avery. "Citizen in Action: The Story of T. R. as Police Commissioner." Theodore Roosevelt Collection, Harvard College Library, Cambridge, Mass. (typescript).

———. "Theodore Roosevelt as Police Commissioner," *New York Historical Society Quarterly* 42 (April 1958), pp. 117–41.

Asbury, Herbert. *The Gangs of New York*. New York: Alfred A. Knopf, 1928.

Astor, Gerald. *The New York Cops*. New York: Charles Scribner's Sons, 1971.

Batterberry, Michael and Ariane. *On the Town in New York*. New York: Charles Scribner's Sons, 1973.

Berman, Jay Stuart. *Police Administration and Reform, Theodore Roosevelt as Police Commissioner of New York*. New York: Greenwood Press, 1987.

Bishop, Joseph Bucklin. *Theodore Roosevelt and His Time*. New York: Charles Scribner's Sons, 1920.

Busch, Noel. *T. R. The Story of Theodore Roosevelt and His Influence on Our Times*. New York: Reynal and Company, 1963.

Byrnes, Thomas. *Professional Criminals in America*. New York: Castle, 1988; reprint of 1886 ed.

Costello, A. E. *Our Police Protectors*. New York: C. F. Roper, 1885.

Davis, Charles Belmont. *Adventures and Letters of Richard Harding Davis*. New York: Charles Scribner's Sons, 1917.

Ellis, Edward Robb. *The Epic of New York City*. New York: Old Town Books, 1966.

Gardner, Charles. *The Devil and Dr. Parkhurst*. New York: Charles Gardner, 1895.

Gosnell, Howard. *Boss Platt and His New York Machine*. Chicago: University of Chicago Press, 1921.

Harbaugh, William. *Power and Responsibility*. New York: Farrar, Strauss and Cudahy, 1961.

Harlow, Alvin F. *Theodore Roosevelt, Strenuous American*. New York: Julian Messner, Inc., 1943.

Howland, Harold. *Theodore Roosevelt and His Times*. New Haven: Yale University Press, 1921.

Iglehart, Ferdinand. *Theodore Roosevelt—The Man as I Knew Him*. New York: Christian Herald, 1919.

Lodge, Henry Cabot. *Selections from the Correspondence of Theodore Roosevelt and Henry Cabot Lodge—1884–1918*. New York: Charles Scribner's Sons, 1925.

Miller, Nathan. *Theodore Roosevelt, A Life*. New York: William Morrow and Company, 1992.

Morris, Edmund. *The Rise of Theodore Roosevelt*. New York: Coward, McCann and Geoghegan, Inc., 1979.

New York Police Department. *Minutes of Police Board, 1895–97*. New York: New York City Archives.

New York, State of, Report. New York City Police Department Investigating Committee (Senate), *Proceedings Before the Lexow Committee*. New York: 1894.

Parkhurst, Charles. *My Forty Years in New York*. New York: MacMillan, 1923.

———. *Our Fight with Tammany*. New York: Charles Scribner's Sons, 1895.

Riis, Jacob. *The Making of an American*. New York: MacMillan, 1901.

———. *Theodore Roosevelt, the Citizen*. New York: Outlook, 1904.

Roosevelt, Theodore. *American Ideals and Other Essays, Social and Political*. New York: G. P. Putnam's Sons, 1897.

———. *An Autobiography*. New York: MacMillan, 1913.

Steffens, Lincoln. *Autobiography*. New York: Harcourt, Brace and World, 1931.

Stone, Jill. *Times Square*. New York: Collier Books, 1982.

Willemse, Cornelius W. *Behind the Green Lights*. New York: Alfred A. Knopf, 1931.

Wister, Owen. *Roosevelt, the Story of a Friendship*. New York: MacMillan, 1930.

Index